PIRATE *Outrages*

For valued colleagues of my days at sea and on shore in Perth, Sydney and London with Macdonald, Hamilton and Company, BP Tanker Company, British India Steam Navigation Company, Peninsular & Oriental Steam Navigation Company, P&O-Orient Lines of Australia, and The Flying Angel Missions to Seamen around the world.

Douglas Sellick was born in Bridgetown, Western Australia in 1936 and was educated in Albany, and later in London at the BishopsgateInstitute and the Coutauld Institute of Art. He worked his passagae from Fremantle to the United Kingdom in 1955 as galley boy on a tanker before joining various shipping companies in London, Perth and Sydney.

After his career in shipping, he worked in publishing in London, New York, San Francisco and Sydney. He is currently a freelance history and literary researcher and anthologist. His recent books, all published by Fremantle Press, are:

Antarctica – First Impressions
Castaway: Remarkable True Stories of Survival
Venus in Transit: Australia's Women Travellers
Survivors: Great Open Boat Voyages

TRUE STORIES OF TERROR

ON THE CHINA SEAS

COMPILED BY DOUGLAS R.G. SELLICK

CONTENTS

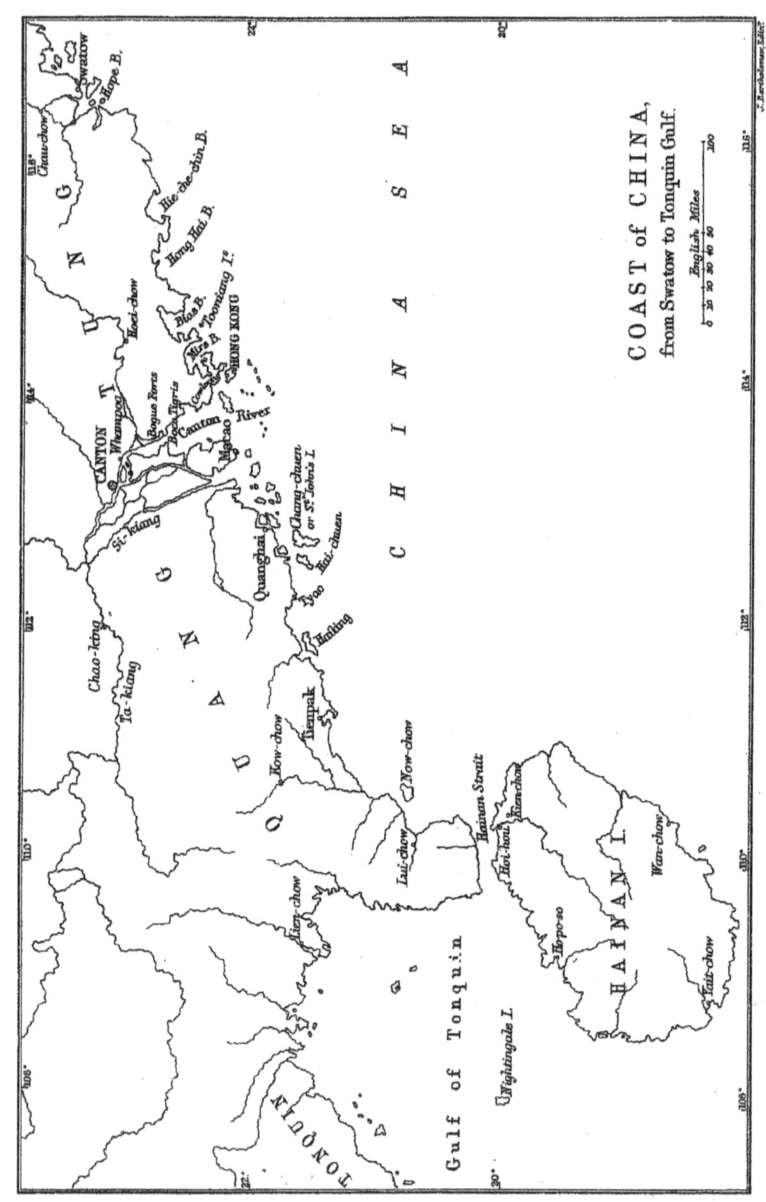
COAST of CHINA,
from Swatow to Tonquin Gulf.
English Miles
Swatow
Hope B.
Chau-chow
Hie-che-chin B.
Hong Hai B.
Hoei-chow
Bias B.
Mirs B.
HONG KONG
Bogue Forts
Boca Tigris
Whampoa
CANTON
Canton River
Macao
Chang-chuen or St. John's I.
Hai-chuen
Quanghai
Si-kiang
Tyao
Hailing
Chao-king
Ta-kiang
Kow-chow
Now-chow
Hainan Strait
Hoi-hou
Wan-chow
Lui-chow
Hopo-so
HAINAN I.
Gulf of Tonquin
Nightingale I.
TONQUIN
CHINA SEA

FOREWORD

Pirates! Piracy!! Of all the great narratives of maritime history – discovery, trade, migration, shipwreck, warfare – piracy occupies an extraordinary place in our collective consciousness. It summons vivid memories of childhood storybooks, swashbuckling film stars and fierce, larger-than-life characters that provide us with ready-made images and imaginings about this topic.

The reality, of course, was – and still is – something quite different. Piracy, possibly as old as seafaring itself, has many contexts. Sometimes it was simply opportune plunder, away from the oversight of authority. Other times it's been part of a wider anarchy, when authority has broken down altogether. Or it's been a response to a dire lack of economic alternatives. Or both, if we think of today's audacious Somali pirates taking on huge ships from their outboard-powered pirogues.

At times piracy has been state-sanctioned aggression against rival states, with privateers doing the work normally associated with navies. And there have been ample times and places when seaborne rebels or resistance fighters have been dubbed pirates by their invaders, and dealt with accordingly.

There's something of all of these contexts in the piracy recounted by this gripping collection of historical accounts, set mostly off the coast of China from the early 1800s to the 1930s. This is of course the period of declining Imperial Chinese power in the face of the West's unstoppable seaborne mercantilism, when Britain joins with the other naval powers of Europe and America to force their way into Chinese ports and markets, quelling resistance with the Opium Wars.

Look at a good map of the waters around Canton, Hong Kong and Macau and the coasts to the north and south where most of these accounts take place, and you'll see what a pirates' paradise they are – indented and strewn with channels, islands and reefs. On this rugged coast with its hundreds of hideaways it's impossible to tell which of the myriad fishing or trading junks is a pirate – until they've hurled their grappling irons and pyrotechnics and are swarming on board with spears and swords and crude firearms!

The breakdown of Chinese authority in the face of Western intrusion is a factor in the lawlessness of these coasts, and much of the piracy here is a seaborne variant of the old protection racket – pay up or we'll plunder and pillage. Most of the victims are Chinese, and we don't hear from them first-hand since most are illiterate fishermen or villagers. The voices we hear are all Western ones, raised in indignation when this plague of piracy spills over and threatens their interests, ships, cargoes and lives.

In this collection you'll hear from admirals and administrators, merchants, customs men and sea captains as they fight back against the pirates. You'll even meet a young Anglican bishop who joins the famous white rajah, James Brooke, to hunt down the Ilanun (sea-Dayak) pirates of Borneo, in the book's only excursion away from the China coast. Enjoying the advantages of steam power and artillery, our bloodthirsty bishop praises the Lord *and* his double-barrelled Terry's breechloader.

Most revealing are the voices of hapless Westerners who survived capture and ransom by the pirates – including the delicate Frenchwoman Fanny Loviot – since they take us closest to the lives of the outlaws. So too the early 20th-century journalist who meets the extraordinary 'queen of the Macao pirates' on the decks of her own junk. It's not quite ethnography – colonial-era prejudices are too ingrained for that – but it allows a glimpse of the renegades as human beings of a sort. It's a welcome counterpoint to the prevailing brutality of the times, dished out by the lawless and law enforcers alike.

A century on from the period covered by this collection – a period that was one of the low points in the power and prestige of the world's oldest civilisation – few will read this book without reflecting on the very different relations between a re-emergent China and the West today. Some might reflect upon how much Western attitudes and assumptions in that earlier period – conveyed throughout these pages – influenced today's China and its view of the West.

Thankfully piracy is nowhere as rampant today – although not all makers of luxury goods, music, films and computer programs would agree!

Mary-Louise Williams, Director
Australian National Maritime Museum

COMPILER'S NOTES AND ACKNOWLEDGEMENTS

The pirate outrages portrayed in this book were carried out by brutal men, except for one, a woman, who was just as brutish. The victims were innocent Europeans and hundreds of innocent Chinese men, women and children.

Over many years ships on voyages to and from Australia feared bad weather and pirates. Sightings of them near Australia have been recorded, however the main cause of trouble was in the China Seas to the north of Australia. In the 1840s it was the Royal Navy, stationed in the Crown Colony of Hong Kong under the Command of Admiral Sir James Stirling, the first Governor of the Territory of Western Australia, who helped to quieten the pirates and directed the famous rescue of Fanny Loviot. Many were not so lucky.

The awfulness of pirates never occurred to me as a boy enthralled with the adventures of Jim Hawkins, Long John Silver, Captain Kidd and others of that period. I was unaware of the true life and times of pirates when I dressed up as a pirate for a least three fancy dress birthday parties. Years later I again dressed up as a pirate for the Fancy Dress Ball held just after Bombay on the last homeward voyage of the P&O *Strathnaver.* I remember the Staff Captain groaning as he cast an eye over my costume and the many other colourful pirates on the dance floor. It seemed everyone had the same costume idea. The Staff Captain told me he was looking forward to his next ship on the P&O Far East Service, where, 'Thank heavens, pirate costumes are banned on that run.' You will soon know why when you read the true stories in this book.

I was unusually fortunate in my preliminary research for historical and literary narratives to discover quite by chance Christie's New York sale catalogue of the important Wichita Driscoll Piracy Collection, sold to benefit the Wichita Public Library in December 2000. One might think that a piracy collection of rare printed books, manuscripts, prints and drawings would have grown up with the smell of the sea in the air. Strange to relate that Charles E. Driscoll did sense the sea; even though he grew up on a Kansas farm, he was able to trace an ancestor who was a pirate on the Spanish Main. The Driscoll Collection contained a particularly fine selection of true first hand accounts of savage piracy relevant to the China Seas. I was able to include two of those stories in this anthology and was guided to others.

A brief note here is necessary in order to explain a few minor but important points about my editing. I have as usual, followed the spelling and punctuation of the original extracts (this is always of interest to many readers), altering them only when it seemed essential to do so for the sake of clearness. Omissions of short passages have been denoted by ellipses (...) in the text. I have used the writer's own spelling of proper names and place names in China, as these have been changed many times since 1949.

I wish here to express my gratitude to the following for their help and encouragement in the preparation of this book and in particular to Middy Dumper, but for whose skilled typing and advice it would never have been written.

Jane Fraser and Naama Amram at Fremantle Press, Mary-Louise Williams at Australian National Maritime Museum, David and Beverley Bird, Hanna and Bella Parsons, Kerry Dowdell, Michael Dumper, Jane Dumper, John Cecil, Kevin Keys, Frank Cascuna, Annabelle Pau, Lee Hulko, Michael Jardine, Brian and Sally Malone, Philip Tan Hai Lee, Andrew Gardner and Darren Delaney have all taken a lively interest in the progress of this book.

The principal sources of which use has been made is also gratefully acknowledged: The Vaughan Evans Library at the Australian National Maritime Museum; The Mitchell Library in the State Library of New South Wales; The Fisher Library, University of Sydney, Newtown; The Reid Library and The Scholars Centre, University of Western Australia; The State Library of Western Australia, Perth; The Chinese Unit, Asian Collections, Printed Books and Newspaper Collections at the National Library of Australia, Canberra; The University of Hong Kong Main Library, The Hung On-To Memorial Library and The Robert Black College at the University of Hong Kong; The Hong Kong Public Libraries at Central and Kowloon; Hong Kong Port and Maritime Board; Merchant Navy Officer's Guild Hong Kong and The Biblioteca de Macau at Macao. The British Library, in London and Boston Spa, together with The Library of Congress in Washington DC, have all been most helpful in supplying copy of rare narrative from their collections.

For reliable general reference I found the following works useful: *The Dictionary of National Biography 1901–1930*, published by Oxford University Press, 1885 to 1980 and the *Supplements* to the present. *Who's Who*, and *Who*

Was Who, Volumes I to VII for 1897 to 1980, together with *A Cumulated Index 1897-1980,* all published by Adam and Charles Black of London. *The Navy List 1815-1918,* The Admiralty, London. *The Royal Naval Biography,* London 1824. William O'Byrne, *A Naval Biographical Dictionary,* London, 1849. Sir W. Laird Clowes, *The Royal Navy: A History from the Earliest to the Present,* London, 1897–1903. *Webster's Biographical Dictionary* for 1963 and 1974, Springfield, Massachusetts. *The Dictionary of American Biography 1928–1955,* Charles Scribner's Sons, New York, 1955. *The American Librarian Association Portrait Index,* Library of Congress, Washington DC, 1908. Carl Crow, *The Travellers' Handbook for China,* Shanghai, 1913. Samuel Couling, *The Encyclopaedia Sincia,* Oxford University Press, 1917. Arthur H. Smith, *Chinese Characteristics,* Canton (n.d.). J. Dyer Ball, *Things Chinese,* Shanghai & Hong Kong, 1936. *The Journal of the China Branch of the Royal Asiatic Society* 1864–1948, and the famous 11th Edition of *The Encyclopaedia Britannica,* the last to be published in England by the University of Cambridge.

I hope you enjoy this anthology of rare stories as much as I did putting it together.

Douglas R.G. Sellick
Lower King, Western Australia
Summer 2010

INTRODUCTION

A SHORT HISTORY OF PIRACY ON THE CHINA SEAS

S. CHARLES HILL

Piracy has always been looked upon as a crime, not merely against the laws of the particular country to which the pirates belong, but also against universal law and, accordingly, pirates are said to be enemies of the whole human race. From this it can be easily understood why all nations are interested in the suppression of piracy and why Great Britain, with her worldwide trade everywhere exposed to piratical attack, has had more to do with the suppression of this form of crime than any other nation ...

This universal concurrent jurisdiction over the whole of the sea has been exercised and is still exercised by all nations. Unfortunately there have been cases in which the men who turned pirates were driven to resort to piracy by circumstances beyond their own control, and thus it will appear that the Chinese and Malay pirates, who were suppressed largely by British, Dutch, French, Spanish, Portuguese and American intervention, looked upon themselves in the first case as patriots and in the second as men waging an ancestral and legitimate war against all nations.

The present article deals with piracy in the China seas; i.e., that portion of the ocean included between China, Japan, the Philippines and the Malay Archipelago. The eastern coast of China is broken by the mouths of a number of great rivers, down which thousands of vessels carried the produce of a rich and fertile country, a mass of wealth which excited the greed of the outlaws who found easy and secure hiding-places in the creeks on the coast itself or in the near-by islands.

Pirates infested the China seas for some centuries, not only plundering vessels at sea but ravaging the coasts of China and Japan indiscriminately. China, however, suffered more than Japan. China was the richer country and offered greater choice of booty. The officials in her seaports were corrupt and ill-treated the Japanese merchants who came to trade, driving them to make reprisals and to ally themselves with the bad characters who swarmed upon the coast.

At this time Japan acknowledged the sovereignty of China, and the Japanese government, eager to establish a legitimate trade, did everything it could to check the Japanese pirates, allowing only such ships to trade as carried Chinese passes and, when it sent ships with tribute, putting on board, for the Chinese authorities to punish, as many Japanese pirates as it had succeeded in arresting. When the prisoners were brought ashore, the Chinese threw them alive into cauldrons of boiling water, a mode of execution which probably accounts for the piratical preference for death to surrender. Since the Japanese ships carried, not only tribute, but a large amount of cargo belonging to their government, they generally flew a flag on which was imprinted the name of their war-god, Hachiman, the characters of which, as read by the Chinese, signified "pirate-ships." Having once been driven from trade to piracy, these Japanese ships did not limit their operations to the coast of China, but cruised as far south as the Straits of Malacca. As late as the year 1605, the fleet of Sir Edward Michelborne met one of them off the east coast of the Malay Peninsula, and John Davis, the famous English navigator, was killed in a fight that occurred on that occasion.

It was on shore, however, that the Japanese pirates did most damage. They came in large squadrons, using Japanese flags and signals. The men, whether Japanese or Chinese, wore Japanese dress – red coats and yellow caps. In parties of fifty or sixty, divided into squads of ten, of whom not more than three were Japanese, they raided the country, accepting battle against any odds and never defeated; for, if overpowered, they fought until the last of them was killed. The Chinese soldiers could not face them man to man, for they were trained to use only one sword whilst the Japanese fought with two; and the Chinese commanders were outwitted by their artfulness in laying ambushes, spreading false intelligence of their movements and baffling pursuit by means of skilfully set decoys of women or booty. The pirates treated with great cruelty the prisoners whom they took in arms but showed so much kindness to the people living round their fastnesses that they were freely furnished with provisions and with information to guide them in their raids. When secure from any danger of attack, they indulged in drunkenness and debauchery, but always paid the strictest obedience to their leaders, who divided, according to the courage and good conduct of individuals, whatever booty had been taken. It was not until 1555 that the depredations of these Japanese pirates came to an end ...

Besides the Chinese and Japanese pirates in the China

seas, there were many of other nations at this time. Arabs and traders from Gujarat, in western India, had trafficked with China for ages, and many of them were pirates. To these were now added the Portuguese, who arrived at Canton first in 1517. They claimed that they wished only to trade and that quarrels arose owing to the attempted extortions of the Chinese officials. Whatever the cause of the rupture may have been, the Portuguese commanders plundered villages and carried off prisoners, whom they sold as slaves. Other Portuguese commanders were pirates pure and simple. For instance, Antonio da Faria, who in 1540 came to take revenge upon a pirate of Gujarat who had wronged him, then turned pirate and attempted to plunder the tombs of the emperors near Peking. So also Fernão Mendes Pinto, who claimed to be one of the three Portuguese who discovered Japan in 1542 and taught the Japanese how to make and use muskets. In revenge for the outrages committed by the Portuguese, the Chinese surprised and destroyed two large Portuguese settlements.

The Spaniards appeared in the China seas almost as soon as the Portuguese. Less piratical in their conduct, they were even more ardent proselytizers and therefore as much hated as the Portuguese. Occupying the Philippines about 1571, they interfered with the Chinese pirates who had been accustomed to resort to those islands. In 1574 on November 30, the Spanish fort at Manila was suddenly attacked by two thousand pirates under one Sioko, the Japanese lieutenant of the famous Chinese pirate Limahon. It was only the fall of Sioko as he led the stormers and the unexpected appearance of Spanish reinforcements and a Chinese fleet that saved the settlement.

So terrible was the state of affairs in the China seas that we find Sir Humphrey Gilbert in 1576 giving it as a chief reason for the search for the Northwest Passage as an alternative route to the East ...

Hitherto the piracy was merely robbery at sea committed by outlaws, but in the seventeenth century the ranks of the latter were swollen by crowds of men who considered themselves to be, not pirates, but patriots. For many years the vast kingdom of China had been slowly overrun and conquered by the Manchus, or Tartars, and now in the far south the Ming princes – the last representatives of the native rulers – were making a final stand against the invaders. Since many of their adherents had in despair taken to the sea, it was only natural that an alliance with the pirates should suggest itself, if only there could be found a pirate chief of sufficient power to control the whole lawless mass.

Such a man was found in Cheng Chih-lung. This extraordinary personage is said to have been born of poor parents. His poverty took him to Macao, where he became a Christian, took the name of Nicholas Gaspard and inherited a large fortune from his Portuguese godfather. After serving the Dutch in Formosa as an interpreter, he went to an uncle in Japan and married a Japanese woman. In one of his uncle's ships he joined a Chinese pirate who, oddly enough for a pirate, devoted much attention to opening up those parts of Formosa that were not occupied by the Dutch. On his death, in 1627, Cheng Chih-lung was elected his successor.

Once in command, he speedily gathered all the pirates under his flag and in a few years was practically in control of all the trade on the southeast coast of China. The Tartar authorities now applied to the Dutch for assistance, which was readily granted; for the Dutch, then the most influential of European nations in the East, resented Cheng Chih-lung's encroachment upon their trade. This official interference on the side of the oppressor ... was the first cause of that hatred for Europeans which has characterized the common people of China up to the present day ...

For the next hundred years the pirates in these seas were simply pirates, known to Europeans as "ladrones" and limiting their attentions to native craft. But all this time, in the mysterious way that appears to be universal amongst subject peoples, there was at work a secret society, formed about the year 1674, to free China from the Manchu control. This was the *Thian-ti-hui*, or Hung League, whose motto was "Obey Heaven and work righteousness." Its leaders were the descendants of Chinese patriots who had fled southward to Tongking and, having no other means of livelihood, had turned pirates, maintaining, however, their connections with their countrymen and enlisting members in all the southern provinces, not only among the seafaring population but even amongst the lower officials in the very offices of the Mandarins on shore. Naturally, however, their influence was greatest amongst the sailors and ladrones, who, finding themselves so well supported, began to show greater boldness. The first attack upon Europeans occurred in 1796, when twenty-six ladrone boats took an English vessel and tortured and killed Captain Roberts and his crew. Only one man was spared and, the ship he was on falling into the hands of the Tartar officials at Ningpo, he was kindly treated and restored to his countrymen, whilst the ladrones, who were regarded as rebels, were put to death. This incident is important, since it shows that at this time the Tartar officials were not hostile to Europeans as such, but that, on the other hand, the ladrone pirates or patriots looked upon Europeans as the allies of their Manchu oppressors.

Towards the end of the eighteenth century, the rulers of Tongking, at the request of the Chinese government, expelled the pirates who had sheltered in their territory. They, with their Tongkingese companions, united under the leadership of a Chinaman named Ching Yih and made their headquarters in the islands of Hainan and Formosa, from which they harassed all ships passing south or north. The Tartar admirals made desperate efforts to destroy Ching Yih, but with so little success that, when he was drowned in a storm, in 1807, his widow succeeded to the undisputed command of his forces.

These were divided into six squadrons, distinguished by their flags; i.e., red, black, yellow, green, blue and black-and-white. The squadrons were massed in two fleets: the red under the widow's favorite commander, Chang Paou, originally a fisher-boy whom Ching Yih had picked up at sea; the black under one Opotae, or Apotsye. The two fleets contained in all from eighteen to nineteen hundred swift and strong-masted vessels, some of which were of five to six hundred tons. Each ship carried twenty or thirty guns and from three to four hundred men, armed with long, curved swords and spears. A favorite device of the pirates, when attacking or repelling boats, was to throw fishing-nets over them so as to entangle the crew. A launch of

H.M.S. *Dover* was nearly taken in this way in 1808.

The desperate resolution of the ladrones attracted the admiration of all foreigners. In 1805, when the brig *Nancy* took a ladrone boat, it was only after the Portuguese commander had cut down the pirate captain with his own hands and half his crew lay dead around him. Even then, three women, wives of the captain, killed themselves rather than be taken.

The wealth of the ladrones was derived not only from the booty taken in fight but also largely from blackmail paid for passes sold to merchantmen by the agents of the pirates in Macao, Canton and other ports. These passes were always scrupulously honored, unlike those granted by the Barbary pirates in the Mediterranean. The ladrones treated their commanders, even when they were women, with almost superstitious reverence, refrained from plundering temples, offered up prayers before going into action and forced their prisoners to make presents to the priests when they were about to be released on ransom. Amongst themselves they observed strict rules, the penalty of the breach of which was invariably death. Thus no pirate might go ashore without permission; the first man to board a prize was to be allowed first choice in the division of booty; all booty was to be registered and equally divided; of money taken, one-fifth went to the captors and four-fifths to the general fund; all provisions and stores taken from the common people were to be honestly paid for; woman prisoners, if not ransomed, were sold to the pirates as wives or concubines, and indiscriminate intercourse with female captives was forbidden; male prisoners were allowed to choose between joining the pirates and being put to death.

On the other hand, the ladrones treated with great cruelty those who refused to supply them with stores or to pay blackmail and those who offered a vigorous resistance. The hearts of the latter they sometimes cut out, cooked and ate with rice. They regarded as enemies, not only the Tartars, but also any of their countrymen who assisted the Tartars and all foreigners who traded with China.

At first the Tartar authorities, too proud to ask officially for European assistance, were satisfied with reporting to court fictitious victories, but in 1809 some Siamese vessels bringing tribute to the court were taken by the ladrones, a misfortune not to be concealed nor repaired by unaided efforts. The Mandarins had, however, noticed the success of the Portuguese vessels in dealing with ladrone attacks and they reflected that, since Macao was in Chinese, and not foreign, territory – it did not become Portuguese until 1845 – they could save their national dignity by demanding Portuguese assistance. An English vessel, the *Mercury*, was engaged by the Portuguese and manned largely by American volunteers. In a fifteen-days' cruise it cleared the Canton River, and then, since the English refused to lend it any longer, the Portuguese manned eight or ten vessels of their own to assist the Mandarin fleets.

The latter were of little use, but the Portuguese did sufficient damage to the pirates to create diffidence, recriminations and quarrels amongst the pirate leaders, which were carefully fostered by government spies and emissaries. Apotsye had long been jealous of Chang Paou and, finding himself in a temporary superiority, destroyed one of Chang's squadrons. Chang's sailors fought to the last, their ships sank with their decks swimming with blood, but Apotsye's fleet was so crippled that, early in 1810, in fear of Chang's vengeance, he surrendered with one hundred junks and eight thousand men to the Tartar authorities. Soon after, the Portuguese destroyed Chang's sacred junk. On it were his priests and a wonderful image, which his followers had been unable to lift from its pedestal in an ancient temple, but which had come willingly as soon as Chang touched it. Chang was so disheartened by his loss that, when he found himself surrounded by the Portuguese and Mandarin fleets and the Portuguese commander agreed to guarantee terms, he persuaded Ching Yih's widow to surrender with two hundred and seventy ships, sixteen thousand men, five thousand women and twelve hundred guns. The pirate fleet sailed up to Canton with flags and colors flying in triumphal fashion. Both Chang and Apotsye received official rank and were set to clear the coast of pirates. As a result, no piratical leader of importance was heard of for some years, and the wild characters of the coast turned from piracy to smuggling.

The most lucrative article to smuggle was opium, and the best quality of opium came from British India. Its introduction was prohibited by the Chinese authorities, partly perhaps on moral grounds, but more in the interests of the native growers and from a desire to hamper the operations of foreign merchants. Constant quarrels resulted between the Mandarins and the Europeans, especially the British, who were most concerned in the opium trade. As is well known, this led to a war between China and Britain, on the conclusion of which, in 1842, China ceded the island of Hongkong, which had for ages been a piratical haunt, to the conquerors.

The British thereupon forbade any Chinese vessels to enter the port without passes from the Chinese authorities, whilst they allowed all vessels registering at Hongkong to fly the British flag. But in China the cession of national territory to foreigners was resented, and the officials were angry because the British flag protected so many vessels from their extortions. The Chinese accordingly refused passes to respectable merchants and hampered trade in every way, whilst they encouraged bad characters to come to Hongkong.

As a result, the ships on the Hongkong register very often abused the protection of the British flag by committing acts of piracy as soon as they were out of British waters, and the opium- and gambling-dens in Hongkong itself, ill controlled by the corrupt and inefficient Chinese police, served as headquarters from which pirates could obtain information about the movements of vessels that they might profitably attack. In short, the main result of the war had been to unite all classes of Chinese against foreigners. It is said that, of all foreigners, the ladrones hated most the Americans, because they had volunteered on the *Mercury*, though the ladrones had not injured them. Next to the Americans they hated the English in consequence of the war. In 1854, when they took the Dutch bark *Paul Johann*, they told the captain that they would not have touched him had he flown the Dutch flag, but that they would have killed every man on board, had his ship been English.

At this time the Hung League was better known as the "Triad Society," or *san-ho-hui*. Its symbol was the Chinese character for the word *wang* (meaning prince), of which the three horizontal lines joined by a vertical line were taken to represent the union of heaven, earth and man. As before, the Chinese authorities looked upon the Triads, as the ladrones were now called, as rebels, whilst they called themselves patriots and Europeans called them pirates. In 1849 two of their leaders became notorious. These were Cheung Shap-ng-tsai and Chui-appoo, the latter of whom, according to a Chinese account, had become a pirate only because the British had put a price on his head for the murder of some British officers who had insulted one of his female relatives. Under these leaders the ladrones did so much damage to trade that the British – assisted later by the Americans – gladly sent war-ships to aid the Mandarins in their suppression. Between May and October, 1849, the British alone destroyed fifty-seven pirate junks and killed nine hundred and four pirates. The ladrones under this pressure retreated south to the Gulf of Tongking, and there Shap-ng-tsai's fleet was destroyed. Though the ladrones showed the most desperate bravery, returning again and again to the junks from which they had been driven, the British did not lose a single man on this occasion. Shap-ng-tsai's vessel was blown up, but he got safely ashore and soon after surrendered with six of his commanders to the Chinese authorities, who pardoned him and gave him an official post. Chui-appoo held out until the next year and then, being defeated, he fled ashore. For the sake of the price set on his head, some of his countrymen seized him in Chinese territory and took him to Hongkong. The court there sentenced him to transportation for life, a punishment which he considered to be an insult, so that he hanged himself in jail in March, 1851.

The British successes had been largely due to information supplied by Mr. Robert Caldwell, who, in September, 1848, had been appointed by Sir George Bonham, governor of Hongkong, to organize a detective department. As a rule, when the ladrones assembled in fleets, Caldwell was able, through his native spies, to pass word to the British war-ships in time to effect a surprise, though on occasion, when they came up with the ladrones, it was only to be informed by a Chinese official that the ladrones had surrendered and were now good subjects. There was, however, a good deal of more serious fighting. In 1854 an expedition against the Triads, financed by some rich Canton merchants, was defeated and five hundred persons were decapitated. In January, 1855, the Triads destroyed forty-four large imperialist war-junks in the Pearl River. On the other hand, in March of the same year, Chinese volunteers from Canton defeated a ladrone chief, destroying ninety-three and bringing back in triumph one hundred and thirty-seven of his vessels. The Chinese traders of Ningpo and Shanghai were so grateful for the destruction of a piratical fleet at Shihpu by H.M.S. *Bittern* that they presented the British officers with $23,000 as well as $5,000 for the widowed mother of the only officer killed and $1,000 for every sailor who had lost a limb in the fight. It was calculated that in this year alone above eighty thousand of the rebels and pirates ashore and afloat were killed in one way or another besides some thousands who committed suicide at places near their homes, to which they were considerately taken by their captors, so that their relatives might give then honorable burial.

About 1853 piracy in the Canton River showed itself

in a new form. This was the seizure of vessels by pirates who went on board disguised as passengers. In July of that year the *Aratoon Apcar* was thus seized three days after she left Hongkong for England. All the Europeans on board were murdered, but the *lascar* crew was allowed to take the plundered vessel back to Hongkong. The packet-boats plying in the river were peculiarly exposed to this danger and, for safety's sake, kept their passengers under armed watch either in the hold or locked in iron cages on the deck.

In 1853 the activity of Chinese and European war-ships was not considered sufficient protection against pirates by the country traders. Their ships were accustomed to sail in fleets under the convoy of armed vessels, generally manned and commanded by Portuguese. These convoymen used to charge somewhat extortionate fees for their services and, not satisfied with what they obtained in a more or less legitimate manner, went so far as to attack and plunder many innocent traders under the pretence that they were pirates. Complaints to the Portuguese authorities at Ningpo and Macao produced no result. It was even said that offenders caught red-handed and delivered to the Portuguese were set free ...

For some time longer the Chinese newspapers were full of accounts of the destruction of pirate vessels and even pirate fleets by British and other European war-ships. The British naturally depended for information on the Chinese authorities, who took a malicious pleasure in misleading them to attack vessels afterwards proved to be only smugglers or even innocent traders, whose only offence was attempting to evade official extortion. So great was the scandal that the British government was forced to issue a strict order to its naval officers not to attack any vessel of whose piratical character they had not previously received incontrovertible proof. Under former circumstances this would have made the suppression of piracy impossible, but, now that steam-vessels had arrived in the China seas, a slight delay in taking action was not of much importance. In Hongkong itself, in the year 1867, Indian police were substituted for Chinese, and the gambling- and opium-dens properly controlled, so that they ceased to serve as centers from which the pirates could obtain intelligence.

From this time, then, it may be said that piracy on a big scale, being very dangerous, as well as no longer lucrative, practically ceased. The common use of steam-vessels makes it improbable that pirate fleets like those of Cheng Chih-lung and Koxinga, Ching Yih, Shap-ng-tsai and Chui-appoo will ever again take the sea, but the success of the German raiders in the World War shows what can be done in single vessels by daring and desperate men. That there are in China men who would seize the opportunity if it were offered, is shown by such incidents as the seizure of the British vessels *Kwang Lee* and *Suian*, on December 15, 1921, and November 19, 1922, respectively, by pirates disguised as Chinese passengers. In the former case the pirates got off with booty worth $120,000; in the latter – and this time the leader of the band was a woman – with booty worth £80,000.

From Pirates of the China Seas: Adventures of East and West in quelling Sea-Roving Enemies of the Human Race by S. Charles Hill, *Asia Magazine*, Volume XXIV, April 1924, New York.

CHAPTER ONE

THE TERRIBLE LADRONES

RICHARD GLASSPOOLE
4TH MATE OF THE *MARQUIS OF ELY*

On the 17th of September, 1809, the Honorable Company's ship *Marquis of Ely* anchored under the island of Sam Chow, in China, about twelve English miles from Macao, where I was ordered to proceed in one of our cutters to procure a pilot, and also to land the purser with the packet. I left the ship at 5 p.m. with seven men under my command, well armed. It blew a fresh gale from the N.E. We arrived at Macao at 9 p.m., where I delivered the packet to Mr. Roberts [ship's agent], and sent the men with the boat's sails to sleep under the Company's Factory, and left the boat in charge of one of the Compradore's men; during the night the gale increased. At half-past three in the morning I went to the beach, and found the boat on shore half-filled with water, in consequence of the man having left her. I called the people, and baled her out; found she was considerably damaged, and very leaky. At half-past 5 a.m., the ebb-tide making, we left Macao with vegetables for the ship.

I had every reason to expect the ship in the roads, as she was preparing to get under weigh when we left her; but on our rounding Cabaretta-Point, we saw her five or six miles to leeward, under weigh, standing on the starboard tack ... Bore up, and stood towards her; when about a cable's length to windward of her, she tacked; we hauled our wind and stood after her ... We soon lost sight of the ship, leaving us in a very critical situation, having no anchor, and drifting bodily on the rocks to leeward ...

At this time not a ship in sight; the weather clearing up, we saw a ship to leeward, hull down, shipped our masts, and made sail towards her; she proved to be the Honorable Company's ship *Glatton*. We made signals to her with our handkerchiefs at the mast-head, she unfortunately took no notice of them, but tacked and stood from us. Our situation was now truly distressing, night closing fast, with a threatening appearance, blowing fresh, with hard rain and a heavy sea; our boat very leaky, without a compass, anchor or provisions, and drifting fast on a lee-shore, surrounded with dangerous rocks, and inhabited by the most barbarous pirates ...

Tuesday, the 19th, no ships in sight. About ten o'clock in the morning it fell calm, with very hard rain and a heavy swell ... found we had drifted several miles to leeward ... Made sail, and endeavored to reach the weather-shore, and anchor with six muskets we had lashed together for that purpose ... and anchored about 1 a.m., close under the land in five or six fathoms water, blowing fresh, with hard rain.

Wednesday, the 20th, at daylight, supposing the flood-tide making, weighed and stood over to the weather-land, but found we were drifting fast to leeward. About ten o'clock perceived two Chinese boats steering for us. Bore up, and stood towards them, and made signals to induce them to come within hail; on nearing them, they bore up, and passed to leeward of the islands. The Chinese we had in the boat advised me to follow them, and he would take us to Macao by the leeward passage. I expressed my fears of being taken by the ladrones. Our ammunition being wet, and the muskets rendered useless, we had nothing to defend ourselves with but cutlasses, and in too distressed a situation to make much resistance with them, having been constantly wet, and eaten nothing but a few green oranges for three days.

As our present situation was a hopeless one, and the man assured me there was no fear of encountering any ladrones, I complied with his request, and stood in to leeward of the islands, where we found the water much smoother, and apparently a direct passage to Macao. We continued pulling and sailing all day. At six o'clock in the evening I discovered three large boats at anchor in a bay to leeward. On seeing us they weighed and made sail towards us. The Chinese said they were ladrones, and that if they captured us they would most certainly put us all to death! Finding they gained fast on us, struck the masts, and pulled head to wind for five or six hours. The tide turning against us, anchored close under the land to avoid being seen. Soon after we saw the boats pass us to leeward.

Thursday, the 21st, at daylight, the flood making, weighed and pulled along shore in great spirits, expecting to be at Macao in two or three hours, as by the Chinese account it was not above six or seven miles distant. After pulling a mile or two perceived several people on shore, standing close to the beach; they were armed with pikes and lances. I ordered the interpreter to hail them, and ask the most direct passage to Macao. They said if we came on shore they would inform us; not liking their hostile appearance, I did not think proper to comply with the request. Saw a large fleet of boats at anchor close under the opposite shore. Our interpreter said they were fishing-boats, and that by going there we should not only get provisions, but a pilot also to take us to Macao.

I bore up, and on nearing them perceived there were some large vessels, very full of men, and mounted with several guns. I hesitated to approach nearer; but the Chinese assuring me they were Mandarin junks [*Junk* is the Canton pronunciation of *chuen*, ship] and salt-boats, we stood close to one of them, and asked the way to Macao. They gave no answer, but made some signs to us to go in shore. We passed on, and a large rowboat pulled after us; she soon came alongside, when about twenty savage-looking villains, who were stowed at the bottom of the boat, leaped on board us. They were armed with a short sword in each hand, one of which they laid on our necks, and the other pointed to our breasts, keeping their eyes fixed on their officer, waiting his signal to cut or desist. Seeing we were incapable of making any resistance, he sheathed his sword, and the others immediately followed his example. They then dragged us into their boat, and carried us on board one of their junks, with the most savage demonstrations of joy, and as we supposed, to torture and put us to a cruel death. When on board the junk, they searched all our pockets, took the handkerchiefs from our necks, and brought heavy chains to chain us to the guns.

At this time a boat came, and took me, with one of my men and the interpreter, on board the chief's vessel. I was then taken before the chief. He was seated on deck, in a large chair, dressed in purple silk, with a black turban on. He appeared to be about thirty years of age, a stout commanding-looking man. He took me by the coat, and drew me close to him; then questioned the interpreter very strictly, asking who we were, and what was our business in that part of the country. I told him to say we were Englishmen in distress, having been four days at sea without provisions. This he would not credit, but said we were bad men, and that he would put us all to death; and then ordered some men to put the interpreter to the torture until he confessed the truth.

Upon this occasion, a ladrone, who had been once to England and spoke a few words of English, came to the chief, and told him we were really Englishmen, and that we had plenty of money, adding, that the buttons on my coat were gold. The chief then ordered us some coarse brown rice, of which we made a tolerable meal, having eat nothing for nearly four days, except a few green oranges. During our repast, a number of ladrones crowded round us, examining our clothes and hair, and giving us every possible annoyance. Several of them brought swords, and laid them on our necks, making signs that they would soon take us on shore, and cut us in pieces, which I am sorry to say was the fate of some hundreds during my captivity.

I was now summoned before the chief, who had been conversing with the interpreter; he said I must write to my captain, and tell him, if he did not send a hundred thousand dollars for our ransom, in ten days he would put us all to death. In vain did I assure him it was useless writing unless he would agree to take a much smaller sum; saying we were all poor men, and the most we could possibly raise would not exceed two thousand dollars. Finding that he was much exasperated at my expostulations, I embraced the offer of writing to inform my commander of our unfortunate situation, though there appeared not the least probability of relieving us. They said the letter should be conveyed to Macao in a fishing-boat, which would bring an answer in the morning. A small boat accordingly came alongside, and took the letter.

About six o'clock in the evening they gave us some rice and a little salt fish, which we ate, and they made signs for us to lay down on the deck to sleep; but such numbers of ladrones were constantly coming from different vessels to see us, and examine our clothes and hair, they would not allow us a moment's quiet. They were particularly anxious for the buttons of my coat, which were new, and as they supposed gold. I took it off, and laid it on the deck to avoid being disturbed by them; it was taken away in the night, and I saw it on the next day stripped of its buttons.

About nine o'clock a boat came and hailed the chief's vessel; he immediately hoisted his mainsail, and the fleet weighed apparently in great confusion. They worked to windward all night and part of the next day, and anchored about one o'clock in a bay under the island of Lantow, where the head admiral of ladrones was lying at anchor, with about two hundred vessels and a Portuguese brig they had captured a few days before, and murdered the captain and part of the crew.

Saturday, the 23rd, early in the morning, a fishing-boat came to the fleet to inquire if they had captured an European boat; being answered in the affirmative, they came to the vessel I was in. One of them spoke a few words of English, and told me he had a ladrone-pass, and was sent by Captain Kay in search of us; I was rather surprised to find he had no letter. He appeared to be well acquainted with the chief, and remained in his cabin smoking opium, and playing cards all the day.

In the evening I was summoned with the interpreter before the Chief. He questioned us in a much milder tone, saying, he now believed we were Englishmen, a people he wished to be friendly with; and that if our captain would lend him seventy thousand dollars 'till he returned from his cruise up the river, he would repay him, and send us all to Macao. I assured him it was useless writing on those terms, and unless our ransom was speedily settled, the English fleet would sail, and render our enlargement altogether ineffectual. He remained determined, and said if it were not sent, he would keep us, and make us fight, or put us to death. I accordingly wrote, and gave my letter to the man belonging to the boat before mentioned. He said he could not return with an answer in less than five days.

The chief now gave me the letter I wrote when first taken. I have never been able to ascertain his reasons for detaining it, but suppose he dare not negotiate for our ransom without orders from the head admiral, who I understood was sorry at our being captured. He said the English ships would join the Mandarins and attack them. He told the chief that captured us, to dispose of us as he pleased.

Monday, the 24th, it blew a strong gale, with constant hard rain; we suffered much from the cold and wet, being obliged to remain on deck with no covering but an old mat, which was frequently taken from us in the night by the ladrones who were on watch. During the night the Portuguese who were left in the brig murdered the ladrones that were on board of her, cut the cables, and fortunately escaped through the darkness of the night. I have since been informed they ran her on shore near Macao.

Tuesday, the 25th, at daylight in the morning, the fleet, amounting to about five hundred sail of different sizes, weighed, to proceed on their intended cruise up the rivers, to levy contributions on the towns and villages. It is impossible to describe what were my feelings at this critical time, having received no answers to my letters, and the fleet under-way to sail, hundreds of miles up a country never visited by Europeans, there to remain probably for many months, which would render all opportunities of negotiating for our enlargement totally ineffectual; as the only method of communication is by boats, that have a pass from the ladrones, and they dare not venture above twenty miles from Macao, being obliged to come and go in the night, to avoid the Mandarins; and if these boats should be detected in having any intercourse with the ladrones, they are immediately put to death, and all their relations, though they had not joined in the crime, share in the punishment, in order that not a single person of their families should be left to imitate their crimes or revenge their death. This severity renders communication both dangerous and expensive; no boat would venture out for less than a hundred Spanish dollars.

Wednesday, the 26th, at daylight, we passed in sight of our ships at anchor under the island of Chun Po. The chief then called me, pointed to the ships, and told the interpreter to tell us to look at them, for we should never see them again. About noon we entered a river to the westward of the Bogue, three or four miles from the entrance. We passed a large town situated on the side of a beautiful hill, which tributary to the ladrones; the inhabitants saluted them with songs as they passed.

The fleet now divided into two squadrons (the red and the black) and sailed up different branches of the river. At midnight the division we were in anchored close to an immense hill, on the top of which a number of fires were burning, which at daylight I perceived proceeded from a Chinese camp. At the back of the hill was a most beautiful town, surrounded by water, and embellished with groves of orange trees. The chop-house (custom-house) [In the barbarous Chinese-English spoken in Canton, all things are indiscriminately called *chop*] and a few cottages were immediately plundered, and burned down; most of the inhabitants, however, escaped to the camp.

The ladrones now prepared to attack the town with a formidable force, collected in rowboats from the different vessels. They sent a messenger to the town, demanding a tribute of ten thousand dollars annually, saying, if these terms were not complied with, they would land, destroy the town, and murder all the inhabitants; which they would certainly have done, had the town laid in a more advantageous situation for their purpose; but being placed out of the reach of their shot, they allowed them to come to terms. The inhabitants agreed to pay six thousand dollars, which they were to collect by the time of our return down the river. This finesse had the desired effect, for during our absence they mounted a few guns on a hill, which commanded the passage, and gave us in lieu of the dollars a warm salute on our return.

October the 1st, the fleet weighed in the night, dropped by the tide up the river, and anchored very quietly before a town surrounded by a thick wood. Early in the morning the ladrones assembled in rowboats and landed; then gave a shout, and rushed into the town, sword in hand. The inhabitants fled to the adjacent hills, in numbers apparently superior to the ladrones. We may easily imagine to ourselves the horror with which these miserable people must be seized, on being obliged to leave their homes, and everything dear to them. It was a most melancholy sight to see women in tears, clasping their infants in their arms, and imploring mercy for them from those brutal robbers! The old and the sick, who were unable to fly, or to make resistance, were either made prisoners or most inhumanly butchered! The boats continued passing and repassing from the junks to the shore, in quick succession, laden with booty, and the men besmeared with blood! Two hundred and fifty women, and several children, were made prisoners, and sent on board different vessels. They were unable to escape with the men, owing to that abominable practice of cramping their feet: several of them were not able to move without assistance, in fact, they might all be said to totter, rather than walk. Twenty of these poor women were sent on board the vessel I was in; they were hauled on board by the hair, and treated in a most savage manner.

When the chief came on board, he questioned them respecting the circumstances of their friends, and demanded ransoms accordingly, from six thousand to six hundred dollars each. He ordered them a berth on deck, at the after part of the vessel, where they had nothing to shelter them from the weather, which at this time was very variable – the days excessively hot, and the nights cold, with heavy rains. The town being plundered of every thing valuable, it was set on fire, and reduced to ashes by the morning. The fleet remained here three days, negotiating for the ransom of the prisoners, and plundering the fish-tanks and gardens. During all this time, the Chinese never ventured from the hills, though there were frequently not more than a hundred ladrones on shore at a time, and I am sure the people on the hills exceeded ten times that number.

October 5th, the fleet proceeded up another branch of the river, stopping at several small villages to receive tribute, which was generally paid in dollars, sugar and rice, with a few large pigs roasted whole, as presents for their joss [Joss is a Chinese corruption of the Portuguese Dios, God]. Every person on being ransomed, is obliged to present him with a pig, or some fowls, which the priest offers him with prayers; it remains before him a few hours, and is then divided amongst the crew. Nothing particular occurred 'till the 10th, except frequent skirmishes on shore between small parties of ladrones and Chinese soldiers. They frequently obliged my men to go on shore, and fight with the muskets we had when taken, which did great execution, the Chinese principally using bows and arrows. They have match-locks, but use them very unskilfully.

On the 10th, we formed a junction with the black squadron, and proceeded many miles up a wide and beautiful river, passing several ruins of villages that had been destroyed by the black squadron. On the 17th, the fleet anchored abreast four mud batteries, which defended a town, so entirely surrounded with wood that it was impossible to form any idea of its size. The weather was very hazy, with hard squalls of rain. The ladrones remained perfectly quiet for two days. On the third day the forts commenced a brisk fire for several hours: the ladrones did not return a single shot, but weighed in the night and dropped down the river.

The reasons they gave for not attacking the town, or returning the fire, were that Joss had not promised them success. They are very superstitious, and consult their idol on all occasions. If his omens are good, they will undertake the most daring enterprizes.

The fleet now anchored opposite the ruins of the town where the women had been made prisoners. Here we remained five or six days, during which time about a hundred of the women were ransomed; the remainder were offered for sale amongst the ladrones, for forty dollars each. The woman is considered the lawful wife of the purchaser, who would be put to death if he discarded her. Several of them leaped overboard and drowned themselves, rather than submit to such infamous degradation.

The fleet then weighed and made sail down the river, to receive the ransom from the town before mentioned. As we passed the hill, they fired several shots at us, but without effect. The ladrones were much exasperated, and determined to revenge themselves; they dropped out of reach of their shot, and anchored. Every junk sent about a hundred men each on shore, to cut paddy, and destroy their orange-groves, which was most effectually performed for several miles down the river. During our stay here, they received information of nine boats lying up a creek, laden with paddy; boats were immediately dispatched after them.

Next morning these boats were brought to the fleet; ten or twelve men were taken in them. As these had made no resistance, the chief said he would allow them to become ladrones, if they agreed to take the usual oaths before Joss. Three or four of them refused to comply, for which they were punished in the following cruel manner: their hands were tied behind their back, a rope from the mast-head rove through their arms, and hoisted three or four feet from the deck, and five or six men flogged them with three rattans twisted together 'till they were apparently dead; then hoisted them up to the mast-head, and left them hanging nearly an hour, then lowered them down, and repeated the punishment, 'till they died or complied with the oath.

October the 20th, in the night, an express-boat came with the information that a large Mandarin fleet was proceeding up the river to attack us. The chief immediately weighed, with fifty of the largest vessels, and sailed down the river to meet them. About one in the morning they commenced a heavy fire till daylight, when an express was sent for the remainder of the fleet to join them: about an hour after a counter-order to anchor came, the Mandarin fleet having run. Two or three hours afterwards the chief returned with three captured vessels in tow, having sunk two, and eighty-three sail made their escape. The admiral of the Mandarins blew his vessel up, by throwing a lighted match into the magazine as the ladrones were boarding her; she ran on shore, and they succeeded in getting twenty of her guns.

In this action very few prisoners were taken: the men belonging to the captured vessels drowned themselves, as they were sure of suffering a lingering and cruel death if taken after making resistance. The admiral left the fleet in charge of his brother, the second in command, and proceeded with his own vessel towards Lantow. The fleet remained in this river, cutting paddy, and getting the necessary supplies.

On the 28th of October, I received a letter from Captain Kay, brought by a fisherman, who had told him he would get us all back for three thousand dollars. He advised me to offer three thousand, and if not accepted, extend it to four; but not farther, as it was bad policy to offer much at first: at the same time assuring me we should be liberated, let the ransom be what it would. I offered the chief the three thousand, which he disdainfully refused, saying he was not to be played with; and unless they sent ten thousand dollars, and two large guns, with several casks of gunpowder, he would soon put us all to death. I wrote to Captain Kay, and informed him of the chief's determination, requesting if an opportunity offered, to send us a shift of clothes, for which it may be easily imagined we were much distressed, having been seven weeks without a shift; although constantly exposed to the weather, and of course frequently wet.

On the first of November, the fleet sailed up a narrow river, and anchored at night within two miles of a town called Little Whampoa. In front of it was a small fort, and several Mandarin vessels lying in the harbor. The chief sent the interpreter to me, saying I must order my men to make cartridges and clean their muskets, ready to go on shore in the morning. I assured the interpreter I should give the men no such orders, that they must please themselves. Soon after the chief came on board, threatening to put us all to a cruel death if we refused to obey his orders. For my own part I remained determined, and advised the men not to comply, as I thought by making ourselves useful we should be accounted too valuable.

A few hours afterwards he sent to me again, saying, that if myself and the quartermaster would assist them at the great guns, that if also the rest of the men went on shore and succeeded in taking the place, he would then take the money offered for our ransom, and give them twenty dollars for every Chinaman's head they cut off. To these proposals we cheerfully acceded, in hopes of facilitating our deliverance.

Early in the morning the forces intended for landing were assembled in rowboats, amounting in the whole to three or four thousand men. The largest vessels weighed, and hauled in shore, to cover the landing of the forces, and attack the fort and Mandarin vessels. About nine o'clock the action commenced, and continued with great spirit for nearly an hour, when the walls of the fort gave way, and the men retreated in the greatest confusion.

The Mandarin vessels still continued firing, having blocked up the entrance of the harbor to prevent the ladrone boats entering. At this the ladrones were much exasperated, and about three hundred of them swam on shore, with a short sword lashed close under each arm; they then ran along the banks of the river 'till they came abreast of the vessels, and then swam off again and boarded them. The Chinese thus attacked, leaped overboard, and endeavored to reach the opposite shore; the ladrones followed, and cut the greater number of them to pieces in the water. They next towed the vessels out of the harbor, and attacked the town with increased fury. The inhabitants fought about a quarter of an hour, and then retreated to an adjacent hill, from which they were soon driven with great slaughter.

After this the ladrones returned, and plundered the town, every boat leaving it when laden. The Chinese on the hills perceiving most of the boats were off, rallied, and retook the town, after killing near two hundred ladrones. One of my men was unfortunately lost in this dreadful massacre! The ladrones landed a second time, drove the Chinese out of the town, then reduced it to ashes, and put all their prisoners to death, without regarding either age or sex!

I must not omit to mention a most horrid (though ludicrous) circumstance which happened at this place. The ladrones were paid by their chief ten dollars for every Chinaman's head they produced. One of my men turning the corner of a street was met by a ladrone running furiously after a Chinese; he had a drawn sword in his hand, and two Chinamen's heads which he had cut off, tied by their tails, and slung round his neck. I was witness myself to some of them producing five or six to obtain payment!

On the 4th of November an order arrived from the admiral for the fleet to proceed immediately to Lantow, where he was lying with only two vessels, and three Portuguese ships and a brig constantly annoying him; several sail of Mandarin vessels were daily expected. The fleet weighed and proceeded towards Lantow. On passing the island of Lintin, three ships and a brig gave chase to us. The ladrones prepared to board; but night closing we lost sight of them: I am convinced they altered their course and stood from us. These vessels were in the pay of the Chinese government, and style themselves the Invincible

Squadron, cruising in the river Tigris to annihilate the ladrones!

On the fifth, in the morning, the red squadron anchored in a bay under Lantow; the black squadron stood to the eastward. In this bay they hauled several of their vessels on shore to bream their bottoms and repair them.

In the afternoon of the 8th of November, four ships, a brig and a schooner came off the mouth of the bay. At first the pirates were much alarmed, supposing them to be English vessels come to rescue us. Some of them threatened to hang us to the mast-head for them to fire at; and with much difficulty we persuaded them that they were Portuguese. The ladrones had only seven junks in a fit state for action; these they hauled outside, and moored them head and stern across the bay; and manned all the boats belonging to the repairing vessels ready for boarding.

The Portuguese observing these maneuvers hove to, and communicated by boats. Soon afterwards they made sail, each ship firing her broadside as she passed, but without effect, the shot falling far short. The ladrones did not return a single shot, but waved their colors, and threw up rockets, to induce them to come further in, which they might easily have done, the outside junks lying in four fathoms water which I sounded myself: though the Portuguese in their letters to Macao lamented there was not sufficient water for them to engage closer, but that they would certainly prevent their escaping before the Mandarin fleet arrived!

On the 20th of November, early in the morning, I perceived an immense fleet of Mandarin vessels standing for the bay. On nearing us, they formed a line, and stood close in; each vessel as she discharged her guns tacked to join the rear and reload. They kept up a constant fire for about two hours, when one of their largest vessels was blown up by a firebrand thrown from a ladrone junk; after which they kept at a more respectful distance, but continued firing without intermission 'till the 21st at night, when it fell calm.

The ladrones towed out seven large vessels, with about two hundred rowboats to board them; but a breeze springing up, they made sail and escaped. The ladrones returned into the bay, and anchored. The Portuguese and Mandarins followed, and continued a heavy cannonading during that night and the next day. The vessel I was in had her foremast shot away, which they supplied very expeditiously by taking a mainmast from a smaller vessel.

On the 23rd in the evening, it again fell calm; the ladrones towed our fifteen junks in two divisions, with the intention of surrounding them, which was nearly effected, having come up with an boarded one, when a breeze suddenly sprung up. The captured vessel mounted twenty-two guns. Most of her crew leaped overboard; sixty or seventy were taken immediately, cut to pieces and thrown into the river. Early in the morning the ladrones returned into the bay, and anchored in the same situation as before. The Portuguese and Mandarins followed, keeping up a constant fire. The ladrones never returned a single shot, but always kept in readiness to board, and the Portuguese were careful never to allow them an opportunity.

On the 28th, at night, they sent in eight fire-vessels, which if properly constructed must have done great execution, having every advantage they could wish for to effect their purpose; a strong breeze and tide directly into the bay, and the vessels lying so close together that it was impossible to miss them. On their first appearance the ladrones gave a general shout, supposing them to be Mandarin vessels on fire, but were very soon convinced of their mistake. They came very regularly into the center of the fleet, two and two, burning furiously; one of them came alongside of the vessel I was in, but they succeeded in booming her off. She appeared to be a vessel of about thirty tons; her hold was filled with straw and wood, and there were a few small boxes of combustibles on her deck, which exploded alongside of us without doing any damage. The ladrones, however, towed them all on shore, extinguished the fire, and broke them up for fire-wood. The Portuguese claim the credit of constructing these destructive machines, and actually sent a dispatch to the Governor of Macao, saying they had destroyed at least one-third of the ladrones' fleet, and hoped soon to effect their purpose by totally annihilating them!

On the 29th of November, the ladrones being all ready for sea, they weighed and stood boldly out, bidding defiance to the invincible squadron and imperial fleet, consisting of ninety-three war-junks, six Portuguese ships, a brig, and a schooner. Immediately the ladrones weighed, they made all sail. The ladrones chased them two or three hours, keeping up a constant fire; finding they did not come up with them, they hauled their wind and stood to the eastward.

Thus terminated the boasted blockade, which lasted nine days, during which time the ladrones completed all their repairs. In this action not a single ladrone vessel was destroyed, and their loss about thirty or forty men. An American was also killed, one of three that remained out of eight taken in a schooner. I had two very narrow escapes: the first, a twelve-pounder shot fell within three or four feet of me; another took a piece out of a small brass-swivel on which I was standing. The chief's wife frequently sprinkled me with garlic-water, which they consider an effectual charm against shot. The fleet continued under sail all night, steering towards the eastward. In the morning they anchored in a large bay surrounded by lofty and barren mountains.

On the 2nd of December I received a letter from Lieutenant Maughn, commander of the Honorable Company's cruiser *Antelope*, saying that he had the ransom on board, and had been three days cruising after us, and wished me to settle with the chief on the securest method of delivering it. The chief agreed to send us in a small gunboat, 'till we came within sight of the *Antelope*; then the Compradore's boat was to bring the ransom and receive us.

I was so agitated at receiving this joyful news, that it was with considerable difficulty I could scrawl about two or three lines to inform Lieutenant Maughn of the arrangements I had made. We were all so deeply affected by the gratifying tidings, that we seldom closed our eyes, but continued watching day and night for the boat. On the 6th she returned with Lieutenant Maughn's answer, saying he would respect any single boat; but would not allow the fleet to approach him. The chief then, according to his first proposal, ordered a gunboat to take us, and with no small degree of pleasure we left the ladrone fleet about four o'clock in the morning.

At 1 p.m. saw the *Antelope* under all sail, standing toward us. The ladrone boat immediately anchored, and dispatched the Compradore's boat for the ransom, saying, that if she approached nearer, they would return to the fleet; and they were just weighing when she shortened sail, and anchored about two miles from us. The boat did not reach her 'till late in the afternoon, owing to the tide's being strong against her. She received the ransom and left the *Antelope* just before dark. A Mandarin boat that had been lying concealed under the land, and watching their maneuvers, gave chase to her, and was within a few fathoms of taking her, when she saw a light, which the ladrones answered, and the Mandarin hauled off.

Our situation was now a most critical one; the ransom was in the hands of the ladrones, and the Compradore dare not return with us for fear of a second attack from the Mandarin boat. The ladrones would not remain 'till morning, so we were obliged to return with them to the fleet.

In the morning the chief inspected the ransom, which consisted of the following articles: two bales of superfine scarlet cloth; two chests of opium; two casks of gunpowder; and a telescope; the rest in dollars. He objected to the telescope not being new; and said he should detain one of us 'till another was sent, or a hundred dollars in lieu of it. The Compradore however agreed with him for the hundred dollars.

Every thing being at length settled, the chief ordered two gunboats to convey us near the *Antelope*; we saw her just before dusk, when the ladrone boats left us. We had the inexpressible pleasure of arriving on board the *Antelope* at 7 p.m., where we were most cordially received, and heartily congratulated on our safe and happy deliverance from a miserable captivity, which we had endured for eleven weeks and three days.

From A Brief Narrative of His Captivity & Treatment Amongst the Ladrones, Bath, 1814, by Richard Glasspoole, 4th Mate of the Honourable East India Company's *Marquis of Ely*.

CHAPTER TWO

AN ADVENTURE WITH CHINESE PIRATES

"MAJOR SHORE"
AN ANONYMOUS CONTRIBUTOR

Taken on the whole, the average Chinaman of the working classes is a plain, thrifty, hard-working specimen of humanity, whose frugal and industrious habits cannot be too highly commended. Side by side, however, there also exists a large criminal class, whose ranks produce the most unmitigated species of scoundrelism which it is possible to imagine, quite unparalleled in any other country. Cunning, low and brutish by nature; ever on the watch for some piece of devilish knavery, and delighting at all times in deeds of savage cruelty.

The period of my story was just after the close of the first Chinese War – commonly known as the "Opium War" of 1841. I was then stationed at Chusan, a small island (close to the coast of the northern mainland); held by us until the indemnity for the cost of the war had been paid. On the occasion referred to, I had just been obliged to make a journey by water to Ningpoo, an important town about a day's sail up the river; and unavoidable circumstances made it imperative that I should return at once. This could only be done by sailing all night, a particularly hazardous proceeding at that time, as the route literally swarmed with pirates. The small craft of these marauders lay hidden in the numerous creeks by day, swooping down at night on any unlucky boat or small vessel that chanced to pass, unless sufficiently well armed to make the experiment undesirable. The boat I had hired carried a mast and the usual two square sails; it was large and roomy, and provided with sleeping accommodation. This was in the waist, and sheltered from the weather by a frame-work of bamboo, covered with straw matting. The bow and stern rose rather high out of the water; on the former was painted a large eye, after the national custom; and the latter supported a small raised platform, used for rowing during the day, under which the crew – consisting of two men and a boy – stowed themselves away at night. It was with considerable difficulty that I overcame their scruples about sailing after dark, and only at length succeeded by the promise of a double fare. I do not think even this would have sufficed – although a Chinaman, as a rule, will almost do anything for money – if it had not been for the great admiration my two double-barrelled guns inspired; they never having seen such weapons before. Their astonishment at my skill in duck shooting on the upward journey was unbounded, and turned the scale in my favor.

The only other passenger was my little boy, a child of seven, whose mother's illness was the sole cause of my journey. I had just left her at Ningpoo under the care of some kind missionary friends, hoping the change of air might perhaps bring back the hue of health to her faded cheeks, on which consumption had already set its fatal mark; and it was with a heavy heart that I was returning to resume my duties. I loaded my two double-barrels with an extra charge of duck shot before turning in for the night. Not that I had any serious belief that they would ever be required, but principally to satisfy the native crew – who watched the operation with expressions of childish delight, giving vent to their feelings in a series of "Hi, Yaws!" – and also partly to satisfy myself in case anything might occur.

I had lingered a short time over my pipe in the clear starlight. A gentle and fresh breeze was blowing, just sufficient to fill the sails, and we were dropping quietly down the river without the fatigue of rowing. Everything looked still and peaceful as I lay down, and I was soon asleep. I woke about midnight, looked at my watch, and saw that my boy was all right. I did the same at three, and had just dropped off again, when I was suddenly roused by one of the boatmen, who was kneeling beside me, trembling all over. He spoke in low tones, though evidently excited, and implored me in broken English to get up at once, as the dreaded *Quy T'zye* (robbers) were coming, and that we should be soon all murdered, and the boat captured. I required no second admonition, but seizing the guns which lay beside me, hurried out at once, having, luckily, not undressed.

The day was just breaking, and the chilly air made me shiver. I looked round, but could see nothing; the light of the stars was waning, and a slight mist, which hid the banks on either side, prevented my seeing far ahead. The mist was, however, lifting fast, and streaks of early dawn already appeared on the eastern horizon. I peered steadily all round for a minute or two, but could discover nothing. I was just about to turn away, thinking it was a false alarm, when my attendant held up his finger in a listening attitude! After a short pause I seemed to hear the faint sound of oars in the distance, which, from their regular swing, appeared to come from a tolerably large boat bearing down on our port bow. He pointed eagerly in that direction, and I shall never forget the expression of his face, which was simply ghastly with terror, as he stood shivering and trembling in the cold grey light. Looking through the haze, I discovered the unmistakable outline of a boat coming rapidly towards us. Turning round, I found my friend fled, leaving me to my own reflections, which were not of the most agreeable nature. That the boat contained a gang of cut-throats, I had no manner of doubt, and their object murder and pillage, was equally patent. But how to prevent it?

I still had a few minutes to reflect before they were alongside, and I began to take stock of the situation. *I was alone!* well knowing that I could expect no help from the cowardly crew, who were lying huddled up in the stern, paralyzed with terror, or, if they had any reason left, were doubtless already devising means of making terms, and thus saving themselves. To surrender, however, would have been madness, knowing well that whatever *their* fate might be, *my fate*, and that of my child (being hated Europeans), would be most certainly sealed. My only hope, therefore, lay in boldly facing them, trusting the surprise and the unexpected warm reception they would meet with from an unseen quarter would lead them to suspect the presence of superior numbers. I was, however, still loath to begin the attack; but the sight of the murderous lot – as I could now more plainly see them – removed any doubts as to their intentions, and lingering qualms that I had hitherto felt.

There they stood, crowding together in the bow of

the boat, naked almost to the waist, the famous pigtails wound round their heads, which together with their partly shaven crowns, served to give an additional air of savagery to features already sufficiently repulsive. The odds were fearful, as from a hasty glance, snatched from behind the bow rail, I saw there could not be less than twenty of them, all standing ready to spring on board. Those in front held long glittering knives unsheathed in their hands, while some at the oars had naked daggers stuck in the folds of their coiled up pigtails. From my knowledge of the Chinese character there was much of mere bravado in all this, something of a theatrical get up – a kind of stage thunder, so to speak, intended to overawe the native crew, as they evidently thought there were no others on board. But at the same time I was well aware that it would be useless to parley with such villains; it would only have had the effect of betraying our weakness. It was a critical moment. Everything was as still as death as I crouched under the rail. I heard my watch ticking quite distinctly, and felt my heart throbbing, and wondered how soon both would cease forever. Instinctively my thoughts travelled to my dear wife's bedside, and to my poor boy, laying all unconscious within a few feet of me. His tender limbs would soon be hacked by those villainous knives. This last thought decided me. Picking up my nearest gun, I placed the other "ready" across my knee, removed the old caps, replaced them by new ones, for I could not afford the chance of a miss fire. A brace of holster pistols that lay at my feet also required similar attention – revolvers and breechloaders, I need scarcely say, being at that time unknown. I knew that at close quarters one man for each barrel might be reckoned on, perhaps six in all; but then, should I not be overpowered before the reloading? My only chance lay, therefore, in preventing their getting on board, by opening fire at just sufficient distance to allow the shot to spread a little, and be thus far more effective.

The boat was now not more than thirty yards off. I was still crouching hidden from sight, and just peeped over to take a final look before commencing operations, when something from behind me touched my shoulder. Looking round, there was the face of my wondering boy, who having missed me, had crawled out to see what was the matter. There was no time to speak, but passing my hand hastily over his face, I motioned him to lie down at my feet. He did so at once, as if by instinct, and mechanically taking up my spare gun, he prepared to hand it up when wanted, as he had been in the habit of doing on previous occasions when shooting on the river. Other game, however, was now in store. I peered over the rail for the last time; the miscreants were now only about fifteen yards off, evidently with no idea of the warm reception awaiting them. The rowers had ceased rowing, the impetus already given being sufficient to bring them alongside. There they stood clustered together, their bare heads almost touching each other, with knives in hand ready to spring. It was now or never.

Dropping on one knee, and pushing the gun at the same time cautiously through the railings, I took deliberate aim, held my breath till their heads were within ten yards of the muzzle, and then, without a note of warning, *let fly both barrels bang in their faces.* Never shall I forget the unearthly yell that followed the report, and startled the morning air. It was not altogether a yell, but a fiendish screech of unexpected agony. The instant the smoke cleared, a shocking sight presented itself. The boat was drifting alongside, but its crew were in the most helpless confusion. Those in the bow were mostly stricken or had fallen down, and lay writhing in agony. Those in the waist were cowering or flying in terror from the unseen and unexpected calamity; while others astern were pressing forward over the prostrate bodies to ascertain the cause of such a sudden collapse. There was no time to be lost, as they would probably soon recover from the panic.

Stifling my emotion, and turning partly away from the sickening sight directly in front, I pointed the other gun at those in the waist and stern, and fired more deliberately this time, pausing slightly between each shot. Again the unearthly yells arose, the confusion increased tenfold, as the boat dropped astern, drifting helpless without guidance or steerage.

Though relieved from immediate danger, I knew it would not be safe to rely much on what would perhaps prove only a temporary panic. I had been obliged to stand up when firing the last two shots, and they must have thus discovered that I was alone in my resistance, and fighting single-handed. It therefore behoved me to prepare to another attack. I had only about half completed reloading, when a ball suddenly whizzed past my head, followed by a loud report, and splintering the mast close by. Springing to the rail, pistol in hand, I saw that the shot had come from a small swivel-gun in the bow of my opponent's boat. The man who had fired was still standing, match in hand, shouting and waving the crew to return again to the attack. Tall and powerful in appearance, he loomed large against the sky line. One arm was outstretched, pointing the lighted portfire in our direction; with the other he grasped an oar and endeavored to induce his cowardly companions to turn round.

I saw at once that he was their leader, and if his act were successful, it would be all over with us. There was no time for hesitation; his purpose was already half accomplished, from the fact that the two boats being allowed to drift, were not more than a dozen yards apart. Cocking and raising my long-barrelled pistol – steadying myself at the same time against the mast – I covered him carefully before firing; and waited until his body became quite steady, as he swung round with the turning boat. At that moment his tall and commanding figure, standing alone in the prow, presented a clear target against the morning sky. The portfire still burned, and blazed for a second, casting a lurid gleam on his upturned face as I pressed the trigger. Bang! Instantly both arms shot upwards, the head sank upon the breast, and tottering forward he fell head foremost into the dark water. The smoking portfire hissed and spluttered for an instant, marking the spot where "the flood closed o'er him."

This was enough; with the loss of their leader, no further attempt was made to rally, but all fled as fast as oars could carry them. I raised the other pistol, with the momentary intention of giving them a parting shot, but dropped my arm, having no wish to inflict further loss now they were beaten off. When I came down and kissed the pale face of my half-dazed boy, the crew came forward, fawning and grovelling, praising my courage *ad nauseam*; I was disgusted, and quickly got rid of them.

It was now broad day, and I saw that we were rapidly nearing the mouth of the river, being then about abreast of Ching Hae. We soon rounded the last point, and the welcome sight of dancing waves sparkling in the morning sun revived my drooping energies. The pure salt breeze seemed never so welcome; and after a cup of hot tea, I threw myself down to get some rest before landing.

Immediately on arrival I reported the circumstance to the proper authorities; and it afterwards transpired that my assailants – who belonged to a well-known gang – were a terror to all wayfarers on the river. The traders passing to and fro were too glad to purchase immunity for their goods on any terms; as these depredators set all authority at defiance, whether native or foreign. It was reported that their chief headquarters was a large junk, moored in one of the creeks not far from Ching Hae; and the boat by which we were attacked was a kind of "tender" to the large vessel. It further transpired, that, out of a crew of twenty or upwards six had been killed outright; several severely wounded – and hardly one had entirely escaped the effects of the scattering duck shot.

Furthermore, it appeared that they had no idea that Europeans were on board, or they would have been more careful in their mode of attack; and would not have exposed themselves so recklessly. As it was, the lesson learnt bore good fruit; no further outrage of a similar nature occurred during our occupation, which was soon after brought to a close.

From *The Living Age*, Boston, November 1895, featured in *The United Service Magazine*, London.

CHAPTER THREE

THE SUPPRESSION OF PIRACY BY THE ROYAL NAVY

OFFICIAL LETTERS & ADMIRALTY DESPATCHES

The following official papers give all the principal particulars relating to the various expeditions up and down the coast during the last two months ... The piratical fleet of Chéung Shap-'ng-tsai has been completely dispersed by the successful movement of Captain John Hay, and this region rid of the most audacious marauder who has appeared since the renowned Apotsai in 1810 ... The immediate cause of the attack upon these piratical fleets so far from Hong Kong was the seizure of a junk belonging to a British subject [a Mr. David Taylor of Canton].

From His Excellency Samuel G. Bonham,
the Governor of Hong Kong
To His Excellency Su, The Chinese Imperial
Commissioner

Government House,
Victoria, Hongkong,
20th September, 1849.

Sir,– I have already upon several occasions addressed Your Excellency regarding pirates: but as long as they remained at a distance and did not interfere with British vessels, I do not consider myself bound to interpose. Lately, however, acts of piracy have been more than ordinarily frequent in the vicinity of this Colony; one junk, the property of a British subject has been seized off Hainán, and there have been rumors that a British vessel, long missing, had been captured by the pirates in that neighborhood. A vessel-of-war was in consequence dispatched to make search, and on the 5th September, in Tienpeh Bay, fell in with a fleet of pirate junks, of which she destroyed five. Upon her report, a second vessel was sent upon the 8th, which also destroyed five. These vessels where undoubtedly piratical, and formed part of the fleet of Shap-'ng-tsai. They were pointed out as such by some of the Chinese whom they had detained at the above place, and the Chinese authorities on the coast, who are all much gratified at our success, also made a statement to that effect.

It is clear that your naval authorities have no power to destroy, or disperse, these marauders. Now, that they have come to the vicinity of this island, I have determined to take steps for the dispatch of vessels to scour the seas in all directions, more especially as I understand that Tsú A-pò, who murdered two English officers in the month of March last: is a leading man among them. I have twice called Your Excellency's attention to this outrage, committed by one of your own countrymen, who afterwards fled from my jurisdiction. He must now be in that of Your Excellency; nevertheless, nothing appears to have been done towards his apprehension: and if, in the attempts which I myself am making to arrest him accidents should happen through ignorance on our part, the blame of those must attach to Your Excellency for not having earlier caused this miscreant to be apprehended. I am aware that there may be some difficulty in effecting his capture; but I feel sure that, if Your Excellency would take the usual steps to secure him, it would be in your power to send him to me to be tried and punished. This murder took place five months ago, but it is still fresh in my memory, and will remain so until satisfaction has been afforded for so abominable an outrage.

Accept the assurances, &c.
S. G. Bonham

THE REPORT OF THE DESTRUCTION OF PIRATE VESSELS

From Captain John C. Dalrymple Hay
To Rear-Admiral Francis A. Collier,
Commander in Chief, Hong Kong

Her Majesty's Sloop *Columbine,*
Typsung Bay,
30th Sep., 1849.

Sir,– I have the honor to inform Your Excellency, that on the evening of Thursday the 27th instant, I left Hongkong in search of a piratical fleet, commanded by the notorious "Cui-a-poo," and proceeded to Harisem Bay, where I arrived at noon on the 28th, and found that after sacking the village there, they had gone to Tysami, off which place, I descried at 11 p.m., the fleet under weigh, consisting of 14 junks formed in two lines, making off for the S.W. The village at this Bay we observed smouldering. I attacked one of the largest I could reach, the wind being very light, at 11.45 and continued engaged with as many as I could bear upon, until calm and their sweeps prevented further engagement. I chased them with sweeps and light airs [wind] through the night, and came up with them again at noon yesterday, the 29th, when to my satisfaction, the wind being still very light, I observed the Peninsular and Oriental Steam Navigation Company's steam vessel *Canton* coming from the eastward, that vessel seeing me chasing as soon as she could, opened her fire, and thereby threw the junks into confusion, when numbers began to jump overboard and take to their boats. Mr. Watkins, who had chartered her for the purpose of looking after the *Coquette* missing vessel, and who carries this dispatch, and who eventually served in our boats, most kindly gave up his charter to admit of Mr. Jamieson, the commander of the steam-vessel, rendering me the assistance I so much needed in getting near the pirates.

I have the satisfaction of acquainting Your Excellency that three junks have been abandoned, and one blown up and destroyed, in these operations, the latter by the boats of the sloop under the command of lieutenant Bridges, senior of the *Columbine*, of which I purpose furnishing Your Excellency more detailed particulars. The remainder of this formidable piratical fleet, ten in number, are now at anchor at the head of Bias Bay near Fan-sokong in sight, and I feel confident, if promptly assisted by the *Fury*, and such other disposable force as Your Excellency may be pleased to send me, can be effectually destroyed; as they show no intention at present of coming out; and I have good information that they purpose repairing their damages where they are. We have destroyed at least 310 pirates since 11 p.m. of the 28th, but I regret to state that our loss has been three killed, one officer and six men wounded. My ship's company having now been 40 hours at the sweeps and quarters, are necessarily much fatigued, and the sick list leaves me not more than 60 effective people on board. Mr. Watkins will give Your Excellency every information of the proceedings of the sloop under my command since noon yesterday, which from my anxiety to put Your Excellency in possession of these proceedings, and to get the *Canton* under weigh for Hongkong, I can not at present furnish. My ammunition is much reduced, but if, to increase my present stock, would detain the expedition, what I have must suffice.

I have the honor, &c.,
John C. Dalrymple Hay, Commander.

From Captain John C. Dalrymple Hay
To Rear-Admiral Sir Francis A. Collier

H.M. Sloop *Columbine*.
Pirate's Cove, Bias Bay,
2nd Oct., 1849.

Sir, – I have the honor to inform Your Excellency that my anticipations have been fortunately realized, and that the piratical squadron of "Chui-a-poo" has been totally destroyed by the force you so kindly and promptly placed at my disposal. Twenty-three piratical junks averaging 500 tons, mounting from 12 to 18 guns, three new ones on the stocks, and two small dockyards with a considerable supply of naval stores have been totally destroyed by fire; and of 1800 men who manned them, about 400 have been killed, and the rest dispersed without resource.

To Commander Willcox of the *Fury*, whose great ability and zeal are already known to Your Excellency, I must give the principal honor of the day. To the *Fury's* unrivaled accuracy of firing, must be attributed the bloodless termination to us of this affair.

The *Columbine* being unable to come close up in the narrow channel where she would have hampered the *Fury's* movements I went on board the *Fury*, to share in the action. The piratical fire was silenced in about 45 minutes, during which time only one man was slightly wounded. The boats of the *Hastings* and *Columbine* under Lieutenants Luard and Bridges, senior of these ships, whom I beg to recommend to Your Excellency, then assisted in completing the destruction, and Lieutenant Holland and the [Royal] marines accompanied me in an expedition to scour the heights, but no opposition was offered to us, the pirates running in all directions. The officers, seamen, and marines employed have conducted themselves in a steady, quiet, and gallant manner, and I am sure, if the resistance had been much larger, similar success would have crowned their efforts. Mr. Caldwell of the [Hong Kong] Police force, who acted as interpreter, has proved himself invaluable in collecting information. I send this at once by a Chinese boat and I hope to succeed in destroying some detached piratical junks of which we have information, in the course of to-day and to-morrow; after which we shall rejoin you.

I have, &c.

John C. Dalrymple Hay, Commander.

From the Governor of Hong Kong
To Su, Imperial Commissioner

Government House,
Victoria, Hongkong,
8th October, 1849.

Sir,– I have again the honor to communicate to Your Excellency the particulars of a successful attack made by two English vessels-of-war upon a large force of pirates.

Information having been received that a large fleet under Tsú A-pò, was at a place called Ping-hoi, in the district of Kweishen, a brig-of-war was dispatched in quest of them on the 27th ultimo. She arrived at noon on the 28th, found that they had sacked the village, and gone to Tysami, on which place she was then about 11 p.m. – fourteen sail in all: the village at this place was also smouldering. The brig continued to chase them the whole night, but the wind was light and she was long in approaching them, until, on the morning of the 29th, an English merchant steamer coming up, towed her close to a large junk, which going into shoal water, the brig's boats attacked and boarded. Two forts on the shore also opened fire upon the junk, and her crew, as soon she was boarded, blew her up, and destroyed some 90 of themselves, while a British officer and three seamen were killed, and seven seamen injured. Of the pirate's squadron, three vessels, abandoned by their crews, were rendered useless by our people; the remaining ten got away and were pursued by the brig. On the 30th, the wounded were sent back in the merchant steamer to Hongkong, with a report of all that had taken place to the naval Commander-in-chief, by whom orders were instantly given to a large man-of-war steamer to proceed to the spot and assist the brig. These two vessels returned to this harbor on the 4th instant, announced the total annihilation of Tsú A-pò's fleet, consisting of 23 piratical junks, averaging 500 tons in burden, and mounting from 12 to 18 guns, 350 guns had been also destroyed; and two new junks on the stocks, at a place in the vicinity; as also two small dockyards, and a large supply of naval stores had been burned. There were besides some 400 pirates killed, and the rest, some 1400, dispersed – with arms, indeed, but without any means of continuing to exercise their dangerous vocation.

As regards Tsú A-pò, who, as I mentioned in my letter of the 20th ultimo to Your Excellency, I had reason to suppose was a leader amongst these pirates, it is stated by a wounded Chinese who was picked up in the water, that he had been wounded in the encounter and carried off by his followers. There would therefore be, I should imagine, little difficulty in discovering him; and the local authorities of the Coast districts will, I trust, receive immediate orders to search for and seize him; and to lose no time in following up this successful attack upon his band, and utterly exterminating them.

I have much satisfaction in communicating these particulars to Your Excellency, and take the opportunity of remarking once more, that our success in completely putting down this nuisance, which is even more hurtful to you than to ourselves, would be sure, if I could prevail upon Your Excellency to concert with me those measures of co-operation, the advantage of which I have so often pressed upon your attention. In my communication of 20th ultimo, above referred to, I said "that I was determined to take steps for the dispatch of vessels to scour the seas in all directions;" and I shall only add that, whether Your Excellency is pleased to co-operate with me or not, I shall accordingly miss no opportunity of destroying these common enemies of mankind, wherever they are to be found in these waters; that the spreading of this evil may be effectually put an end to.

Accept the assurances, &c.
S. G. Bonham

A true translation of the reply from Su to the Governor of Hong Kong:

[Your Excellency]
I am in receipt of Your Excellency's letter of the 22nd of the 8th moon, (8th October), and have fully acquainted myself with the contents of it. My mind is most anxiously concerned about the injuries which the men and officers of your honorable nation engaged in the extermination and capture of the pirates have suffered from the ignition of the powder to which the latter, in their desperation, set fire. The civil and military officers to the Eastward had reported that on the 10th of the 8th moon (26th September), certain pirates, whose vessels were in the harbor of the military station of Ping-hai, had fallen upon Tá-ngáu (Tai-ò), a village within the creek. Shin, the chief magistrate of this district of Kwei-shen, acting in concert with the military authorities, had put himself at the head of troops and volunteers, and from the fort

of Cheh-tsang, had sunk three and burned one of the vessels of the pirates, of whom upwards of 100 were killed: some ten of the troops and volunteers being at the same time wounded. The pirates now made for Shan-wi (Saumi), and being there again beaten off by the troops and volunteers stood out to sea, where they fell in with the cruisers of your honorable nation, on being attacked by whom they got away to the harbor of Tun-tau. Here the commandant of Hwui-chau, the chief magistrate, and an officer of the rank of captain, opened upon them from the forts, and having, by the cross fire of these, set one of the ships in flames, they took alive 18 of the crew as they were making their escape ashore, and as soon as they had extracted from them all they had to say, forwarded them to the city.

The destruction of the whole fleet of the pirates and the death of some 400 of them, of which I am informed in the letter now under acknowledgment, will greatly gladden the hearts of all men.

Upon the receipt of the reports from the Eastward, I had already sent as express [a message] to the civil and military officers along the coast, with orders to make search and to seize in all directions, in the hope that (the pirates) might thus be swept clean away, and utterly extirpated.

As Sú-A-páu (Tsú A-pò) was wounded, he would, I imagine, have difficulty in flying to any distance. If he be not yet dead, as soon as he shall be taken he shall of course be punished with the utmost rigor; there shall be no possibility of his resuming his evil career (*lit*, no sprout however small, which might again flourish, shall be left).

While thus replying to you, I avail myself of the opportunity to wish that the blessings of the season (autumn) may daily increase to Your Excellency.

A necessary communication addressed to Mr. Bonham, *H.B.M. Plenipotentiary, &c., &c.*,
Taukwang, 29th year, 8th moon,
25th day. (11th October, 1849.)
T.F. Wade, Assistant Chinese Secretary.

From Captain John C. Dalrymple Hay
To Rear-Admiral Sir Francis A. Collier

H.M. Sloop *Columbine*,
Chokeum, Cochinchina,
23rd Oct, 1849.

Sir,– I have the satisfaction to report to Your Excellency the great success of the expedition you did me the honor to place under my command; 58 piratical vessels, mounting about 1200 guns, and with crews of 3000 men, have been totally destroyed by fire; and, by the blessing of God, without the loss of one life of the officers and men under my orders.

After leaving Hongkong on the 8th October, I searched the harbors of "Concock," "Sattei," "St. John's," "Mong," "Mamee," "Sungyue," and "Tien-pak," and proceeded to "Now-chow." From information received there, I determined to proceed to Hoi-how in Hainan, inside the shoals, and through the junk passage, for I found good pilots, and junks with 14 feet draught going through, and we drew little more than 15 feet; moreover Shap-'ng-tsai had boasted he would go where English ship dared not follow him. This vaunt, I determined to belie. We reached Hoi-how on the 13th, and found the admiral (Ho), whom I visited at the capital, in great fear of the pirates, and with a most friendly feeling to the English nation. He immediately ordered a Mandarin named Wong to proceed with me, taking with him eight war-junks, and I gave him a passage, to prevent delay, on board the *Fury*. On the 16th we reached "Chook-shan," which the pirate fleet had left five days before, and we found the same sad story of towns destroyed, men murdered, and women taken away, that mark his track along the coast. On Thursday, the 18th, we fell in with one of his lookout vessels, which having got into shallow water, was overtaken by the *Phlegethon*, and destroyed by her boats, under the command of Mr. Simpson, first officer. On the 19th, we reached Hoo-nong, his reported haunt, and found he had gone about 12 miles further, and I feared we had lost him; but that invaluable officer, Mr. Daniel R. Caldwell impressed me so strongly with the correctness of his information, that I decided on a reconnaissance in the *Phlegethon* in spite of our shortness of fuel; and proceeding in to Chokeum for that purpose on Saturday morning the 20th, saw 37 of the fleet under weigh. From 7 a.m. until 4 p.m., like terriers at a rat-hole, we hunted for the channel. Then a pilot managed to escape from the shore. I proceeded in *Phlegethon*, with *Fury* astern and *Columbine* in tow, over the bar 14 ft. (mud), and at 4.40 p.m. had the pleasure of finding all the ships warmly engaged. At 5.05 p.m., Shap-'ng-tsai's junk blew up with a tremendous crash, and at 5.30 they had ceased firing. Before 8 o'clock, 27 were in flames, and the squadron in position to blockade the river. On the 21st October, the steamers and boats destroyed 24 more; and nine of them gave lieutenant George Hancock in a paddle-box boat of *Fury*, assisted by Captain Moore, R.M. and Mr. Close, acting mate, with Mr. Leao, an opportunity of distinguishing himself. Two large junks turned to bay, to defend the retreat of the rest, but Mr. Hancock so handled his boat and her gun, that after an hour and twenty minutes he had beaten them from their guns, and carried them by boarding without loss, and then pursued and destroyed the other seven. Mr. Hancock's boldness in attacking, and correct judgment in managing this affair, are worthy of the highest praise; and Captain Moore, R.M., Mr. N.N.C. Leao, a Brazilian lieutenant, and Mr. F.A. Close, acting mate, gave him the greatest assistance. On Monday the 22nd, I proceeded in *Phlegethon* and boats to destroy all that were left; we found that the Mandarins had destroyed four, and we finished two others. The low flat islands at the mouth of the river were at times covered with men deserted from the junks, yet afraid of the Cochinchinese, who had assembled in great numbers to attack them. The ships' boats and small-arm men harassed and destroyed many by a constant fire of shell and grape, whilst the Cochinchinese destroyed and captured the rest. From the best information it appears that the fleet consisted of 64 vessels of war and 3150 men.

Of these, 2 small of the 3rd class and 4 of the 4th class have escaped with Shap-'ng-tsai, but without much ammunition; and the Mandarin assures me he will shortly destroy him – now an easy prey. He took with him about 400 men, – so that 1700 having been killed; about a thousand more remain to be finished by the Cochinchinese, who have already sent some prisoners to the authorities.

I shall now proceed to Hongkong with all dispatch. I have the pleasure of mentioning the exceeding good conduct of the officers and men during these laborious and hazardous operations. Their unanimity, willingness, and cheerfulness have made it a most pleasant service, and no plunder, rapine, or misconduct, has tarnished their honor. Major-general Wong, the Mandarin, proved himself a gallant, active and efficient ally, and I trust his own government may reward him for his good services. To have Commander Willcox with me, is, I feel, to have success. As a friend and an officer he is unequaled, and his ship is in such good order that I believe there is nothing he could not do. His judgment and gallantry are on an equal footing. Mr. Niblett of the *Phlegethon* has handled his ship in a bold and determined manner, and has given me every assistance. As I was frequently obliged to be in the steamers, the command of this sloop has devolved upon lieutenant J.H. Bridges, senior lieutenant, and he conducted her into action on the 20th with much ability. Lieutenant Darnell, senior of the *Fury,* in command of her boats, has also rendered good service. Captain Moore of the *Hastings'* marines has assisted me most materially in command of that body. Lieutenant Hancock, and Mr. Chambers, acting mate, in command of the respective detachments of the *Hastings'* men, have given me much satisfaction, and Mr. Rathbone, midshipman of the *Fury,* has brought himself into notice for his zeal. I had also to notice the name of Mr. Algernon Wootton, midshipman, a most promising young officer, who has acted as my aid-de-camp, and been very useful on every occasion. I have the honor to enclose a list of the officers employed in the boats, who I have no doubt would equally have distinguished themselves if they had had the opportunity.

I inclose a journal of my proceedings since leaving Hongkong, together with some hydrographical remarks compiled by Mr. Thomas Kerr, acting master of this sloop, which will I trust be of service to commerce and navigation in the Gulf of Tonquin, hitherto so little known. Mr. Kerr, during all this very hazardous navigation, has proved himself a careful and judicious officer.

Mr. D. R. Caldwell of the police force, has again proved his talent as a linguist, his intimate knowledge of the Chinese character, and the thorough correctness of his information. To him in a great measure our success is to be attributed.

Mr. Soames, Master of the Hongkong Company's steam vessel *Canton,* did his work well as a pilot, as far as he was acquainted with the coast.

I have the honor to be, Sir,
Your most obedient humble Servant,
John C. Dalrymple Hay, – Commander.

From *Journal of Occurrences, The China Mail* and *The Hongkong Register*, Hong Kong, November 1849.

CHAPTER FOUR

TWELVE DAYS AMONG THE PIRATES

BY FANNY LOVIOT A FRENCH WOMAN

On the 7th of July we set sail [from Rio Janeiro] once more for California. Seeing our little schooner depart on so long a voyage, the Brazilians proved themselves quite as discouraging as our evil prophets of Havre. "The *Independence*," said they, "can never weather the tempests off Cape Horn!" My sister implored me not to continue our voyage; but, although I partook of all her fears, I remained inflexible ...

Once more at sea, and, this time, for two or three months at the least. We talked, it is true, of touching at Lima, but on this head there was nothing certain ... For a whole week we had the finest weather imaginable ...

Now the weather began to grow colder, and the sea, become more boisterous, no longer rocked us like a kindly nurse, but flung us rudely to and fro. Our embroidery, our loto, our singing came abruptly to an end, and we found ourselves subjected to all the miseries of a maritime journey ... Thus several long weeks went by, and, day by day, the cold grew more severe. At length we came in sight of Cape Horn, clad in ice ... For twelve days we remained tossing to and fro without making any appreciable progress. On the thirteenth, we doubled the Cape. Soon after this, we sailed into a warmer latitude, and crossed the line for the second time.

And now the provisions became more and more scanty, wherefore we all complained bitterly of the shipowner. Eight or ten days more must, perforce, elapse before we could arrive at San Francisco ...

At sight of San Francisco, our passengers forgot all the sufferings of the journey, and began dreaming once again of the good fortune which awaited them. My sister and I followed the general example, and, for us, the present wore all the pleasant colours of the future. Poor France! thou wert soon forgotten, and we already opened our arms to this inhospitable land where gold is the only true God.

After eighteen months of Californian life, a circumstance occurred, which changed, not only my position, but my prospects. I became acquainted with one Madame Nelson, a French lady who, like myself, was engaged in commercial speculations. It was, at this time, her intention to leave California for Batavia, in the Island of Java ... She proposed that we should travel together, and share the profits, as well as the fatigues of the enterprise ... But, while I was yet hesitating, an event took place which summarily decided it for me. One of those destructive fires so common in San Francisco broke out next door to us, in the dead calm of a lovely summer's night, and made such rapid progress that we with difficulty escaped. Startled from sleep, we had but time to collect a few valuables which we flung into a portmanteau, and threw out of the window. Scarcely had we gone twenty paces from the house, when staircases and flooring fell in with a tremendous crash. Three hours later, fifty-two houses were entirely destroyed. This fire cost us more than four thousand piastres, since we rescued nothing from our stock.

My sister, being utterly out of heart, made up her mind to return to Eureka, where commercial affairs were said to be unusually prosperous. As for me, I decided to accompany Madame Nelson; for, notwithstanding the pecuniary advantages which I hoped to derive from the journey, my love of novelty was in nowise abated.

We then drew up the following programme of our route: – Directing our course through the Chinese seas, we proposed touching at Canton, Macao, Hong-Kong, and Batavia, where we hoped to remain about two months. These matters settled, we had but to prepare for our departure.

On the 14th of June, 1851, we embarked on board the *Arcturus,* bound for China. Our fellow-passengers consisted of four French artistes, going to Calcutta on a musical speculation. In addition to these, we carried thirty-five Chinese in the steerage.

On the fifteenth day of our voyage, we came in sight of the Sandwich Islands. My companion, who up to this time had proved herself an excellent sailor, became all at once languid and melancholy. Two of our Chinese passengers were professed fortune-tellers. Finding that they could both speak a little English, and hoping thereby to amuse Madame Nelson, I summoned them to an exhibition of their talent. Half laughing, half incredulous, my friend offered her hand to their scrutiny. Silently and sadly they looked at it, hesitated, and consulted together. Becoming impatient of this delay, Madam Nelson pressed them for an explanation. "We pause," said they, "because we fear to afflict you." "You are wrong," said she, "for I have no belief in your art." Annoyed, perhaps, by this observation, they framed and evil prophecy. "You have been wealthy," said they (and this was true), "but you seek in vain to accumulate fresh riches. Your days are numbered." Speaking thus, they gazed earnestly upon her, and seemed to read the future in the lines upon her brow.

Painfully impressed by this prediction, my friend yielded to a despondency which I tried in vain to dispel. I then regretted what I had done, and strove to conceal my uneasiness by consulting the necromancers on my own account. The second prophecy made up in a measure for the dreariness of the first. The markings of my hand, said they, were especially favourable. I was destined to prosperity, and should one day become rich. One of them then pointed to a line upon my forehead. "A great misfortune awaits you," said he; " but it will not affect your future prosperity." I only laughed at these predictions, and endeavoured to cheer my poor friend by every means in my power.

Within eight days from this time the state of Madame Nelson's health had become truly alarming. We had no medical man on board, and my anxiety grew daily more and more insupportable ... A violent delirium seized her, during which she raved of the Chinese and their prophecies. The delirium was succeeded by spasmodic paroxysms. I bent sorrowfully over her; I drew her head to my bosom; and, seeing that death was close at hand, imprinted a farewell kiss upon her lips. She looked up, smiled languidly, as if to thank me for my love, and gently breathed her last.

The death of Madame Nelson left me almost broken-hearted. Far from my friends and my country, I felt more than ever desolate, and lamented the fatal day which bore me from my native land. What was now to become of me, friendless and alone, in a strange and savage country? Alas! what would I not now have given to turn back; but I could not change the course of the ship, or turn the currents of the winds. Go on I must, and submit to my destiny.

The navigation of the Chinese seas is rendered more than commonly hazardous by reason of the sunken rocks which there abound. Threading these securely, we came, one glorious day, upon the Bashee Islands. In three days, said the captain, we should probably arrive at the end of our journey. Just, however, as we were congratulating ourselves on this pleasant intelligence, we were overtaken by a frightful storm of wind and rain. Huge black clouds traversed the sky, and we saw more than one water-spout in the distance. When the tempest at length abated, it was succeeded by a dreary calm, which lasted for nine days. A faint breeze occasionally sprang up, only to die away again, and leave us more impatient than ever. At length, after beating about the Chinese shores for more than twenty days, the captain informed us that our sea-stores were almost exhausted. Hereupon the sailors refused to work, unless some of their number were allowed to take a boat, and venture in search of Hong-Kong, which, we calculated, could not be distant more than thirty miles. The captain despatched eight men. We then cast anchor amid a group of islands, and there awaited the return of these brave fellows who had undertaken to risk their lives for our safety. Twenty-four hours after, they returned with a steamer, which towed us into the Hong-Kong roads, on the 29th of August, after a sea voyage of seventy-six days. Summoned to the French Consulate to attest the death of my unhappy friend, I made the acquaintance of our vice-consul, M. [George L.] Haskell, and explained to him all the discomfort of my present position. He advised me to relinquish an enterprise so unfortunately begun. I replied that my only desire was to get back to California. "Suffer me," said the vice-consul, "to make all the arrangements for your return; and I trust that my influence may be sufficient to ensure you every attention during the voyage." I thanked him for his kindness, and from this time became better reconciled to my Chinese expedition.

The island of Hong-Kong contains twenty thousand Chinese, and one thousand European inhabitants. It is situated at the foot of an immense mountain, and is built in the form of an amphitheatre. On entering the principal street, the traveller is surprised to find himself in the midst of elegant European buildings. The houses are very large, surrounded by verandahs, and fitted up with jalousies [shutters] – a very necessary luxury in all tropical climates ...

There are but two hotels in Hong-Kong, and both lodging and provisions are quite as expensive as in California. As might be expected, the accommodation is far inferior; and even the cleanest and best regulated houses are infested with frightful insects. Everywhere, on the furniture, in the presses, hidden in your shoes, clinging to your curtains, and ensconced in your portmanteaus, you find spiders, beetles, and mosquitoes. If you take out a garment for use, two or three of these disgusting creatures are sure to be lying in the folds of it. The beetles, however, are the most annoying of all; and at night, when the candles are lighted, become almost unendurable. One falls on your head;

another alights upon your nose; and in the morning, when you wake, you are sure to find half-a-dozen lying drowned in your wash-hand basin, or served up, struggling, in your tea. At table you meet with them constantly in the gravy, or the vegetables; but this is a matter of course, and cannot be avoided.

The vegetation of Hong-Kong is the most luxuriant in the world, and the flowers are redolent with a perfume more sweet and more penetrating than those of Europe. Admitted to visit the garden of a Mandarin, I scarcely knew which was the greater, my delight or my astonishment. It was an artificial world in little, interspersed with grottoes, rocks, rivulets, and miniature mountains. There was not a straight path in the place, and at each turn I came upon some fresh point of view. Here were fantastic kiosks with windows of coloured glass; rustic suspension bridges; and tranquil shrubberies, musical with birds. It is only in balmy solitudes such as these that the Chinese ladies can, with their pinched and mutilated feet, enjoy any kind of out-door recreation.

Taking advantage of the time that still remained to me, I agreed to join my fellow-travellers in a visit to Canton. Just at this period the insurrection of 1854 was at its height, and, although the city itself was tolerably tranquil, the neighbourhood all around was up in arms. Under these circumstances, we could hardly hope to make any lengthened stay.

In this enormous city (only two streets of which were then accessible to Europeans), factories, English counting-houses, and extensive warehouses abound. There is not a single hotel in the place. At the houses where you wish to transact business, you send in your card. The retail dealers are classed as a separate body of tradesmen. One quarter of the city is wholly occupied by the porcelain-sellers, another by the tea-dealers, a third by the silk-merchants. I was never weary of admiring these magnificent warehouses, where are displayed specimens of the most exquisite handiwork imaginable. Lacquered furniture, ivory fans, carved jewel-cases, silken tapestries, and resplendent stuffs, distract the attention of the stranger at every step. The thoroughfare called New China Street is bordered by these superb stores, each of which has its flat roof decorated with parti-coloured balls, and its upright sign, where golden letters on a scarlet ground proclaim the name and trade of the merchant. The streets are filled by a busy, noisy crowd: strolling vendors, with their strange guttural cries; grave and solemn citizens, with their flowing robes and perpetual parasols; and, now and then, one or two women of the poorer class, hurrying along with children in their arms ...

During the three days that I stayed at Canton, I witnessed a fracas amongst the Emperor's soldiers. A Chinese army is the most ludicrous affair imaginable. How shall I describe these absurd warriors, dignified by the titles of "War-tigers," and "Mountain-splitters?" Standing on a lofty terrace, I was quite near enough to distinguish all their proceedings. Armed with lances and cumbrous matchlocks, they crowded along in the greatest disorder, and almost every soldier carried an umbrella, a fan, and a lantern; all of which forcibly reminded me of the Chinese burlesques that I had seen in the theatres at San Francisco.

The perpetual thundering of cannon, the brawling and skirmishing of the insurgents, the frequent encounters which took place beyond the walls, and the false alarms by which we were continually harassed, all combined to hasten my return to Honk-Kong.

After I had been resident about a month in China, our vice-consul informed me that a ship was about to sail for California. He was so extremely kind as to interest the captain in my favour, and this officer, whose name was Rooney, promised to pay me every attention in his power. Having thanked M. Haskell for all the interest which he had taken in my affairs, I hastened to my hotel with a light heart, and prepared forthwith for my journey.

Towards four o'clock in the afternoon, on the 4th of October, 1854, I went on board the brig *Caldera*, which, under a Chilean flag, was about to set sail that evening for California. Such was the honesty and frankness of the captain's face, that I was immediately prepossessed in his favour. Mr. Rooney was a man of about thirty-five years of age, neither short nor tall, and, to all appearance, a thorough sailor. His countenance betokened an energetic character, and I would have staked my existence upon his courage and good- nature. My first care was to visit my cabin, and arrange my luggage. Soon after this, we weighed anchor, and put out to sea. Once on the way, I was seized with a listless melancholy, for which I found it impossible to account. This melancholy, which might have been a presentiment, seemed all the stranger considering that I was returning to America, to my sister, and my friends. Resolved, somehow or another, to shake it off, I left my cabin and made the tour of the ship. It was a handsome three-masted brig of eight hundred tons burthen, well rigged, and gracefully built. I visited the saloon, the cabins, the captain's parlour, and another which belonged to the supercargo of a commercial house at San Francisco, the heads of which had a valuable cargo on board. The saloon was lighted from above, and elegantly fitted up with panellings of white and gold. So clean and orderly was every corner of the vessel, that it seemed as if nothing adverse could take place to interrupt our course; and I almost fancied that we might all be allowed to sleep away the three long months which must elapse before our arrival in California.

Of one of my fellow-travellers I shall often have occasion to speak. He was a Chinese of about fifty years of age, and an inhabitant of Canton. He had a commercial house at San Francisco, and was carrying with him a large stock of opium, sugar, and coffee. His name was Than-Sing. His features were of the type common to his nation, and deeply scarred by the small-pox. Though plain, however, he was not unprepossessing; for good-nature was expressed in every line of his countenance, and his smile was kindness itself.

We sat down four to dinner, and found that no two of us belonged to the same nation. The captain was English, the supercargo American, Than-Sing Chinese, and I French. I am thus particular in defining our several nationalities, in order to prove how much our difficulties must have been increased, in any case of peril, by the differences of language. Than-Sing spoke English as I did, that is to say, indifferently; but not one of the party spoke French. It will hereafter be seen how Than-Sing, who alone spoke

Chinese, had it in his power to save and serve us all. Our crew consisted of seventeen men of various nations.

Awakened next morning by the hurrying to and fro of the sailors, I became uneasy, dressed in haste, and went on deck. A sailor had fallen overboard, and the ship was lying-to. His head was just visible above the waves, and we had already left him far behind. He followed us, swimming gallantly, and, in the course of about twenty minutes, came alongside, and was hoisted upon deck. His comrades greeted him with acclamations; but he replied roughly enough, as if he were ashamed of his misfortune.

Trifling as this incident was, it left an unpleasant impression on my mind; for it seemed as if our voyage had begun badly. The song of the sailors augmented my melancholy. It was a fantastic and monotonous melody, very unlike the cheerful airs sung by our French mariners. Going back sorrowfully to my cabin, I amused myself by feeding two charming little birds that I had brought with me from Hong-Kong. I kissed them tenderly; for they were all that I had to love.

The breeze was mild; we had land in sight all day, and made but little way. Towards evening the barometer fell with alarming rapidity, a strong wind sprang up, and the sea grew boisterous. Anticipating the coming storm, the captain made rapid preparations, and furled all sail. It was well he did so; for we were soon to be at the mercy of the typhoon. The typhoon is a dangerous wind, much feared in the Indian and Chinese seas. On the sea, as on the land, it carries with it death and destruction. It is neither a north wind nor a south wind, and blows as much from the east as from the west. It is, indeed, a combat between all four, and the great ocean is the scene of their warfare. Woe, then, to the ship which has to contend against this fearful strife! Tossed and tormented, driven on from behind, and driven back from before, neither sailors nor steersmen avail to guide her.

For long hours the *Caldera* remained the plaything of this fearful wind. We were every moment threatened with destruction. Before the tempest had lasted two hours the mizen-mast and main-mast were both broken half-way, and the top-gallant masts laid along the decks, with all their cordage rent. Two of our boats had been carried away by the waves. Below, everything was broken, and we had two feet of water in the cabins. Added to all this, the waves broke against us with a noise like thunder, and out timbers creaked as if the ship would go to pieces.

Every now and then, the captain came down to console me. His hair and clothes were wet through; but, in the midst of all this danger, he never lost his cheerfulness for an instant. "You're afraid," said he, in his rough but kindly tones. I denied it; but my pale face betrayed my fears, for he shook his head compassionately as he left me.

I must confess that I endured an agony of terror. Everything was rolling about, and my poor little birds, hanging from the ceiling in their wicker cage, shrank down together, trembling and stupefied. For my part, I had taken refuge in my berth; for the motion was such, that I could no longer keep my footing. All at once a frightful crash resounded overhead, and I was flung out upon the floor. I covered my face with my hands – I believed that the ship was going to pieces, and that our last moments had arrived. This crash proved to be the fall of the mizen and top-gallant masts. I marvel now that the *Caldera* should have lived through the storm. She did live, however, and after fourteen hours of distress, the tempest gradually abated. Towards mid-day, the wind died quite away, and, if the sea continued to be somewhat agitated, that agitation, after what we had lately gone through, seemed like a delightful calm.

About four o'clock in the afternoon, I left my cabin and went into the saloon. It was flooded with water, and strewn with a chaotic mass of broken furniture and crockery.

I then proceeded upon deck. There, indeed, the tempest had done its work. It was with difficulty that I could make my way from one end to the other. Cables, chains, and broken masts lay about in all directions. The sea was muddy, and the sky was low, and a thick haze hung over the distance. The sailors look weary, and one of them had been severely wounded by a falling mast. Added to our other misfortunes, fifty-two fowls and six pigs had been killed during the night. We were still within sight of land, and the captain, whose object was to get back to Hong-Kong as soon as possible, had with difficulty hoisted a sail to the foremast. To return was imperative, since it would take at least six weeks to repair the damage that we had sustained. A dead calm now reigned around us, and we remembered for the first time that we were all very hungry. Our dinner was the dreariest meal imaginable. We were all profoundly silent. The captain's face betrayed his anxiety, and I afterwards learnt that he was thinking at that very time of a misfortune which happened to him only two years before. Falling into the hands of Indian pirates, Captain Rooney had seen all his sailors killed before his face, and, being himself bound to the mast of his ship, was cruelly tortured. For three months they kept him prisoner, at the end of which time he effected his escape.

So dismal a countenance as that of the supercargo I never beheld. He had been in mortal fear of death all through the night, and acknowledged that he had trembled almost as much for his cargo as for his life.

As for Than-Sing, his was the face of a man who openly rejoiced in his safety, and his calm smile contrasted strangely with the general uneasiness.

For my part, I could not so readily forget the sufferings of the last eighteen hours. "What more can I know of the horrors of the sea," I asked myself, "if it be not to make it my grave?"

The captain ordered us early to rest. I was so weary that I could have slept upon the floor as contentedly as upon a feather-bed, and my berth appeared to me the most delightful place in the world. I hoped to sleep for at least ten or twelve good hours, and had no sooner laid down than I fell into a profound slumber.

It might have been midnight, or perhaps a little later, when I awoke, believing myself to be the victim of a horrible nightmare. I seemed to hear a chorus of frightful cries, and, sitting up bewildered in my bed, found my cabin filled with a strange red light. Believing that the ship was on fire, I sprang out of bed and rushed to the door. The captain and the supercargo were standing each on the threshold of his cabin. We looked speechlessly at one another, for the savage yells grew every instant louder, and a shower of missiles was falling all around. Pieces of stone and iron came crashing down through the skylights, and rolled heavily about the decks, and strange flashes of fire were reflected from without.

I clung to the captain – I could not speak – I had no voice, and the words died away upon my lips. "Captain!" I faltered; "captain! fire! – the ship is on fire – do you hear? – what noise is that?" But he stood like one petrified. "I do not know," said he; and, rushing into his cabin, came back with a revolver in his hand. That revolver was the only weapon of defence on board. At this moment the mate came running down. I could not hear what he said, but, dreading some terrible misfortune, I went back into my cabin, and climbed up to the window that overlooked the sea. By the lurid light without, I beheld a crowd of Chinese junks. Beside myself with terror, I flew back to the captain, crying, "Oh, they are pirates! They are pirates!" And they were indeed pirates – those terrible pirates which scour the Chinese seas, and are so famous for their cruelties. We were utterly in their power. Three junks, each manned by thirty or forty ruffians, surrounded the *Caldera*. These creatures seemed like demons, born of the tempest, and bent upon completing our destruction. Having boarded the *Caldera* by means of grappling-hooks, they were now dancing an infernal dance upon deck, and uttering cries which sounded like nothing human. The smashing of the glass awoke our whole crew, and the light which we had taken for a fire at sea was occasioned by the bursting of fiery balls which they cast on deck to frighten us. Calculating upon his method of alarming their victims, they attack vessels chiefly in the night, and seldom meet with any resistance. The captain, the supercargo, and the mate, made an effort to go upon deck. I followed them instinctively. Driven back by flaming balls, we were forced to beat a retreat, and narrowly escaped being burnt. It seemed strange that they should risk setting fire to the ship, when plunder was their evident intention. The captain, having but his revolver for our defence, recommended that we should keep out of sight as long as possible. Useless precaution! Accustomed as they were to predatory warfare, they were sure to find us as easily in one place as another. Fear, however, left us no time for reflection. We fled precipitately between decks, and hid ourselves as best we might. Five of the sailors were there before us, and none of us knew what had become of the rest of the crew – perhaps they were already taken prisoners. As to Than-Sing, he had not been seen since the evening before.

These savage cries, and this still more savage dance, went on overhead without cessation. Through a crack in the partition which concealed us, we witnessed all their proceedings. Seen by the red firelight, they looked unspeakably hideous. They were dressed like all other Chinese, except that they wore scarlet turbans on their heads, and round their waists broad leathern belts garnished with knives and pistols. In addition to this, each man carried in his hand a naked sword. At this sight my heart sank within me, and I believed my last hour was at hand. Creeping on my hands and knees, I crouched down behind the captain, and we hid ourselves amid the merchandise, about twenty feet from the entrance. Further than this we could not go, on account of the goods which were there piled to the level of the upper deck. Scarcely able to breathe, we heard them come down into the cabins, and upset everything on which they could lay their hands.

Soon a well-known voice reached our ears. It was the voice of Than-Sing, whom they had just discovered. A loud dispute then took place between him and the pirates. They doubtless demanded where the rest of the crew had hidden themselves; for he called to us in English several times, saying, "Captain, captain! where are you? Are you below? Answer! Come here! Come quickly!" But nobody stirred.

The captain grasped his pistol, and vowed to shoot the first pirate who came near us; but I entreated him to do no such thing, since the death of one man could in nowise serve us, and might, on the contrary, incline our enemies to a wholesale massacre. He seemed to see the justice of my fears, and hid his weapon in his bosom.

It was not long before we were discovered. I shudder still when I recall the sound of those approaching footsteps. They raised the trap on deck, and let down a lighted lantern. We crowded together in a vain effort at concealment; but the light came lower and lower, and we were seen at last. In another instant five or six pirates, armed to the teeth, leaped into the hold, and advanced towards us. The captain then rose up and went to meet them. Smiling, he offered them his revolver. They drew back, as if to defend themselves; then, seeing that he held the butt-end turned towards them, and that we made no effort at resistance, came eagerly forward, and glared at us with savage delight. Two of them then went up on deck, and made signs that we should follow them. More dead than alive, I remained crouched behind some bales. I saw my companions going, one by one. I would have followed them, but had to strength to stir. When the last had disappeared, and I found myself left alone with these monsters, I rose up by a despairing effort and fell at their feet. Seeing that I was a woman, they burst into exclamations of surprise and joy. Dreading every instant lest they should seize me, I rushed to the door, and in another moment found myself on deck.

Surrounded by a crowd of pirates armed with sabres and pistols, I saw every eye fixed eagerly upon the few jewels that I wore. To pull off my rings and ear-rings, and throw them at their feet, was the work of a moment, for I dreaded lest I should become the victim of their impatience. Those who were nearest clutched them greedily. An angry scuffle ensued, and but for the interference of their captain, a sanguinary quarrel would probably have followed. They then pushed me towards the stairs leading to the upper deck, and there I found my companions loaded with chains. The sea was still agitated, and huge black clouds, last remnants of the tempest, scudded hither and thither across the sky. The poor *Caldera,* riding helplessly at anchor, swayed to and fro like a mere log upon the waters. A thick fog froze us with cold, and a dead silence, which was only interrupted by the groans of the sailor who had been hurt the night before, reigned all around us. Torn by a thousand fears and regrets, I longed to weep, but could not shed a tear.

Meanwhile the pirates, who numbered, perhaps, a hundred men, were searching for plunder. Two or three of them came up, and made signs to me to observe the chains with which my companions were fettered. Thinking that they wished to treat me in the same manner, I submissively held out my hands; but they shook their heads. One of them then passed the cold blade of his sabre along my throat, whilst the others made signs expressive of their inclination to behead me. I stirred neither hand nor foot, though my face, I dare say, indicated the depth of my despair. Once more I extended my hands to be tied. They seized hold of them angrily, and passed their fingers round and round my wrists, though for what purpose I could not imagine. What could they want? Was it their intention to cut off my hands? In this moment I recognized all the horrors of my position. I closed my eyes, and leaned my head against the bulwark. The sight of these monsters was alone sufficient to make death welcome, and I awaited it with entire resignation. I was still in this state of semi-stupefaction when Than-Sing came up, and touched me on the shoulder. "Be not afraid," said he; "they do not mean to harm you. Their only object is to frighten you, lest you should attempt to set your companions at liberty."

He was now sent for by the pirate-chief, who was a small wiry-looking man, with a countenance more intelligent and less ferocious than the others. Than-Sing, although not fettered, was a prisoner like ourselves, and, being the only Chinese on board, acted as our interpreter.

Captain Rooney was next sent for. Calm and disdainful, he seemed to despise the success of his captors and his own personal danger. "Is he English?" asked the chief. Than-Sing, luckily remembering the feud then existing between China and Great Britain, replied that the captain was a Spaniard, and the crew composed of various Europeans. This proved, indeed, to be a fortunate inspiration; for the pirate instantly replied that, had we been English, our throats should all have been cut upon the spot. He then enquired respecting the number of persons on board, and the amount of money which we carried, and ended by asking if I were the wife of Mr. Rooney. Having satisfied him on the two former points, Than-Sing replied that I was a Frenchwoman, journeying to California, a stranger in China, and quite without friends or relatives in this part of the world. The excellent Chinese was careful to impress this fact of my loneliness upon them, hoping thereby to moderate any expectations which they might have formed respecting the amount of my ransom.

Captain Rooney's hands were then released, and he had to submit to the humiliation of accompanying the chief through every part of the ship. He was even obliged to furnish an exact inventory of his cargo. For our lives we were already indebted to the generous misrepresentations of Than-Sing; but it was yet possible that the pirates might change their minds, and although they had promised to save our lives, we scarcely dared to depend upon it. Besides all this, more pirates might arrive to dispute the prize, and we be sacrificed in the strife. Such were my reflections during the absence of the captain. A scene of plunder was at this moment being enacted before my eyes. The cabins were first dismantled; and I beheld my own luggage transported on board the junks. Everything was taken – even my dear little birds in their wicker cage. "They survived the tempest," said I, "only to die of cold and neglect!" And, with this, the tears which had so long refused to flow, coursed hotly down my cheeks.

I was aroused from this melancholy train of thought by the return of the captain. Our sailors were now unchained to work the ship, and the pirate-chief gave orders that we should weigh anchor, and put into a neighbouring bay. At the same time our men were all given to understand that, at the least token of revolt, we should all be slaughtered without pity. As for Than-Sing, the supercargo, and myself, we were left on the upper deck in company with the wounded sailor, since none of us could be of use in the management of the vessel.

At this moment one of the robbers came up with a parcel of jewels and money, which he had just found. In one hand he held a silver fork, the properties and uses of which seemed mightily to perplex him. He paused, looked at me, and raised the fork to his head, as if to ask me whether it were a woman's comb. Under any other circumstances his ignorance might have amused me; now, however, I had no strength to reply to him even by a sign. Than-Sing then came to my assistance, and the pirate, having received the information he desired, went away. I hoped that we had got rid of him, but returning almost immediately, he held a handful of silver before my eyes, pointed towards a junk which we had in tow, and endeavoured, by his looks and gestures, to arouse me from my apathy. It was not difficult to interpret these signs, and I saw with a shudder that he wanted me to fly with him. Than-Sing, who had been silently observing this scene, now took pity on my distress, and addressed the man in Chinese. He doubtless threatened to betray his treachery to the chief; for the pirate hung his head, and went silently away.

The weather was now misty, and much colder; and, half-clothed as we were, we suffered intensely. It was but fair, however, to say that our captors were not wholly insensible to our miseries, and that they had at least the charity to cover us with a few rugs and pieces of sail-cloth.

Shortly after this, we heard a sound of falling chains, and the anchor was cast once more. Alas! was that anchor ever to be weighed again, or was it destined to rust away throughout all the ages of time, in the spot where it was now imbedded? Heaven only knew! ...

Day broke, and the last shades of night faded and fled. The pirates assembled us on deck, counted us over to see that none were missing, lifted the hatches at the foot of the mainmast, and lowered us, one by one, into the hold. Some of them followed us down, and kept a savage watch upon our every movement. This last proceeding struck us with a mortal terror. Believing that our fate was just about to be decided, we sat down mournfully among the bales of goods, and waited like condemned criminals. Our jailers seemed now to be more cruelly disposed than ever. Every moment, and without any kind of provocation, they struck our poor sailors with the handles and flats of their sabres, and amused themselves by flourishing these weapons round my head and that of Captain Rooney. Presently they took to examining our wrists, and laughed to see the wounds which our chains had left upon them.

Hearing a noise on deck, they, by and bye, left us; having first taken the precaution of battening down the hatches above our heads. Plunged into utter darkness, and almost suffocated for want of air, we endured this captivity for more than an hour. The hatches were then lifted, a flood of blinding sunlight poured in upon us, and the friendly voice of Than-Sing greeted us from above ...

It was now decided by the pirate-chief that our crew should be set to work to unlade the vessel. The valuable freight of opium which we had on board was the property of Than-Sing, who was accordingly sent below with Captain Rooney to assist the pirates in clearing out these stores. The sailors then passed the packages from hand to hand; the pirates formed a chain from junk to junk; and the bales of sugar, rice, coffee, and other goods were speedily transferred.

Forgotten in the midst of this excitement, I sat alone and watched the work of spoilation.

After about an hour's labour, our sailors were allowed to rest for a few moments, and received a scanty ration of biscuits and water. Several of the poor fellows offered me a share of their food; but, although I eagerly drank what water they could spare me, I found it impossible to eat a morsel. For long hours my throat and chest had been on fire, and I suffered cruelly from thirst.

Soon after this, Than-Sing and the captain came in search of me. Thankful was I, indeed, to see them; for the pirates had of late been thronging around me with gesticulations which filled me with uneasiness. My friends then led me to a cabin, at the other end of the vessel, where I hoped to be left without molestation. Crossing the deck, I saw that we had anchored close in shore, and were surrounded by an immense amphitheatre of wooded hills. At any other time I should have been charmed with this exquisite scene; but the sight of the *Caldera,* now a mere wreck, usurped all my attention. Her broken masts were lying along deck – fragments of doors and windows lay scattered all about – the compass had been carried away, and the helm was broken. Add to this the ferocious cries of our barbarian captors, and the picture is complete.

I was glad to hurry away from this sight; but our pretty cabins were no longer recognizable. Lying upon a large green velvet sofa, which was the only article of furniture left entire, I yielded to an access of the profoundest melancholy. Every moment the pirates kept passing to and fro, or coming in to cast lots for such of the booty as was yet unshared amongst them ... I recalled some frightful stories read in times gone by, and dreaded lest I should become the victim of their brutality. Sooner than this, I resolved to throw myself into the sea. That I should now be living to write these lines – that I should now be relating the long story of my sufferings – seems, if I may dare to say so, like a special manifestation of that divine goodness which measures the trial by the strength of the sufferer.

Our provisions, with the exception of some rice and a few biscuits, had all been carried on board the three junks. Our sailors had been allowed no rest. Groaning under fatigues, which were enforced with the sword, they laboured on till night-fall, and even then, but for the intercessions of Than-Sing, would have been allowed no sleep.

My companions slept in the cabin adjoining mine, and we were allowed to close our doors for the night. Having eaten nothing all day, and being kept awake, moreover, by the vociferations of the pirates, whose numbers had lately been increased by the arrival of fresh junks, I passed a miserable night. Many a time, during these long hours of wakefulness, I opened my little window and leaned out into the air; but each time that I did so, my terrors were increased by the sight of these demons quarrelling over their booty. Day dawned, and a sudden rumour spread all at once throughout the ship. Starting from their sleep, our sailors rushed on deck, and two or three came down crying, "The pirates are leaving us! The pirates are leaving us!" A wild and sudden hope possessed us. We believed that help was at hand, and that the moment of our release had arrived. Could it be the approach of a steamer which caused the flight of our captors? A single glance, however, was sufficient. Alas! that which we had supposed to be a deliverance, proved to be but an added danger. Our pirates were indeed leaving us, but a new flotilla was bearing down upon us with all sail set! For more than a quarter of an hour we were left alone in the wreck, and Than-Sing explained to us that the small junks were making off with their booty, for fear it should be wrested from them by the new comers. These second enemies were, then, fiercer and more numerous than the first! What would they do with us? What would now become of us? What had we to expect? We counted the minutes as they passed, and the junks drew rapidly nearer. I felt my very heart sink within me, and all the horrors to which I might be subjected rushed across my mind. "Oh, captain," said I, "I shall die with fear! Can you not help to disguise me? Let me be dressed as you are! What shall I do? I am a woman, and these monsters are coming! Have pity on me! Have pity on me!" "Yes, you are right," said Captain Rooney, kindly and compassionately. Having on two pairs of trousers, he then gave me one. We next found a shirt and a Chinese jacket, and one of the sailors gave me his cap, beneath which I gathered up my hair. I had but one hair-pin left, and on my naked feet a pair of slippers. Hastening into my cabin, I dressed rapidly, and had scarcely completed this transformation when loud shouts proclaimed the approach of our new enemies. The small junks, which had fled before the others like startled water-fowl, were already far away. We hid ourselves in one of the after-cabins, and the captain grouped his men in such a manner as might best conceal me. He and Than-Sing stood before me, and in another moment the pirates were on board. About forty junks now surrounded the *Caldera,* each junk carrying from twenty to forty men, and the large ones being mostly mounted with ten or twelve cannons.

The pirates of the Chinese seas make their junks their homes, and carry their wives and children with them on every expedition. The women assist in working the ships, and are chiefly employed in lading and unlading the merchandise. As for the children, they carry them upon their backs in a kind of bag, till they are able to run alone. Each junk is commanded by a chief, and such is the terror of the pirate-name, that, in a country which numbers three hundred and sixty million inhabitants, they ravage the seas with impunity. It sometimes happens that they have feuds among themselves, and many a piratical sea-fight takes place, in which the victory rests with the strongest.

Hidden as we were in a lower cabin, we heard these barbarians rush upon our decks, with the force of a torrent that had burst its flood-gates. The first junks having carried away but a small portion of our cargo, these new pirates found an ample prize remaining. They therefore employed themselves in pillaging the ship, without taking the trouble to seek for us. Presently, such of the junks as were sufficiently laden, dropped away, and set sail for those villages along the coast, where they were in the habit of taking refuge. In the meantime, despite the indifference with which they treated us, fresh fears assailed us. We dreaded lest they should exhaust our store of provisions, and found ere long that these apprehensions were but too well grounded. Soon, a sack of rice, and a small bag of biscuits alone remained, and even these they would have taken from us, but for our urgent supplications. We were now utterly destitute. For two days and more, we could scarcely be said to have eaten anything, and faint, with exhaustion, we abandoned ourselves to despair. As if animated with the very spirit of destruction, the pirates demolished everything which came in their way. The panellings in the saloon, the looking-glasses, the windows, the doors, and such of the furniture as was not already destroyed, they smashed into a thousand pieces. They carried away the very hinges and fastenings from off the doors, and even the green velvet divan, which had hitherto been left on account of its size. The deck was strewn all over with, tea, coffee, sugar, biscuit, fragments of broken glass, and merchandise. We were constantly obliged to turn out our pockets, in proof that we kept nothing back; and these monsters pressed around us, every now and then, in such numbers that we could scarcely move or breathe. My dress, which I had hidden as best I could, was found and carried off like everything else; and Than-Sing, who had chanced to take off his slippers for a moment, saw them snatched up and appropriated in the twinkling of an eye. The poor man was more annoyed by this loss, than by all his previous misfortunes; for the slippers were made after the fashion of his country. Hereafter, one of our sailors, who was indifferently skilful in such matters, contrived to make him a new pair, out of some fragments of leather which he found about the deck.

Cast upon the mercy of these savages, our situation was inexpressibly horrible. They were not deceived by my costume; for they surrounded me with eager curiosity, and asked Than-Sing if I were the wife of the captain. These questions filled me with terror, and I entreated Mr. Rooney to let me pass for his wife. They gathered round us in brutal mockery, asking if we wished to go to Hong-Kong; and then, finding that we were silent, laughed in our faces. Some of them, who seemed more savage and cruel than the rest, seized our sailors by the hair, and flourished their sabres threateningly before their eyes; whilst I, sinking, and sick at heart, shrank down in a corner, and hoped to be forgotten. Slender indeed was the tenure upon which we now held our lives! Who knows what might have happened had one single drop of blood been actually shed?

That same day, one of these men came, when none of the rest were by, and talked for some time with Than-Sing. I saw the merchant's face light up as the conversation progressed, and the breathless eagerness with which he replied. The pirate was offering, as I afterwards learnt, to effect our escape; and Captain Rooney, by help of Than-Sing, agreed on the amount of our ransom. We were to be landed at Hong-Kong, and, meanwhile, were desired to hold ourselves in readiness for the first chance of escape. Two others came shortly after upon the same errand; but, whether the reward which we offered was insufficient to recompense them for the danger, or whether they dreaded the discovery of their treason, I know not – at all events, not one of the three kept his word, and we saw them no more.

Towards the evening of this day our sailors complained bitterly of hunger. We feared being left to all the agonies of starvation; but, in the midst of our distress, help came whence we had least reason to expect it. Amongst these robbers there was one who seemed actuated by sentiments of compassion. He came to us every now and then, appeared to sympathize with our distress, and, by and bye, pointed out his wife and children on board a neighbouring junk. Pleased to observe the interest with which we looked upon his family, this pirate, at the very moment when we were deploring our hunger, came back with a dish of rice and a huge bowl filled with some kind of Chinese *ragoût,* dressed after the Chinese fashion, with a thick saffron-coloured sauce. Our poor fellows, little used to dainties, devoured it eagerly. But I could only just touch it with my lips, for the odour of it disgusted me. I contrived, however, to alleviate my hunger with a few spoonfuls of the rice. Towards night, the junks let go the grappling-irons, and put out to sea. It seemed scarcely probable that they would return again in equal numbers, since our plundered state must soon become known throughout the pirate-villages which line that coast.

On the following day our sailors set to work gallantly. To repair the jolly-boat would take, at the least, eight or ten hours of hard labour, and our only hope lay in the continued absence of our enemies ... for hours and hours no sail was visible on the horizon. Once more we had the *Caldera* to ourselves; but she was now a mere shell, dismantled, melancholy, and motionless – a floating mass of utter ruin! We fixed ten o'clock at night for the moment of our escape, and throughout all the day toiled on without any kind of food or rest.

To fit a mast to the boat, and construct some kind of rude sail out of the rags that lay strewn about our decks, occupied the men up to a late hour of the evening. As all our rigging had been either carried away, or cut to pieces, they even contrived to make some bamboo canes serve in the place of ropes. This done, we prepared to leave the ship, and were just about to lower the boat, when two junks came into sight, and bore down straight upon us. Stowing away all that could be hidden of our preparations, we hastened to take refuge in our cabins, and there awaited whatever might happen.

It was not long before they hove alongside, and they had no sooner leapt on board, than they came down in search of us. Two of the pirates carried lanterns, by the light of which they examined us one by one, as if to make sure that none were missing. Arrived where I lay hidden behind some of my companions, they laughed, and called to each other with every mark of satisfaction. One made signs to me to rise, but I could only look up imploringly, and had no strength to stir. Another, irritated, perhaps, by my languor, threatened me with his sabre, which only added to my terror, and left me more helpless than ever. But for an agonized cry, which just then drew their attention from me towards one of their number, who had missed his footing and fallen into the hold, I hardly know now how this scene might have ended. Having pitched from the deck to the very bottom of the vessel, the Chinese was brought up by one of our sailors. More dead than alive, he lay and groaned piteously, and the pirates, being occupied with his sufferings, and pleased, to all appearance, with the ready help which our men had afforded him, tormented and threatened me no more.

Our alarms, however, were not yet ended. These barbarians seemed to delight in our terror; and, not content with all that they had already done, now took it into their heads to carry lighted torches into the hold, and all about the cabins, thereby scattering a shower of sparks in every direction, and more than once setting fire to the chips and rubbish that lay heaped around. Had not our sailors followed, and stamped out the sparks as they fell, the wreck must soon have been in flames. Weary at length of this ferocious pastime, the pirates returned to their junks, put out to sea, and left us once more in peace.

Thankful to be released from their presence, our brave fellows flew to work again, and rigged the jolly-boat afresh. She was still somewhat leaky; but we had made up our minds to sink or starve at sea, sooner than to die at last by the hands of the pirates ... meanwhile, the weather, which had hitherto been all that we could desire, became less favourable to our purpose. The sky, last night so serene, grew low and cloudy, and the wind, which had up to this time been blowing to the shore, shifted quite round, and seemed to forbid our progress. Seeing these signs of bad weather, the captain shook his head doubtfully; but our minds were made up. We had resolved to go, and would not be delayed.

It had now become a matter of some difficulty to get down into the boat; for, being gutted of her cargo, the *Caldera* necessarily drew but little water, and floated so high above the sea-level, as to leave an immense distance between the ship's deck and the jolly-boat. A wounded sailor and I were then lowered by means of cords, and the others, being more agile, contrived to clamber down in safety. The captain then placed himself at the helm; the supercargo, the Chinese merchant, the sick man, and myself were seated near him: the sailors grasped the rude oars which they had themselves constructed; and, twenty-two in number, we put out to sea. From the first moment of our starting, two sailors were constantly baling out the water that made its way through the bottom of the boat; and, as Captain Rooney had already anticipated, our sail soon proved to be worse than useless, and had to be taken down.

Struggling against a contrary breeze, and driven back by every wave that met us, we made but little progress ... Then, after four hours of super-human effort, our sailors confessed that they could do no more ...

The current, which had been hitherto our greatest enemy, bore us back, almost without an effort on our part, to the very spot from which we had started. The rope by which we had been let down, was swinging to and fro as we had left it. The others caught hold of it and climbed easily enough, but it was with the utmost difficulty that the invalid and I were hoisted on board.

I no sooner found myself standing, once again, upon this fatal deck, than everything swam before my eyes, and I fell heavily to the ground. Pain and hunger were fast doing their work upon me ... it was long before I recovered my consciousness, and, when I opened my eyes, I found that I was laid upon a bench and surrounded by kindly faces. Every man had deprived himself of some article of clothing to warm and cover me. Having but water to give, they gave it. Such cares as were in their power to bestow they lavished on me and so called me back to life at the very moment when it would have been most sweet to die. Some of them wept. Perhaps, looking at me, they thought of the wives, the mothers, the sisters, whom they had left at home ...

The next day was [Wednesday] the 11th of October. I had slept and this brief rest had for awhile effaced the remembrance of my sufferings. Starting up, however, in the early morning, I had no sooner opened my eyes than all the dread reality was brought before me. There, close beside me, stood a group of armed Chinese, and, in the midst of them, Than-Sing, eagerly conversing. He who seemed to be their leader, pointed towards me with his finger. I looked on in speechless stupefaction. Captain Rooney then came up, and Than-Sing, who still acted as our interpreter, explained the nature of the conference. "Captain," said he, "the chief [pirate] is about to carry you and me, and this French lady, to Macao, where he hopes to get a heavy ransom for us." ... I was immediately lifted by some two or three pirates and carried upon deck; but I scarcely comprehended what had been said, or whither they were taking me. Than-Sing went first; and I, being helped down a wretched ladder, followed him. I then looked up, expecting to see Captain Rooney next on his way; but found, to my horror, that the pirates had snatched the ladder away, and pushed off without him! No words can depict the shock with which I beheld this last act of treachery. Leaving Canton, I had been recommended to his care, and in all our troubles he had watched over me with the gentlest solicitude. He was my protector – my friend; and, parted from him, I believed myself lost beyond redemption. I held out my arms in a token of adieu, and saw the stony wonder in his face.

"Take me with you!" he cried, passionately; "Oh, take me with you!"

Then, seeing that it was useless, he covered his face with his hands and wept bitterly.

We were summoned, some few minutes after, to the cabin of the pirate-chief, who told Than-Sing that Captain Rooney was presently to be forwarded to Hong-Kong or Macao, there to negotiate for our ransoms and his own ... The pirates then lifted a kind of trap [door], about two feet square, and pushed us down into a narrow dark hole below deck, where we had no room to stand upright, and could with difficulty lie at full length ... Thus two frightful hours went by; and then the trap-door was suddenly raised, and the blessed sunlight flowed in once more upon us ... They crowded round the opening, laughing and pointing at us; and then, when their curiosity was satisfied, would have closed it up again, but for the prayers and representations of my companions. They consented to leave about two inches open ... and we breathed, at least, a less polluted air.

Towards evening they brought us a small bucketful of water, with which we washed our hands and faces; also some dried fish, some rice, and a little tea. So weak was I, that my head seemed too heavy for my body, and I now loathed the very sight of food. But Than-Sing ate eagerly, and implored me to partake of some little nourishment. Above all, he counselled me not to seem mistrustful of our foes, or of the food they gave us. Thus urged, I contrived to eat half a saucer of rice, and drink a little tea; but even this cost me a painful effort, and a degree of emotion for which

I find it difficult to account ...

When it was quite dark, the pirates summoned Than-Sing upon deck. Coming back some few minutes after, they told me that I also might go up to take the air. We were now anchored not far from land, in the neighborhood of several other junks, the crews of which were all at prayer ... This moment of brief liberty was inexpressibly delightful ...

One of the pirates now brought us a light, which consisted of a little wick in a saucer of oil. Feeble as it was, it yet sufficed to light up the walls of our narrow dungeon. Scarcely had I looked round, when I uttered a cry of horror. Ceiling, walls, and floor were peopled by a multitude of huge velvety spiders, enormous beetles, and monstrous wood-lice, horned and shiny. In another instant, three or four great rats rushed out of a corner, and ran between my feet. Seeing my disgust, Than-Sing offered to put out the light; but I preferred the sight of these reptiles to the torture of hearing and feeling them in the darkness of night ...

Not long after daybreak, we were again supplied with provisions, and with a bucket of water, in which we washed our hands and faces. Than-Sing then informed me that the Chinese never eat till they have performed their morning's ablution. As before, our food consisted of rice, fish, and tea. With these they sent us two pairs of tiny chop-sticks, each about a foot in length, and as thick as an ordinary pencil. The Chinese hold them as we hold a pen, and handle them with the utmost dexterity. Notwithstanding all the patience and skill with which Than-Sing endeavoured to teach me the use of these little sticks, I found them so impracticable as to be obliged at last to give up the attempt, and eat with my fingers.

To-day, again, the pirates came to watch and mock us. One of them, more insulting than the rest, pointed first at me and then at Than-Sing, and represented the action of two persons embracing. This cowardly insult pained me more than all their previous cruelties. I felt myself become scarlet with shame and anger, and gave way to a passion of tears. In the midst of my distress the pirate-captain happened to pass by, and, as if moved by my affliction, ordered the trap-door to be closed above our heads.

This chief, unlike his men, had something not wholly disagreeable in the expression of his countenance. He alone inspired me with neither disgust nor terror. His ugliness was, so to say, individual. His face was long and thin; he had high cheek-bones, a wide mouth, a short flat nose with open nostrils, dark eyebrows, and very large black eyes. His head was closely shaved, excepting on the crown, whence grew a long thick tress, which he wore sometimes clubbed on the nape of the neck; sometimes plaited, and bound round his head like a coronet; and sometimes hanging down his back, a yard or more in length. Transformed as he was by these various styles, his face always preserved a certain pleasant character. His consideration on the present occasion inspired me now with some hope for the future.

Than-Sing, partly to amuse me, partly to set my mind at rest, repeated to me the questions and observations which the pirates had addressed to him. They had asked him the number of his wives, which, in China, is a standard of wealth; and then added that if our ransoms were not sufficiently heavy, they would make a pirate of him, and give me in marriage to one of their companions. Seeing me now look more distressed than ever, the good merchant explained that the men of his country were not permitted to intermarry with aliens, and that these threats were only feints to draw him into conversation. "Be careful, however," said he, "never to lay your hand upon me in their presence. It is contrary to our custom, and they might repeat it to my disadvantage." To all their other questions he had replied that he was only a poor man, about to seek his fortune in California, and gave them to understand that he was working out a cheap passage on board the "Caldera." He was, therefore, careful to avoid any allusion which might lead them to conjecture the extent of his means. Had they supposed him wealthy, they would not only have quadrupled his ransom, but might even have put him to the torture. He then spoke to me of his family. He had but one wife, he said, and his home was Canton. He was the father of three daughters, of eight, eighteen, and twenty-five years of age, the eldest of whom was married. He seemed to love them tenderly, and wept when he spoke of them. He scarcely hoped ever to see them again, and had but little belief in our ultimate deliverance. I often enquired of him, at this time, respecting the manners and customs of the pirates; to which he always replied, shudderingly, that they were not to be depended upon depended upon, and were dangerously fond of decapitating their prisoners ...

It was now the 13th of October. The junk still coasted along close in shore ... On the morning of the 15th, we came up with several other pirate-junks, and joined them in giving chase to a merchant-junk, plying between Hong-Kong and Canton with goods and passengers. All was now excitement on board ... When the evening came, we were fastened down in our dungeon more closely than ever. It might have been about ten o'clock at night, when we once more heard the frightful war-cries ... These cries were followed by a dropping cannonade. Two shots were then fired from our own junk ... four junks then surrounded the merchant-vessel, which, taken by surprise, offered but a feeble resistance.

Amid the silence that ensured, Than-Sing contrived, with much difficulty, to raise the trap-door; for we had been a long time shut in, and the heat had become insufferable. Scarcely, however, had he succeeded, and looked out, than he drew precipitately back, and closed up the entrance. His terror and agitation alarmed me; but he refused to describe what he had seen. Some hours later, however, I learnt all that had taken place.

Having boarded and pillaged the merchant-junk, the pirates, it seemed, proceeded to interrogate the [Chinese] passengers. Several of these unfortunates unluckily confessed that they came from California [the goldfields], which was alone sufficient to expose them to every kind of ill-usage. In order to wring from them a full avowal of their riches, the pirates had put their victims to the torture. Bound by only one thumb and one toe, these wretched captives were suspended from the masts, and swung violently backwards and forwards. As if this were not sufficient suffering, their agonies were, from time to time, augmented by heavy blows, and their shrieks were inconceivably distressing. Although these scenes were not taking place on board our own junk, Than-Sing guessed but too plainly the species of torture which the barbarians had chosen to inflict.

Day broke, and the dreary silence which succeeded to the horrors of the night was only disturbed by the slow plashing of the waves, and the dipping oars of the rowers, who were transporting the booty in small boats from junk to junk.

We had hoped that the day would, as usual, bring us some little liberty and fresh air; but the pirates were too busy to heed us. Absorbed in the pursuit of gain, they were all day occupied in negotiating the sale of their plunder, and for that purpose received on board those traders whose special line it is to buy up stolen goods. Bathed in perspiration, racked with acute cramps, and half stifled by the long-confined air, I suffered horribly. My skin, too, was covered with a painful eruption, and I had become so weak that, although my companion strove to amuse and cheer me, I was no longer able to reply. By and bye, we heard the pirates counting their gold, and then the splashing oars that bore the purchasers away. This done, our jailers at length remembered our captivity, and opened the trap-door. It was time they did so; for we had lain there upwards of four-and-twenty hours! The delight which it was once more to breathe that fresh night-air, I shall remember to my dying day.

The next day was the 17th, and a glorious morning dawned. To our surprise, the pirates came at sunrise, and quite removed the trap-door. They seemed almost pleasant, and, when the hour of breakfast came, brought us not only an abundance of food, but even some wine. This liquor, which is extracted from rice, is as transparent as water, and by no means unpalatable. The flavour or it, indeed, is not unlike that of new Bordeaux.

The junk was now coasting beside an uninhabited shore, and the pirates, assured that we could not here be observed, left our cell uncovered throughout the day. They even suffered Than-Sing to remain for some time on deck, and behaved towards us with an amazing degree of good-humour ... I ventured to stand up in my place, and look around at the land and the sea. Oh, how delicious seemed that sight! After having lived for seven long days in a dark and filthy den, I now beheld the bright broad ocean and the verdant shore! The sight of this landscape intoxicated me. I fancied myself once more in sight of my own dear France, and wept as I have seldom wept before or since.

At this moment the pirate-chief passed by ... Motioning to me to be calm, the chief then said that he had long despatched Captain Rooney in a junk to Macao; that Captain Rooney was empowered to treat there for our ransoms; and that he had expected yesterday to meet the junk on its return. Should five more days elapse, however, without further tidings, it was his intention, he said, to transfer us on board another vessel. This vague reply troubled us more than ever. Transferred to another junk, what might not be our fate? After all, the interpretation of the thing was plain enough. They were not disposed, somehow, to put us to death; but should they find it impossible to extort a ransom for our liberty, they would get rid of us to those who might not be so scrupulous. Even supposing that we had come across a steamer by the way, what had we to hope? Would not our captors sooner throw us overboard, than be taken in the fact of piracy and kidnapping on the high seas?

The pirate-captain now gave me leave to walk awhile

on deck, and I gratefully availed myself of the permission. So happy was I in the enjoyment of light and liberty, that I forgot all my former tortures, and learnt to look upon these lawless men with feelings that were almost friendly. They were very busy this morning, bustling to and fro, chatting familiarly together, and dividing the spoil of the previous evening. I confess with shame that I scarcely remembered by what means they had wrung that spoil from their miserable victims, and could think only of my present freedom. It was not often that the pirates took any notice of me; but, strange to say, whenever they did look at me, it was with an expression of good-nature of which I should scarcely have supposed them capable ...

It seemed incredible that these men should forego their native ferocity in my favour; but perhaps my patience and my weakness touched their hearts. On the other hand, I owed much, doubtless, to their cupidity. When I recall the length of my imprisonment, the character of my jailers, and all the circumstances of my capture, I can scarcely credit, even now, the evidences of my own memory.

Having been on deck for about two hours, I went back voluntarily to my cell. Long confinement had incapacitated me for any kind of exertion, and I fell down upon the floor, utterly wearied and exhausted. At the same time, I felt better than for many days past, and the weight at my heart was lightened.

Gazing languidly around the four dreary walls within which I had spent so many frightful hours, I observed an old book lying in one corner, covered with dust and dirt. I had seen it before, but had not till now the heart to take it up. It was a German work, and printed in German text.

Ignorant as I was of the language, I turned the pages over with delight, for they reminded me of Europe and of home. At the end of the volume were some three or four blank leaves, still tolerably clean. "Oh," thought I, "had I but a pen, to record something of my story!" It then occurred to me that I had one hair-pin left, and that I might contrive to write with the point of it. My success surpassed my hopes, and the following words, thus traced upon the page, were sufficiently legible:–

"I have been captured by Chinese pirates, and am kept prisoner by them. I am a French-woman, and was a passenger on board the *Caldera*. This is my seventh day in the junk. –17th of October, 1854. – *FANNY LOVIOT.*"

I then wrote the same thing in French upon another page. As for the pirates, they kept passing backwards and forwards, and glancing down every now and then, to see what I was doing. They never guessed, however, that I was writing words which might, some day, hang every man among them!

Having recorded these three sentences, I lay down and rested ... Profiting by my present privileges, I soon rose and went again on deck. The pirates were still friendly, and encouraged me to walk where they were at work; which I did, though not without misgivings. Some of them were busy launching a little boat, and Than-Sing explained to me that they were going to put off on an oyster-dredging expedition, which they presently did. It seemed that their first haul was fortunate, for they soon came back with the boat half full of enormous oysters, larger than any which I ever remember to have seen before.

The cook to-day was fully employed with his stewpans

and braziers, and appeared to be giving himself airs of no little importance. A feast was evidently in course of preparation, and he well knew that on his skill depended the success or failure of the entertainment. First of all, he opened and shelled the oysters, and put them over the fire in a huge saucepan. He then fried a quantity of delicious little fishes, besides attending, every now and then; to a quarter of pork, which was browning before a fire close by. The sight of all these good things sharpened our appetites, and we asked each other if we had any chance of sharing the feast. When the hour of repast came round, Than-Sing and I went back to our dungeon, scarcely hoping to be remembered till the best of the dishes were eaten. How much, then, were we surprised, on finding the pirates assemble and seat themselves all round about our cell, while the cook, ladle in hand, went round, and helped the company to saucerfuls of smoking oysters. Of these, Than-Sing and I received as large a share as the rest, and although I was at first somewhat doubtful of the sauce in which they were floating, I soon came to the conclusion that I had seldom tasted anything more savoury. After the oysters came the pork, and after the pork, wine, tea, and fish fried in rice. We were liberally helped to all these dishes. Indeed, it seemed as if the pirates wished to show us how sociable they could be, and for this day, at least, we were treated less as prisoners than guests. They enjoyed the dinner immensely themselves, and more than once asked Than-Sing how I liked their cookery.

Towards the close of the feast, just as I was anticipating the comfort of a few hours' rest, a large merchant-junk came in sight to the leeward. Every man was on his feet in an instant, the remains of the dinner were cleared hastily away, the flags were hoisted to the mast-head, and the pirates, running eagerly hither and thither, prepared for fighting. Plunder was once again the order of the day, and we, crouched silently in our little den, awaited whatever might take place. The merchantman, however, made too much way for us, and the pursuit was presently relinquished. I was inexpressibly thankful that this comparatively happy day was not destined to end in bloodshed and pillage.

The merchantman was soon out of sight, and we were shortly overtaken by a flotilla of pirate-junks, the captains of which proceeded to make exchanges of merchandise and provisions. Amongst other things, our chief bought a quantity of live ducks. As night fell, the junks all dropped away, and we continued our solitary route ... To-night I observed that, instead of anchoring for several hours, as we had hitherto invariably done, we were sailing rapidly on, under press of canvas. Going back to our dungeon, I lay as usual on the floor, and fell asleep. Waking from time to time, I heard the wind whistling through the cordage, and the rapid gliding of the waters as our keel ploughed onwards.

The next day was Wednesday, October 18th, 1854 – a heaven-sent day, never to be named unless with prayer and thankfulness! It might have been about four o'clock in the morning, when we were awakened from our sleep by the sound of hurrying feet and eager voices. After having sailed fast all night, the junk was now riding at anchor, and the trap-door was closely fastened above our heads. I could not conceive what our captors were about, or why they should be thus active at so early an hour. The more I listened, the stranger it seemed. Having waited and wondered for some time, I tried to compose myself to sleep; but sleep would not come again, and, somehow or another, a strangle restlessness possessed me. I turned to Than-Sing, who was awake and listening also, and asked him what he thought could be doing overhead? He laid a finger on his lip, and, bending breathlessly forward, paused for some moments before replying.

"Hush!" said he, at length. "They are going. I tell you, they are going. It is a steamer in pursuit. The pirates have seen a steamer, and they are escaping to the mountains." ... I listened. A profound silence reigned around us, and I heard only a sound of murmuring voices, which became, every moment, more and more distant. I strove to raise the trap-door, but Than-Sing pulled me back. At that instant, a heavy footstep echoed overhead, and the trap-door was lifted from without. It was the ship's cook, who, with startled face and hurried gestures, looked in upon us.

"Fear nothing," said he. "It is a steamer! You are saved!"

And with these words he also fled, and we were left alone. Quick as thought, I jumped up and sprang upon deck. A feverish strength possessed me, and I uttered cries of frantic joy. It was indeed true. We were alone, utterly alone, on board the junk, which, having anchored somewhat too close in shore, was left half stranded by the ebbing tide, and could not be pushed off. They had ventured here in search of fresh water, and it was not till daybreak that they found themselves in such close neighbourhood with the steamer. This latter, it seemed, was also lying at anchor, and had been partly hidden by a jutting tongue of land. Terrified, then, by the imminence of the danger, and finding it impossible to put off to sea, the pirates had preferred flight to fighting, and were, at this moment, abandoning their vessel. Having waded through the shallow water that lay between the ship's side and the land, they were now in the very act of climbing the steep precipices which here start, as it were, from the very verge of the sea. We could see them distinctly, and even the plunder with which they had loaded themselves.

No language can describe the emotion with which I beheld the flight of our enemies ... In the meantime, those on board the steamer had not yet observed us, or put off a boat to our rescue ... I looked [again], and there indeed were three boats rounding a point of land, and making directly towards us ... I could distinguish the blue jackets of the rowers ... All at once the rowers ceased to row, and sat in the boats with uplifted oars ... I rushed to the prow, and showed myself. I pulled off my cap – I waved it wildly to and fro – I tried to shout aloud, and immediately a prolonged "Hurrah!" broke from every lip, and told me that a crew of English sailors were our deliverers! They waved their hats in reply to my signal; then bent to their oars again, and cleft the waters as an arrow cleaves the air. They had recognized me now, and we were saved at last!

Overwhelmed with joy, I staggered back and fell upon the deck. The boats were within a yard or two of the junk ... My strength was all gone now, and I wept profusely. I could not speak and when our friends came climbing up the sides, and leaping on deck, I had no greeting to give them. They were chiefly soldiers and officers of the Royal

Marines, and were accompanied by some blue-jackets and Royal Naval officers. Captain Rooney was with them. He could scarcely contain his joy on seeing me again; and they all crowded round me with every mark of interest and good-will. As for poor Than-Sing, he was at first mistaken for a pirate, and had some half-dozen fists shaken in his face; but I ran and stood beside him, and Captain Rooney told them how he had saved us all, and how nobly he had behaved from first to last.

Finding that I was not too weak to be moved, the sailors then carried me down into one of the boats, and I left the junk for ever. While we were on our way, the officers explained to me that the removal of my cap left my light hair visible, and Captain Rooney recognized me ... I also learnt that every one in Hong-Kong believed either that I had been killed, or that I was carried up into the country and sold. They, themselves, they said, had long since given up all hope of saving me ...

When I was calmer, and had rested awhile, Captain Rooney told me all that had happened to himself and the crew since we parted. Scarcely three hours had elapsed, he said, from the time of our departure, when another junk came up and took him on to Macao, leaving the crew with the wreck. An agreement was made upon the price of our ransom, and the pirates (confident of their own safety, since Than-Sing and I remained as hostages in the hands of their companions) sailed straight into port, and landed openly. Two of their number then followed Captain Rooney into the town, believing that he would immediately proceed to raise money among his friends. Captain Rooney, however, did no such thing, but presented himself before the [Portuguese] governor, gave his two attendants into custody, and petitioned for immediate succours of men and arms, in order to rescue his crew, his passengers, and his ship, from the hands of the pirates ... in Hong Kong he went on board H.M.S. *Sparta*, then lying in harbour, under command of Captain Sir William Hoste. Nothing could exceed the promptness and generosity with which this gallant officer hastened to place twenty-four Royal Marines at their immediate disposal; or the courtesy with which the Peninsular and Oriental Steam Navigation Company lent the *Lady Mary Wood* for their conveyance.

By six o'clock the next morning everything was in readiness, and they steamed out of Hong Kong harbour, taking the two prisoners with them and an interpreter skilled in the Chinese dialects. During the greater part of the day they saw not a single sail. It almost seemed as if the pirates had anticipated pursuit, and purposely abandoned their accustomed haunts. Meeting, however, with some floating fragments of charred wood, they came upon the track of the *Caldera* and found but a few burnt fragments of her hull remaining ... The steamer then continued to coast close in shore, and landed at every village, on the chance of learning something definite ... Having as yet heard nothing of us, and seeing but little likelihood of coming up just yet with any pirate-junks, the captain of the *Lady Mary Wood* prepared to return to Hong-Kong. Scarcely had they put the helm about, when they met a merchant-junk, with the whole of the crew of the *Caldera* on board, [who had been picked up at sea soon after escaping in a small boat] ... The steamer then went back to Hong-Kong, without having yet discovered any traces of Than-Sing or myself.

Scarcely had the first expedition returned, when a second was organized. Another steamer, named the *Ann*, set off in search of us on Tuesday, 17th October, 1854. Accident alone led the captain to steer in the direction of that very mountain under the shelter of which our captors had chanced to anchor. The steamer *Ann* and the junk must have even reached the same spot much at the same time, and anchored within a couple of miles of each other, under cover of darkness. It was not till morning that they perceived and rescued us; and the date of my deliverance was Wednesday, October 18th, 1854.

From Fanny Loviot, *Twelve Days Among the Pirates*, 1858, London.

THE ROYAL NAVY TO THE RESCUE

From George L. Haskell, Vice-Consul for France
To Captain Sir William Hoste

Hong Kong
October 16th, 1854.

Sir,– The *Lady Mary Wood* having been obliged to return to this place this morning without having succeeded in rescuing the French lady passenger on board the bark *Caldera* seized by the pirates to the south of Macao, I would ask if you could allow another force from your vessel to go down to the resort of these pirates in a steamer that the agents of the insurance companies (interested in the cargo of the bark) are to send down to-morrow morning for the purpose of saving what cargo they can, that is now lying in the houses on shore at that place, and to renew the search after this unfortunate person. I am desirous of leaving no means untried to rescue this lady, and I shall feel much obliged if you can accede to my request.

I have, &c.,
George L. Haskell, Vice-Consul for France.

From Captain Sir William Hoste
To Rear-Admiral Sir James Stirling

Her Majesty's Ship *Spartan*
Hong Kong,
October 20th, 1854.

Sir,– My letter of the 17th inst. will have informed you of the return of the *Lady Mary Wood*, and the unsuccessful result of her cruise, as far as the rescue of the French lady taken by the pirates from the bark *Caldera* was concerned. In consequence of a requisition from the Vice-Consul of France that I would permit another force to proceed in the steamer *Ann* for a further search, I again despatched 85 seamen and marines, under the command of Lieutenant Palliser, with orders to search for the French subject above-mentioned, and to effectually destroy the piratical settlement in the island of Symong.

The force returned this day, having been most successful; the French lady has been recovered, and the piratical forts and settlements of Coo-choo-mee, from which our boats were fired upon on the 15th inst., completely destroyed. I herewith enclose Lieutenant Palliser's report.

I had given to Lieutenant Palliser directions to destroy the town of Coulan, should he obtain certain information of the inhabitants being concerned in the plunder of the *Caldera*. On his entering the bay the boats were fired upon by 20 large junks and several batteries of heavy guns. Lieutenant Palliser, seeing that any attack with the force he had would be useless, most judiciously retired. There can be no doubt that Coulan is the stronghold of a large piratical fleet that has infested this neighbourhood, and committed great depredations for the last seven months. No ship thrown on the coast or passing its vicinity is safe. They detach small parties to plunder in this neighbourhood, who carry their booty to Coulan, where they consider themselves impregnable. I am of opinion that no boats could successfully cope with them; but it appears, from the soundings taken, that a steamer might be got within range, and a large force landing at the same time might effectually destroy the place.

Lieutenant Palliser speaks in high terms of the conduct of the officers under him. The conduct of the men, who worked for 12 hours under a burning sun, was most exemplary, and, though exposed to great temptation in the shape of liquor, no case of drunkenness occurred. I cannot conclude without bringing to your Excellency's notice the judgment and gallantry of Lieutenant Palliser, by whose judicious arrangements the object of these two expeditions have been most satisfactorily attained. This is the fifth occasion within four months in which Mr. Palliser has been employed successfully in command of the boats of this ship against pirates. And when it is taken into consideration that on the two latter occasions the steamers were unable, from their draught, to come within nine miles of the shore; that Lieutenant Palliser was left entirely to his resources, opposed to a very superior force; that he captured three forts mounting 17 guns, and completely destroyed a large piratical settlement. I hope I shall not be considered presumptuous in requesting your Excellency will be pleased to bring his conduct to the favourable notice of my Lords Commissioners of the Admiralty.

I have, &c.,
W. HOSTE, Captain.

P.S.
Detail of force belonging to Her Majesty's Ship *Spartan*, employed in the destruction of a piratical fort and settlement on the Island of Coo-choo-mee, 18th of October, 1854, Lieutenant Palliser in command:–

Barge, 12-pounder howitzer, Lieutenant Palliser.
Pinnace, 12 pounder howitzer, Lieutenant Morrell.
Jolly boat, Mr. Sarratt, Second Master.
Fifty-five seamen, small arm men; Lieutenant Stokes, 2 corporals, and 18 privates, Royal Marines.

W. HOSTE, Captain.

In consideration of the gallant conduct, as well as judgment, displayed by Lieutenant Palliser on the above occasion, the Lords of the Admiralty have promoted that officer to the rank of Commander.

From Lieutenant Wray Palliser
To Captain Sir William Hoste

Her Majesty's Ship *Spartan*
Hong Kong,
October 26th 1854.

Sir,– According to your directions I proceeded, at 7 a.m. of the 17th inst., with 85 seamen and marines of this ship, in the barge, pinnace, and jolly-boat to the steamer *Ann*. On the evening of the same day we anchored near the wreck of the *Caldera*. The next morning I observed some suspicious-looking junks working to windward; we immediately went in chase with the barge, pinnace, and jolly-boat. On our approach they made for the shore, threw their guns overboard, the crew succeeding in escaping before we could come up with them, leaving their vessels aground.

I am happy to inform you that the first junk I boarded had on board the French lady whom we have been in search of; also a Chinese merchant, who was taken in the *Caldera*. I immediately sent them to the *Ann*, in the jolly-boat, burnt the junk, and subsequently two others.

We then pulled up to the villages of Coo-choo-mee and landed, having previously burst some shrapnel shell over the town. We carried down to the boats all the cargo that was not damaged that we could find – viz., 43 bags of sugar and 40 chests of tea – and burnt two separate villages. While employed embarking the cargo we discovered another village in an adjacent valley, guarded by a battery, with men standing at the guns. I immediately collected our men and went to the attack. Not knowing the road, we had to force our way through a thick jungle till we came in face of a battery, which opened fire on us with four guns and five wall-pieces at about 80 yards. At the same time we received a shower of rocks and stones from a height that commanded the path, which knocked down several men. We immediately charged and cleared the battery, killing and wounding several, and the rest fled into the jungle, where many were shot. We then burst the village, which contained many houses, principally built of brick. Four of the guns and two of the wall-pieces we carried off; the rest we destroyed, and, after having burnt 17 boats on the beach, we returned to the *Ann* at 7.30 p.m.

Early the next morning we left the *Ann*, in the boats, and pulled into Coulan Bay. Immediately on rounding the point we were fired upon from several batteries, situated in different parts of the bay; also, from 20 large junks hauled up broadside on to the beach, mounting heavy guns, from which they fired upon us with very fair precision, at a distance of 1,000 yards. Near these large junks there was a battery from which they fired some shell that burst short. After having satisfied myself as to the force and position of this strong place, I retired behind the point, as I considered that, from the very strong position taken by the pirates, any attempt that I could have made with the force at my disposal to attack the place would be useless. I therefore returned to the *Ann*, and arrived in this harbour at 8.30 a.m. this day.

I take this opportunity of expressing to Lieutenant A. Morrell my thanks for his able advice and assistance throughout the expedition. To Lieutenant Stokes, who commanded the marines and assisted me greatly, my thanks are also due. I have great pleasure in informing you of the exemplary conduct of the men throughout. I herewith enclose a plan (by Mr. Henry D. Sarratt, second master) of the Bay of Coulan, which appears to be the stronghold of the pirates, and I am happy to state no casualties occurred.

I have, &c.,
W. PALLISER,
Senior Lieutenant, Her Majesty's Ship *Spartan.*

THE PIRATES IN THE CHINA SEAS

The following despatches have been received at the Admiralty from Rear-Admiral Sir James Stirling, Commander-in-Chief on the East Indian and China station, reporting operations of boats of the Spartan, under Lieutenant Palliser, of that ship, in pursuit of pirates:–

From Sir James Stirling
To the Lords of the Admiralty
Received Jan. 6, 1855.

Her Majesty's ship *Winchester,*
at Hongkong,
Nov. 8, 1854.

Sir,– I have the honour to transmit herewith, for the information of my Lords Commissioners of the Admiralty, the copy of a letter I have received from Captain Sir William

Hoste, Bart., of Her Majesty's ship *Spartan*, dated the 20th ult., with its enclosures, reporting the operations of a detachment of seamen and marines in the boats of that ship, under the orders of Lieutenant Wray Palliser, which their Lordships will perceive happily resulted in the recovery of a French lady who had been seized by the pirates, and part of the cargo of a vessel they had plundered, as well as in the destruction of three forts mounting 17 guns, the piratical settlement, and 20 piratical junks, without the loss of a single man.

I have on two former occasions (letters Nos. 48 and 58) expressed my opinion of this officer's conduct on similar services, and now again feel it my duty to draw their Lordships' attention to the judgment, gallantry, and discretion evinced by Lieutenant Wray Palliser on the present occasion, and to the important assistance rendered to him by Lieutenant A. Morrell R.N., Lieutenant Stokes, R.M., Mr. Oliver, mate, Mr. Rogers, second master, and the other officers, seamen, and marines employed under him.

I have, &c.,
James Stirling,
Rear-Admiral and Commander-in-Chief.

From *The Times*, London, Monday, 8th January, 1855.

CHAPTER FIVE

BREAKING UP OF THE CHINESE PIRATES' STRONGHOLD AT KULAN

A SUPPLEMENT TO *THE OVERLAND FRIEND OF CHINA*

H.M.S. *Baracouta*, Captain Parker, returned this morning from the Island of Tylo, where, at Kulan, the expedition under Captain O'Callaghan, which left this on Saturday last, has been completely successful in destroying three formidable batteries that kept up a steady fire on the boat squadron for upwards of half an hour yesterday, until fairly shelled out from the boats: which could not get nearer to the Chinese guns than seven hundred yards. There has been only one serious casualty, that of the death of an American seaman (Morrison), who was shot through the brain.

Altogether 340 men landed, viz.: – British 280, Portuguese 25, Chinese Braves 20, Americans 15.

Twenty guns: (12s. – 18s. – and 24s.) were taken from the long battery by the Chinese Braves, after it was silenced. Three guns were found in another battery, and seven guns and two gingalls about a mile inland, the Chinese keeping up a fire there until driven out by the Marines' musketry.

Ten Chinese were made prisoners. Fifty-one junks destroyed, and three piratical nests burnt. Number of killed among the hills unknown, supposed to be fifty at the least. H.M.S. *Baracouta* returns immediately, with further instructions regarding a fleet of piratical junks said to be at anchor at Ty-kam. It was known, prior to the despatch of the last mail, that H.E. the Naval Commander-in-Chief [Sir James Stirling] had been in correspondence with the Governor-General of the Two Kwang regarding the notorious pirate haunt at Kulan, on the Island of Tylo, a place about forty miles south and west of Macao; Admiral [James] Stirling, being anxious to obtain the co-operation, or rather the direction, of the Chinese authorities, before undertaking an expedition which, by some, might not be deemed altogether necessary by reason of any particular attack on British vessels; although the plunder of the Chilean ship *Caldera,* opposite Kulan, whilst commanded by a British subject, (a native of La Belle France [Fanny Loviot] being there also subjected to a good deal of annoyance and peril of life) gave perfect reasonable warranty for the interference really necessary. In our issue of the 11th it was stated that a party of pirates had joined the Imperialist service for an attack on Fatshan; as many as fifty West Coast Junks being passed by one of the local steamers *en route* to that place. Be the previous pursuit of these vessels whatever it may have been, the Chinese Governor readily, as we before stated, gave the required sanction, and issued orders to the Commodore of the Taipung Division to hold himself in readiness to proceed with the foreign vessels to wherever lawless characters might be found, and especially to destroy Kulan, a fortified place which for four years has successfully resisted all attempts of the Chinese Government to take it.

H.M.S. *Baracouta* was, in accordance with the sense of this reply, promptly despatched, with Mr. Caldwell on board, to bring H.E. the aforesaid Chinese commodore and suite down from the Bogue to Hongkong; and arrangements being completed, as the *Baracouta*, returned at 8 a.m. on Saturday last, a squadron, consisting of H.M.S. *Encounter*, 14 guns, Captain O'Callaghan, (as Commodore) *Baracouta* 6 guns, Commander Parker, and *Styx* 6 guns, Commander Woolcombe, were ordered to hold in readiness for immediate movement. It should have been mentioned that H.M.S. *Spartan,* Commander Sir William Hoste, was sent to lie off Macao and the Broadway on the previous Wednesday, in order to watch the motions of any vessels towards, or from, the beforementioned Island of Tylo; and that service having been effected so far as necessary, the *Baracouta* was ordered off, whilst her steam was up, to tell Commander Hoste to return to Hongkong, the *Spartan* giving, however, a pinnace, with Lieut. Palliser, to proceed on towards the intended place of action.

In addition to the vessels named the U.S.N. *Queen*, Lieutenant Preble, with a party of men from the U.S.N. *Macedonian*, and the P. and O.S.N. Co.'s steamers *Canton* and *Sir Charles Forbes* added to the number of the squadron; the *Canton* towing H.M.S. *Winchester*'s launch, and a full crew under the command of Lieutenant C. Fellowes.

On board the *Forbes* was the party [Chinese businessman] who paid the expense of the two smart P. and O. steamers; the Chinese who lost wives, children, and some $60,000 on a recent occasion on his way from Canton, and who was now prompted to follow the pirates into their stronghold, not so much with the expectation of recovering his household goods, as to view a bloody vengeance on the desecrators of his happiness. The final signal for starting was made about half-past four p.m., and a little before sunset the vessels were fairly under weigh, the *Encounter* towing the flag-ship and tender of the Chinese Commodore, H.E. Cheong-yok-tong, who, in virtue of his rank, was saluted with three guns. The order of sailing for the night was as follows – *Encounter* leading – followed on the starboard quarter by the *Canton* – on the port by the *Forbes* – the *Queen* as whipper-in – the *Styx*'s place being regulated, apparently, by various signals. The wind outside was found fresh from the northward and eastward, with somewhat of a swell, causing the heavy vessels to roll about rather more than was pleasant. By midnight the steaming and progressive powers of the various vessels seemed fully ascertained, each doing its work very well. About that time the land was well in the rear, and a course was shaped for Tylo, distant 70 miles from Hongkong, and bearing about S.W. from the southwest end of Lantao. At daylight the high land of Tylo was right ahead, but was passed, Captain O'Callaghan determining on getting to the other side of the island by the safer channel between the island of Kow-kok and Ty-kam ... At 10.30 a.m., three suspicious looking junks were observed in a bay on the west side of Kow-kok, and signal was made for the fleet to anchor; the Mandarin suggesting that they should be destroyed, for no honest vessel he asserted could be found in that place.

The launches were accordingly prepared, and taking one of the Chinese Commodore's officers and Mr. Caldwell (who accompanied the expedition as interpreter) in the *Winchester*'s boat, Lieut. Fellowes proceeded in towards the junks to examine them. But evidently anticipating what was in store, the crews of the junks lost no time in removing their armament and everything of value, the gun carriages being left to float about the beach, rice, fish, rattans, &c. formed the bulk of what was found on board these vessels, with large quantities of powder and stink pots, and amongst other things some rolls of English canvas, which Mr. Rooney (late master of the plundered ship *Caldera* who accompanied Lieut. Fellowes) identified as part of one of his topsails. Several Triad passes were also found, and quite sufficient evidence to warrant the Mandarin's assertion that they were pirates. Between the *Winchester*'s and the other boats' crews, the junks, from 50 to 100 tons burden each, were effectually set on fire, and the Mandarin then landed to inspect the Joss house, and two or three small houses, off which the junks lay; but every thing of utility or value had been removed from them by people who were seen in the distance struggling up the hills. A quantity of charcoal was found for the manufacture of gunpowder, in rear of the ruins of half a dozen good-sized houses; and on the hills an English shirt and trousers, with a California gold digging license. A few half starved dogs and cats were the only living occupants of the place, which the Mandarin said was called Ho pow shan. By 2 p.m., the boats had returned (the *Styx*'s boat towed out by the U.S.N. *Queen*) and at half-past two, with the *Winchester*'s boats astern, Captain O'Callaghan being on board, the *Canton* weighed and steamed up to reconnoitre Kulan, and ascertain the depth of water, off the entrance of Kulan Bay, about opposite the village of Cho ko me, where so much of the *Caldera*'s cargo was found on the *Lady Mary Wood's and Ann's* trip. At 3.45 p.m. observed a long English looking boat pulling away from the stockade running across the mouth of Kulan valley, – off which seven junks were counted; the others afterwards seen being hid by the headland. Captain O'Callaghan with the cutter then left the steamer which had anchored, intending to try the water further in, but the breeze was too fresh, and current too strong, to effect such a service, so that the cutter shortly returned, and at 4.15 p.m. the *Canton* weighed and steered back towards the squadron, distant about nine miles, the signal being made to weigh and approach. At 5 p.m. a lorcha was seen coming down before the wind, and by her firing a gun she was concluded to be the [Portuguese] armed vessel, *Amasona,* expected from Macao, her assistance in the expedition having been tendered by H.E. Governor Guimaraens. At 5.20 p.m. the lorcha, which proved to be the *Amasona,* was observed firing at the Kulan stockade, and as the signal to weigh had been seen, and was being acted on, Captain O'Callaghan determined on running back towards Kulan again. At 5.45 the water shoaling to a quarter less three, the *Canton* anchored in a safe position for the heavy vessels to lie for the night, and shortly afterwards Lieut. Scarnichia, commanding the *Amasona,* came on board and reported that the Chinese at Kulan fired at him before he discharged his guns. The *Amasona,* which had 40 men and 10 marines from the Portuguese corvetta *Dom Joao* on board, brought intelligence, which had reached Macao, of 16 junks that had left Kulan a day or two before, and were believed to be at Ty-kam, the island at the sou'west end of the channel. A blue light was burnt shortly after the squadron had anchored, and the respective senior officers came on board the *Canton,* when it was determined that the *Canton* (towing the *Amasona*), the *Forbes*, and *Queen* should take up a position off Kulan, and prevent the escape of any of the junks. A rocket was fired for the *Forbes* to close, and at 7 p.m. the *Canton* weighed, anchoring with the others off Kulan Bay at 8.20 p.m – the *Amasona* running well in shore. Boats then rowed guard. At midnight L. Fellowes, in charge of the night blockade, proceeded with Mr. Soames, of the *Forbes*, right into the bay, and ascertained the best passage for the boats to take on the following day. At 2 a.m. Monday, the *Forbes'* boat returned, without having been observed by the people on shore. At 4 a.m. the *Forbes* got up anchor and ran back to the *Encounter*, distant about four miles, for Captain O'Callaghan. At 6.30 a.m. the *Canton* weighed and stood towards the shore – 7 a.m. *Canton* anchored, and the Kulan men fired a shot which fell short. At 7.15 the pirates were observed hoisting their flags, the principal of which were triangular, of a slaty white color, with blue border, studded with high sounding Chinese characters, descriptive of the opinion the pirate chiefs wished the world to entertain of their bravery. Other flags were red, with black borders. At 7.20 pirates again opened fire at the *Amasona*, which had gone into within gunshot range in most gallant style; but in accordance with the previous orders of Captain O'Callaghan no return was made. At 7.30 a.m. Captain O'Callaghan arrived on board the *Canton*, and directed all the boats to rendezvous at the *Forbes*, whilst the *Canton* returned to bring up the Mandarin and a party of Kwantung braves, it being Capt. O'Callaghan's intention, according to the instructions given by H.E. Admiral Sir James Stirling before starting, to make no aggressive movement without the express desire of the Chinese Commodore. The firing and bravado of the pirates, however, rendering official parley unnecessary. At 9.30 a.m. the *Canton* arrived back, and Lieutenant Fellowes commanding the starboard division, received orders to proceed to the Portuguese lorcha and tell Captain Scarnichia to open fire as hot and heavy as he pleased. The first gun fired was from the *Queen*, but the ball fell short of the shore, her metal being too light. The Portuguese guns, however, told beautifully. The boat squadron under Captain Parker, H.M.S. *Baracouta*, [was arranged to have seven 12 pounder carronades and two 24 pounder carronades].

The Marines (50), under Lieutenant, Burton, R.M., of H.M.S. *Winchester*. Small arm Party (50), under Captain Woolcombe, of H.M.S. *Styx*, and field piece and rocket party, under Lieutenant Montgomery, of H.M.S. *Encounter*, with an Assistant-Surgeon, from each ship, followed close in to the shore on the left hand, where a landing, it was found could be effected; Drs Babington and Jenkins being in the *Canton* to attend to such casualties as might occur. The heavy launches could not get closer than within seven hundred yards of the pirates' battery, from which a fire was maintained with excellent precision, the shots striking and ricocheting right up to the *Amasona*. The spirit and coolness with which the pirates served their guns gave every promise of a hard day's work; but the round shot and shell, from the various launches as they took up their respective positions, and which were seen to fall right in amongst them, took the natural effect; and not long after the *Winchester*'s launch had anchored, and trained her guns towards the battery, the fire was observed to slacken.

Particular mention is made of the *Winchester*'s launch, it being that on board which the narrator took passage to the shore, and which had the good fortune of a few minutes' start from the *Amasona* directly the orders were given. The other boats being kept to the *Forbes* until it was evident what those orders were by the launch's bow gun (trained by Mr. Gilmore) stirring the dust up in the battery. But as it is not possible, or fair, to attempt to give a detail of the services of each boat, the clearest way to continue the account of the rest of the day's work appears to be to print such notes as were at the time hastily jotted down.

At 9.40 a.m. Dr. Sanders took the helm. Firing general – Captain Parker came alongside – Boat aground – Shot pitching pretty close – 10.05 anchored – *Queen*'s boat came up – a shot had just passed between General Keenan, sitting with Messrs. Moses and Alvord in the stern sheets, and splintered the blade of one of the oars – got them to land me on the rocks, to where some of the marines had proceeded – 10.15 got my glass to bear on the batteries, but the men previously observed waving flags were not to be seen – concluded that they had run for it – Captain Parker and Lieutenant Fellowes, in the *Baracouta*'s cutter, hailing the launches to up anchor and try for deeper water on the other side, towards where Lieutenant Palliser's party were wading through water up to the hips – Chinese retreating up the hills.

At 10.40 counted nine Chinese as they were being made prisoners one previously shot by Captain Rooney as he was aiming with a gingall at him;

11 a.m. reached the end of the creek, party of Portuguese came up, observed heavy firing on the left, where there

were two or three white flags; marines and small arm men well up. Captain Parker and Lieutenant Fellowes racing neck and neck, to get up to the guns; Chinese retreating up the hills, the blue jackets in pursuit; saw one man's brains beat out with butt end of musket, got up to the deserted battery, found a creek in front, and 7 guns of small calibre, with two gingalls. Marines and blue jackets up the hills in pursuit. Captain Parker's party gone on up the valley in pursuit ...

11.40 came up to the large village which the Mandarin had desired might be spared. It was a beautiful place, in an amphitheatre of wooded hills, the houses running up, flight by flight, thirteen or fourteen terraces deep, from fifteen to twenty in each row.

11.50 came up with the marines and *Winchester*'s men drawn up in file for breath, and waiting the report of scouts sent ahead to reconnoitre an artificial pass through the hill at the head of the valley, which, properly guarded, might have barred further progress for some time. Plenty of people on the hills, but out of gun-shot range.

Noon – Dr. Tronson, of H.M.'s ship *Baracouta* and scouring party came up, reporting the defile clear from end to end – Capt. Parker directed Lieut. Fellowes and party to proceed to the village in the valley opposite the large one, and search for evidence of piratical occupation – Captains Parker and Woolcombe, Lieutenant Burton, R.M., and the Marines and small arm men, accompanied by Lieutenant Scarnichia with some of the Portuguese marines and others, then proceeded through the pass, a gap cut about twenty feet deep, just wide enough for one or two abreast, for a length of eighty paces, and running for some three hundred paces further over a very narrow outlet to the head of another spacious valley, at the extremes of which houses could be seen among clusters of cocoa nut and other trees, about a mile and a half distant, with a wide sandy beach in front, forming the south eastern side of Tylo.

12.45 p.m. reached some half dozen fishing huts surrounding a little temple, dedicated to the Queen of Heaven ... Nothing of a suspicious nature was found in the huts, which were all deserted ... Capt. Parker gave orders to destroy nothing (excepting the cocoa nuts on the tree in front of the temple.) By an accident however, the thatched roof of the weather house caught fire, and so speedily did the others ignite that some who were resting in them out of the sun had barely time to escape – one of the marines' minie's [an elongated bullet rifle, recently invented] being left in the blaze, the barrel of which was only got out after the stock was consumed. The temple being built of brick did not catch fire, although the flames licked the tiled roof of it pretty clean.

1.40 p.m. returned by the opposite side of the valley; – examined a little farm house, also deserted, but containing nothing suspicious.

2.45 reached back to the bay, taking one prisoner, an old man, by the way. Found the cluster of houses outside the inland battery all in a blaze. All the junks had been set fire to, and were burning furiously, as well as the village on the opposite side of the valley, in which were found some more of the *Caldea*'s tea, and an empty mathematical instrument case, with a silver plate on the top of it, on which was engraved "To Captain Matthew Rooney, from D.O.B." and immediately identified by Mr. Rooney as part of the

Caldera's plunder. The *Caldera*'s bills of lading were found in one of the 335 houses, we heard – Just as the boats were shoving off, observed four men coming down to the junks carrying shields and swords: marines returned towards, and had a shot at them, when they scampered back and hid themselves – Launches gave them a parting salute of shell, which appeared to burst right over their locale. Between five and six, all hands being on board, or in tow of the steamers, returned to the squadron; the *Baracouta* being directed to get ready by mid-night to return to Hongkong with dispatches for the Admiral.

We have only to regret, in furnishing the foregoing statement, that we have not had ample time to condense and exhibit its main features with more glowing color. The expedition of whose work we have now only given a partial tale, is not only the most complete of its kind ever sent from this colony, but is also singular as one of the phenomena of the age. Here were English and Americans, Portuguese and Chinese, hand in hand together, heartily engaged in putting down a common enemy ... During the voyage, however, we were brought in contact with those who had no interest in making the matter appear otherwise than it really stood; and, amongst them, the party who pays for the charter of the P. and O. steamers, who, as well as the Canton Mandarin, denied most distinctly the possibility of any connection between the Kulan-ites and the legitimate Red heads. It was, as we said in the commencement of the narrative, an expedition to destroy a hold which for a period of four years has successfully defied the endeavors of the Provincial Government to subdue. Nor even now would it have been carried so speedily, with all our arms, had not fortune and good judgment for once combined.

Kulan Bight, in Tylo Bay, is peculiarly adapted for a pirate haunt. At its embouchure, it must be some four hundred yards or so across; the hills running abruptly down on each side, and lined at their bases with small oyster sprinkled rocks, covered with the sea even at low water, so rendering a landing on them a work of much difficulty at any time ... Most fortunate was it that the large piratical squadron attached to this place were out on one of their cruises, and now likely to be destroyed in detail. Not one casualty, nor one hundred, would have sufficed in the carrying of this celestial Bomarsund. There is no doubt but the forty-eight junks found in the natural dock inside, and which could only come out at high-water, would soon have been equipped for sea. The mischief they then might have done can hardly be calculated.

From a Supplement to *The Overland Friend of China,* Monday, 27th November, 1854.

CHAPTER SIX

COMBINED NAVAL FORCES H.M.S. *RATTLER* AND U.S.N. *POWHATAN* ENCOUNTER PIRATES

FROM THE *PEKING GAZETTE* AND *THE CHINA MAIL*

Last week we mentioned that a lorcha and three junks, under convoy of the steamer *Eaglet,* had been cut off by pirates, who displayed such a formidable battery and determined front that Captain Caldwell was unable to rescue them, and had to apply to Captain Fellowes, of H.M.S. *Rattler,* for assistance. This was readily granted, and the *Rattler,* with Captain Caldwell on board, started for Kulan, near which they sighted the pirates, and followed them as far into the bay as the depth of water would permit. The pirates, quite aware of their advantage in light draught, and conscious of their ability to resist successfully any attempt that might be made on them by the boats of the steamer, fired a few harmless broadsides in defiance, and stood in towards Kulan. Captain Fellowes thereupon returned to Hongkong, and invited the co-operation of the U.S.N. *Powhatan,* now in this harbour under repair; when it was determined that the *Rattler,* with three boats and a hundred officers and men of the American steam frigate should form the expedition, Captain Caldwell volunteering the use of his steamer to tow the boats up the bay. Accordingly the *Rattler,* with the *Eaglet* in tow, and the

Powhatan's boats astern of her again, left the harbour on Friday, about three o'clock, first Lieutenant Pegram of the *Powhatan*, with Lieutenant Jones and his marines, taking passage in the *Rattler*, and the blue jackets in the *Eaglet*. The steamers arrived close to Kulan before midnight, the *Eaglet* anchoring a couple of cable's length in-shore of the man-of-war. At five next morning the launches were sent alongside the *Rattler* for the marines; and then, with the *Powhatan*'s cutter, and three boats from the *Rattler*, besides the captain's gig, made fast astern of the *Eaglet*, which, everything being ready, steamed slowly up the bay.

At Kulan only one junk was to be seen, and it was feared the birds had flown; but Captain Caldwell described a lorcha at anchor at the head of the bay, and steered in that direction. The lorcha got under weigh, apparently with the intention of escaping, when Captain Fellowes despatched the *Rattler*'s pinnace at *Powhatan*'s cutter ... The British marines having been first transferred to the American launches – to intercept her, and these had unfortunately got beyond recall before the pirate fleet with their prizes, numbering in all some thirty-six sail, were observed at anchor in the narrow and shallow passage from which the lorcha had started. As the steamer approached, the junks hoisted their sails, but without getting under weigh, until several congreve rockets, discharged from the *Eaglet*'s quarter deck by Mr. Pine the gunner and two marine artillerymen from the *Rattler*, and two or three well directed shots from her 32-pounder, fired by Mr. Randall, her chief officer, startled them from their fancied security; for up to that time the pirates had either not observed the boats, or thought they would not have the temerity to attack them. In this, however, they soon discovered their mistake; for the boats, which at first had made for a narrow neck of land, bore up for and rounded the point – and then from the deck of the steamer was witnessed as bold an attack as was ever witnessed in these waters.

The pirate fleet formed a dense mass, the larger and heavier armed junks bringing up the rear, every now and then yawing round and firing their broadsides at the boats, from which, in reply, tiny puffs of smoke arose, as the howitzers in their bows discharged their more deadly contents, the shrapnel bursting over the junks, and making frightful havoc amongst their crews. The boats soon neared the pirates, Lieutenants Pegram and Rolando, with the launches of the *Powhatan*, first, by volleys of musketry, clearing the decks of the two largest, then boarding and driving the pirates overboard at the point of the bayonet. This, however, was not done without a hard struggle, for the miscreants fought with the fury of despair; but they had of course no chance against the marines and blue-jackets. Meanwhile the other boats were far from idle, and though small in comparison with the launches, performed their share of the work with the utmost gallantry, officers and men vying with each other for the post of danger and of honour, so that five or six more junks were soon secured. Mr. James, the boatswain of the *Rattler*, particularly distinguished himself, having, with five seamen and a few marines, in a whale-boat dignified with the title of second cutter, boarded and carried a junk that seemed fully a match for either of the launches. Lieutenant Pegram, in the first launch, was hastening to their assistance, but seeing the battle nearly won, would not interfere with their well-earned laurels, and turned his attention elsewhere. The pirate chief's junk, after being shelled by the first launch, was boarded almost simultaneously by her crew and that of the *Rattler*'s gig, and Captain Fellowes was fortunate enough to secure the chief's flag. The chief himself – Lee Afyee, a principal leader of the Whampoa "patriots" was shot by an English marine who had jumped on deck from the *Powhatan*'s launch, and four women threw themselves overboard, and were drowned. The ammunition on board the pirate fleet may be judged of from the fact, that this junk alone is believed to have had nearly 100 kegs of English gunpowder, besides stinkpots, cartridges, and loose powder.

Up to this time only one serious casualty had happened to the attacking force, a young American marine named Adamson having been shot with a musket-ball in the groin; but two other fatal accidents followed in quick succession. The *Rattler*'s first cutter, in charge of Paymaster Brownsdon, ran alongside of a large junk. Several stinkpots thrown at them missed, but at last one hove from the raised poop of the pirate by a woman with a child slung to her back, fell into the boat, and being followed by others, the crew were compelled to jump overboard, where two were speared, and a third was wounded and drowned. One of these, a marine, who had been wounded by a spear-thrust, called to his comrade to save him, and the other being an excellent swimmer, got hold of him for that purpose. The Chinese then threw a mat over them and the marine, still holding on by his wounded friend, dived below, and came up clear of the mat; but as soon as he was observed, several stinkpots were pitched at him, one of which struck him on the head, and though not much hurt, he was stunned for a second or two, and lost sight of the man he had displayed such a determination to save: the brave fellow's name is William Robinson. The other fatal accident was the blowing up of a junk which for a time had offered the most determined resistance to the gig, in which were Captain Fellowes and Assistant Surgeon Wilson with five men, but which was ultimately taken possession of by Lieutenant Rolando and his launch. Either a train had been laid before the crew left, or some determined scoundrel fired the junk, for she blew up with a tremendous explosion, and both officers and men were hurled into the water. Three of the men were killed, and several others frightfully scorched, one of whom died the same night, while another is not expected to live; but the officers miraculously escaped, though Lieutenant Rolando was burnt, and Captain Fellowes injured by the falling spars. The survivors were, however, all picked up by Mr. Craig, master's mate of the *Powhatan,* who had luckily gone into the boat the moment before the explosion took place. In this junk was an immense quantity of treasure, said to amount to 200,000 dollars, and the desperation with which her crew fought may be judged of from the fact, that even after the Americans gained the deck, they were encountered hand to hand. One man made himself particularly conspicuous, and, notwithstanding several wounds, continued to throw stinkpots, but ultimately ran below, and is believed to have fired the train which blew up the vessel.

The time thus occupied in securing the larger junks enabled sixteen smaller ones to get so far ahead as to render pursuit hopeless; while but for the unfortunate absence of the pinnace and cutter, as above mentioned, the whole would probably have been captured. The men in these boats tugged manfully at the oars, and pulled a distance of fifteen miles in three hours; but notwithstanding their utmost endeavours, arrived too late to take part in the fight, though they assisted in destroying the captured junks, while the other boats returned with their wounded men to the *Eaglet*. There Dr. Pritchard, with Mr. Pine the gunner, were prepared to receive them, and everything was done by the three surgeons (Pritchard, Schriver, and Wilson) that humanity could devise or medical skill perform.

Ten junks were destroyed, five of which more than ordinarily deserve notice. They were built of the most substantial materials evidently for war purposes, as they differ in many respects from the common trading junks. They carry every large guns, 32, 24 and 12 pounders – a 68-pounder was found in one of them. Another had no less than 21 guns mounted, the weight of one of which, carrying only an 18-pound shot, was estimated at not less than 50 cwt. Two lorchas and seven junks that had been detained by the pirates were released – two of which, however, had to be burnt to prevent their falling again into the hands of the piratical junks that escaped; time and an adverse wind and tide not allowing them to be brought away. The officers employed estimate the number of guns taken at 200, large and small, and the pirates at 1000, 500 of whom were killed.

From *The China Mail*, 9th August, 1855 and the *Peking Gazette*, Wednesday 15th August, 1855

CHAPTER SEVEN

ELI BOGGS' TRIAL FOR MURDER AND PIRACY

GEORGE WINGROVE COOKE SPECIAL CORRESPONDENT IN CHINA

Hongkong, July 8, 1857.

Lord Elgin has arrived.

It was quite time that something should happen to break the dreary monotony of existence here. The last mail did not arrive, and we have only just learnt that the *Erin* steamer was wrecked. The *Shannon*, which brought Lord Elgin, brought us no news of any description, except that the *Simoom* was gone on to Calcutta with the troops from the Mauritius.

The sickly season is doing its work. Of the 600 men who now form the strength of the 59th, there are 150 in hospital. The proportion is still greater among the blue-jackets and marines up the river. Happily, however, the Hongkong fever has not reappeared in its old terrible malignity. Although fever, dysentery, diarrhoea, and ague are rife, deaths are not numerous. There is plenty of hospital-room, and the surgeons can hold every case well in hand. Precautions also are multiplied with a praiseworthy minuteness. Every sentry has sherry and bitters given him to fortify his stomach against the night miasma; the ships are alternately moved down to the healthy islands at the Bogue; and the expulsion of our old friend, the Mandarin of Chuenpee, was because his fort was wanted for sanitary purposes.

The few officers and civilians who are daring enough to go out in the sun, try to escape from themselves by a voyage round the island, or a trip to Macao ... It is a voyage of forty miles round this little island.

It is scarcely more to Macao, and, although the fate of the *Thistle* and the *Queen* has rendered the perils of that passage more notorious, I doubt whether there are more pirates lurking in the archipelago between Victoria and Macao than in the islets at the back of Hongkong. While we gaily steamed along in our little toy steamer several times did some vicious-looking junks stand down towards us, their large mat-sails looking like the wings of a bird of prey, and heavy cannon frowning mischief from their deck. But they always stood off again when they found we were a party of eight Englishmen, with revolvers in our belts and rifles lying close at hand. We grow used to precautions in this land ...

The passage-boats to Macao are little armouries. There are cannon upon deck and revolvers in every belt. But so it was on board the *Queen* when the cannon was turned round and fired into the cabin upon the passengers absorbed in tiffin. Further precautions, however, are now taken. In the *Fei ma* the Chinese passengers are put down into the hold, twelve feet deep, and the ladder is taken away. A sailor keeps guard over them with a drawn cutlass. One of the Yankee ships has an iron cage on deck, into which the Chinese passengers are invited to walk, and are then locked up. The Peninsular and Oriental [Steam Navigation Company] boat has a better but more costly precaution; she carries no Chinese passengers. Easy, cosy people at home, who fear nothing but the gout or an easterly wind, may laugh, or may even, perhaps, be very indignant, at these precautions. But two boats out of five have been already taken, and the passengers put to death. Death at the hands of those simple sons of civilization is not an easy transit. The *Bustard* gunboat only a few days since, on taking a pirate, found two men nailed to planks, each with a stinkpot tied round his neck and slow matches burning. By what torments the prisoners taken in the *Queen* perished we do not know. She was carried up to that very Fatshan creek where the battle of the 1st of June took place. Pieces of machinery, marked by fire, were seen on a point near the fort; some revolvers were found in one of the junks; and Captain Corbett obtained a Portuguese flag from a Mandarin boat which afterwards blew up. These circumstances do not absolutely prove, but they strongly suggest, that some scene of horrors was enacted in this spot, and that the fleet we destroyed were spectators of the tortures. Every man in that fleet has been a pirate, and there would be no lack of proficients in the art of producing agony.

While I am upon this subject of piracy, let me mention that an American, named Eli Boggs, was tried at Hongkong on Wednesday last for piracy and murder. His name would do for a villain of the Blackbeard class, but in form and feature he was like the hero of a sentimental novel; as he stood in the dock, bravely battling for his life, it seemed impossible that that handsome boy could be the pirate whose name had been for three years connected with the boldest and bloodiest acts of piracy. It was a face of feminine beauty. Not a down upon the upper lip; large lustrous eyes; a mouth the smile of which might woo a coy maiden; affluent black hair, not carelessly parted; hands so small and so delicately white that they would create a sensation in Belgravia: such was the Hongkong pirate, Eli Boggs. He spoke for two hours in his defence, and he spoke well – without a tremor, without an appeal for mercy, but trying to prove that his prosecution was the result of a conspiracy, wherein a Chinese bumboat proprietor and a sub-official of the colony (both of whom he charged as being in league with all the pirates on the coast) were the chief conspirators. The defence was, of course, false. It had been proved that he had boarded a junk, and destroyed by cannon, pistol, and sword, fifteen men; and that, having forced all the rest overboard, he had fired at one of the victims, who had clutched a rope and held on astern. No witness, however, could prove that he saw a man die from a blow or a shot struck or fired by the pirate. The jury, moved by his youth and courage, and straining hard their consciences, acquitted him of the murder, but found him guilty of piracy. He was sentenced to be transported for life.

I record this trial, not because this young ruffian is a dandy as well as a cut-throat, but because the subject of piracy is of great importance while dealing with this country, and must form an article of our new treaty. Where I now write there are 200 junks lying in the harbour before me, and every one of them is armed with at least two heavy guns – some have twelve. Probably one quarter of these are pirates, who live principally by piracy, and adopt the coasting trade only as a cover to their real profession; at least one other quarter are not proof against temptation and a weak victim. It requires great charity or credulity to believe that all the junks that compose the other half are honest traders. The opinion here is that an armed Chinese junk is always a pirate when opportunity offers.

This state of things cannot be tolerated. Every one of these vessels must be disarmed, and some arrangement must be made whereby the cruisers of the Chinese government shall be distinguishable by, and be made to act in concert with, the cruisers of the European powers. Every country is bound to protect its coasts.

From George Wingrove Cooke, *The Times* Special Correspondent, China and the Years 1857–1858, London, 1859.

CHAPTER EIGHT

PIRACY AND MURDER ON BOARD THE *NORTH STAR*

FROM *THE CHINA OVERLAND TRADE REPORT*, HONG KONG

The pirates infesting these seas have made another successful attack, and on this occasion on a British vessel, in which murder and robbery have been committed. The British brig *North Star* was brought into harbour on the morning of 14th May, having left Hong Kong only the morning (bound for Nagasaki, in Japan) previously, by an officer belonging to H.M.S. *Pearl* and the report is taken from a crew member.

"The vessel had just been put round. The wind had fallen very light. The captain, who had gone forward, told the men to rest while they could, as the vessel would be making short tacks during the night and their services would therefore be required. Whilst forward he was superintending the lashing of a carpenter's bench abreast the bow of the long-boat, on the port side. In the meantime a boat came alongside. This boat is described as being a size larger than the ordinary two-masted boats used chiefly by captains of vessels in this harbour, and had mat sails. We conclude that she was a pilot-boat, the description comes nearest to that kind of craft. The man at the helm was first attacked, and, we believe, was actually burnt to death by stinkpots which were hove on board previous to the pirates boarding, as we did not observe any severe wounds from sharp instruments about him. The men were down in the forecastle, and their attention was attracted by the Chinese passengers rushing down below to their quarters. They came up and saw smoke aft. Saw the captain cut down. Saw the chief officer and Mr. Lariski fighting, and finally overpowered. Saw the cook (a European) stabbed aft, in the waist, and saw him driven forward to the windlass, where he was again stabbed. Observed a burning stinkpot lying on the helmsman, who was then stretched before the house on deck; he it appears must have passed through the mate's cabin, and through the main cabin, to the fore part of the house, in his endeavour to escape from the stinkpots. Mr. Marks we can hear no tidings of whatever; we cannot discover where he was at the time, no one seems to have seen him. Three young men made for the jibboom, and one seaman and the carpenter for the port fore rigging. The seaman got up the rigging; but the carpenter was stabbed, and went overboard, more of his own accord than being thrust over. The Chinese followed the boys out on the jibboom as far as the fore stays, when they went in again. The captain was struck over the head and breast by six of those pirates, when going aft, and struck down. The pirates then went aft, and it is our belief that if all could have kept forward of the mainmast none would have been hurt. They clearly knew that treasure had been put on board the ship, and it was for that they came. Mr. Marks had engaged the captain's stateroom, and the money (about 4,000 dollars) was there in two boxes. They quickly placed the boxes in the boat, took the chronometer, but did not touch the cargo. In fact, the whole affair did not last ten minutes. The captain had discharged his revolver a few minutes before the disaster, in order to clean it, so that accounts for its being unloaded at the time of the attack.

The boat containing the men that boarded the *North Star* had been observed the whole day cruising about, only one man and two boys being visible. It is suspected that the compradore who attended the ship (Ty-kee it is said), the steward, a Chinese boy, placed on board by the compradore, and the pilot had concocted this vile scheme. It was particularly observed that the pilot was very anxious to get away from the ship sooner than is usual, and that he was very nearly going without his fee. The boy actually assisted the pirates, by showing them where the valuables were to be found, and finally decamped with them.

When they were gone the man and lads who were aloft, and on the jibboom came in. Two boys manned the gig, and went on board the Siamese barque *Four Stars,* (Captain Butcher), who was passing at the time, for assistance. Now, we hope it is not true, that Captain Butcher not only saw and knew what had occurred, but that when the boys applied to him for assistance he refused, and sent them away with a letter to a man-of-war. Captain Butcher may have thought that he was studying the interests of his Chinese friends by proceeding on the voyage; but we think that, under the circumstances, he might have taken some pains to have inquired more into this sad affair, particularly as night was coming on. The boat then pulled for the harbour, and boarded the *Pearl,* where they met with ready assistance, in the shape of a doctor, and men to take charge of the vessel.

About seven p.m., two hours after the disaster, the pirate was seen returning, when the two men remaining on board put the brig before the wind and outsailed them. They managed to get the brig inside Green Island before they were boarded by the *Pearl*'s boat crew.

It will be a caution to masters of small vessels, we should imagine, for the future, to take care, in the first place, when they are going to carry any treasure, to take it on board as secretly as possible; and, in the second place, to be provided with some weapon of defence which could be got at easily. The *North Star* had only a few muskets on board, which were taken away by the pirates. The seaman who has died since her arrival in the harbour, defended himself as long as possible with a handspike.

On the 14th, the chief officer of this unfortunate vessel died at the hospital. We are happy to inform the public that Mr. [Henry] Marks, the passenger supposed to have been taken away by the pirates, has turned up. We hear that he went overboard, but, with the assistance of several spear handles that were floating about, he fetched a rock, after being in the water about eight hours. With great difficulty, he induced a fishing-boat, for the sum of $200, to bring him into the harbour."

Below we publish a letter received from Mr. Marks, late a passenger in the unfortunate *North Star*:–

To the Editor of the Daily Press.
c/– H.M.S. *Pearl,* Hong Kong.
Monday, May 20, 1861.

Sir,– I beg leave to hand you a short account connected with the piracy committed on board the brig *North Star,* no particulars mentioned below being as yet noticed in your valuable paper. Some portions of the statements of the disaster hitherto published are also not quite correct.

The pilot left us about two o'clock; we had a very light wind, and at about half-past three o'clock the brig was put about. The captain told the seamen to 'go below and sleep.' There then remained on deck the man steering, the cook, and three seamen; also my fellow passenger Mr. Lariski, and myself. We were sitting on a cane-bottomed sofa in front of the cabin. All of a sudden a large boat came alongside, which was the weather side, unnoticed, and immediately six or seven 'stinkpots' were thrown on board, and at the same time twenty or thirty men jumped overboard with drawn swords, and commenced to kill and wound all the Europeans they met, and during the same time 'stinkpots' were coming on deck very fast. The captain, Mr. Lariski, and myself retreated to the cabin, and each one of us armed ourselves with an empty single barrel musket. At the same time the captain said, 'My God; where is my pistol? I left it on the sofa,' I ran out for it, and was attacked by three men with long boarding pikes. I ran abaft, and was knocked overboard by a blow from the butt end of one of them, and when I arose to the surface of the water I had three spears darted at me, but they did not reach.

I dived under the brig's bottom, and when I again arose to the surface I saw the carpenter knocked overboard; he was in the water with me half an hour, and he then sank, after catching me by the hair, when I had a fearful struggle to get clear of him. I then made for the land, which was ten miles distant, and after being in the water thirteen hours, and with the assistance of the three spears, wind, and tide,

I was thrown on a rock the next morning at about half-past four o'clock. I had considerable difficulty in raising myself out of the water, but a heavy sea coming in raised me to a place of comparative security, and there I remained until five o'clock in the afternoon.

There I was exposed to the rays of the sun, with only a small flannel on, which I wrapped round my head to prevent sunstroke.

The position of the rock on which I was thrown was about 400 yards from a small bay, where I saw the pirates run into after they had attacked the brig. I did not see the pirate vessel leave the bay during the time I was on the rock, and as I had a good view of the bay, I do not think they could have left it without my observing them. At last a boat came out of the same bay, and, after a consultation of about four hours, and laughing at me when I endeavoured to excite their compassion, they at length agreed to take me to Hong Kong for 300 dollars.

When I got on board the boat I was treated as a prisoner, and compelled to lie on my back, covered over with a mat and an old piece of cloth. When I endeavoured to look up I was brutally kicked. All this I submitted to until I got close to the shipping at Hong Kong, when I jumped up and struck one of them and made them pull me towards the brig. I must also here remark that when we got near Green Island one of the boatmen suddenly disappeared, – he going on board another boat. I had great difficulty in getting them to put me on board the brig, and since then I have neither seen nor heard anything of them, and I have every reason to believe that they were not only fishermen, but in league with the pirates who attacked the brig, as they seemed to avoid the brig as much as possible. I must apologise for encroaching on your valuable time;

and remain, sir, your obedient servant.

Henry Marks.

Captain Voight, of the *North Star*, died on the 16th, in the hospital, of his wounds, and was buried last evening at five o'clock. Should Mr. [Henry] Marks be well enough to-day, we hear he will proceed in a gun-boat to what he supposes to be the place where the pirates disappeared. The inquest held on the bodies of the murdered men belonging to the *North Star* has just been closed (May 23). The verdict returned was "Wilful murder against the steward, and persons unknown."

The following is from a letter written by Mr. Marks to his relations in Melbourne, and received by the *Benares* and printed in *The Argus* of Melbourne on Friday, 19th July, 1861:–

Hong Kong,
Monday, May 27,. 1861.

I take this opportunity of writing these few lines to you, to inform you I had a narrow escape from death. I took my passage to go to Japan in an English brig, named the *North Star*, with my cargo. When we were about thirty miles from Hong Kong we were attacked by Chinese pirates, and they killed every person on board, except two, and plundered the ship. Thank God! I lost no goods, only all my clothes, gold watch and chain, and my ring. I was in the water thirteen hours, as you will see by the enclosed pieces of newspaper; and I was on a rock one day, naked, and when I was taken off I had lost my speech for two days, and I also lost the use of my legs for four days. I was taken on board of a man-of-war, and was under the doctor's hands fourteen days, and treated very kindly. The admiral sent a man-of-war to look after me. I swam ten miles, and I am a curiosity in this place. The pirates killed the captain, chief mate, second mate, a gentleman passenger, and the sailors. It was a dreadful slaughter, and all Hong Kong is up in arms. The admiral treated me very kindly, and I have this day returned from a four days' search in a man-of-war for them, without any success. I am sorry to say the reason for their attacking our vessel was because she had a lot of dollars on board, as freight for Japan.

Thank God, I have recovered, and I am quite well. I leave here in a few days, in another vessel, for Japan.

I remain, &c.,
H. Marks.

From *The China Overland Trade Report*,
Hong Kong, reprinted in *The Argus*, Melbourne,
Friday, 19th July, 1861.

CHAPTER NINE

A DESPERATE PIRATICAL ATTEMPT TO CAPTURE THE *IRON PRINCE*

FREDERIC BRINE

To the Editor of *The China Mail*, Canton, China,
On Board the *Spark*,
Wednesday, May 7, 1862.

Sir,– The following are nearly the correct particulars of this dastardly attack. Captain Harris, on arrival this evening at Hong Kong, will be able to furnish more detailed accounts:–

The *Iron Prince*, screw passenger steamer, of 200 tons and thirty-five-horse power, with a crew of fifteen, and thirty-one passengers, carrying also, in addition to two boxes of specie, sixty cases of opium, the latter being worth over $40,000, left Hong Kong as usual yesterday morning at eleven, for Macao, a distance of over forty miles. After starting, the captain, remarking that some of the Chinese passengers had come with him on the steamer's previous voyage from Macao, took the precaution of taking six of the twelve muskets that were in his cabin in the centre of the ship to the small after-cabin on the starboard side, and mentioned his suspicion that all was not right to the mate. In this after-cabin, where there were previously six muskets, he loaded the six which he had taken from his own cabin. There was also in the cabin a loaded five-barrelled Deane's revolver, and he had about his person a small five-barrelled loaded revolver. He further had the sense to take all the ammunition and caps out of his own cabin. Of thirty-one passengers, twenty-six were Chinese, including one woman; the rest, consisting of a French doctor, a Mr. Hyeem; one Parsee, one Jew, and one Irish lady, a Mrs. Dunn, who arrived at Hong Kong from Singapore, on Tuesday, and was going to join her husband at Macao. Of the crew of sixteen, including the captain, eight were Chinese, the rest being the captain, an Englishman; the mate, Portuguese; and the engineer, Moorman; one Lascar, one Malay, one Moorman, and two Manillamen. After passing "The Brothers," nearly halfway to Macao, the captain, finding none of the passengers required luncheon, sat down at about two o'clock, by himself, in the small saloon in front of his cabin. Just as he was in the act of commencing his tiffin, he noticed some of the Chinese passengers looking in at each of the two doors. He immediately jumped up, and told his boy to bring his lunch aft, and drew the attention of the mate to two Chinese junks near at hand, which apparently had no decided course, and were crowded. In about a quarter of an hour a third junk appeared, when suddenly a yell was given, stinkpots were thrown into the captain's cabin and engine-house, and the attack commenced. The first thing the captain did was to call all the crew and passengers aft. In less than a minute the engineer was shot through the right arm, the mate stabbed near the captain's cabin door and disabled, one of the Manilla crew killed and thrown overboard by the pirates. Mrs. Dunn, while rushing from the captain's cabin aft, was wounded about the neck and shoulders, and the Lascar was killed when in the act of getting a musket from the cabin. The captain, while in the act of preparing for defence, in the after-cabin, received likewise a slight sword-cut across the forehead and fingers. At this stage the captain shot dead the man who struck him, and likewise in the back the two men whom the pirates had placed, one after the other, at the wheel, to change the steamer's course. The pirates, who had now possession of the vessel, and continued to keep it for three-quarters of an hour, began to cut the rigging, and by throwing wood and rope overboard endeavoured to foul the screw. They likewise made signals to the third Chinese junk; but, odd to state, she sailed away, like the other two. In the meantime the captain made one of his crew go to the wheel, and posted two of the passengers on the starboard side, and two of the crew on the port, about midship, who kept firing towards the bows at any of the pirates who showed themselves in the fore part of the vessel. The captain kept reloading the muskets as they were fired off, being aided by the engineer and Mr. Hyeem, while Mrs. Dunn handed them out, and received them back. The pirates now seeing all was up, first threw their dead comrades overboard, and then began to jump over themselves, and many of them were afterwards killed or wounded when in the act of swimming. Of course, all who jumped into the sea must have been either killed or drowned, as by this time the junks were out of sight. Two hours had now elapsed since the commencement of the attack. The captain mustered all on board, when only twelve, including the Chinese woman, of the twenty-six Chinese passengers, made an appearance. Four of the former he put in irons, having proof, he believes, that they took part in the affray. The mate was found mortally wounded, and the Lascar found dead in the captain's cabin. The French doctor, Parsee, and Jew were likewise slightly wounded.

The steamer now pursued her course to Macao, which she reached at half-past five p.m. On arrival, the agent of the steamer, Mr. Carneiro, and the Judge (Acting Governor) of Macao, went on board, where the four prisoners were taken to Macao gaol. The mate and dead Lascar were removed to the Military Hospital. At three o'clock this morning the mate died, leaving a widow and eight children. Both he and the Lascar will be buried this evening. Last night I met Captain Harris at the Agent's home, when I totally coincided with them that, as this attack took place on the high seas, in a ship carrying an English flag, the prisoners ought to be brought to an English port. Accordingly, they will arrive at Hong Kong this evening in the *Iron Prince,* in charge of six Macao policemen, and I have informed the superintendent of the Hong Kong police of their probable arrival. The decks, cabins, &c., of the *Iron Prince* will, as far as possible, be left in the same state as they were found after the attack, two clerks and four policemen being put on board of her last night.

The mate, from his arrival at Macao, never spoke, and, I am told, would not look at anyone. His body this morning showed two fingers cut off, one stab in the chest, and two wounds in the head. The Lascar's body showed two stabs in the back, two fingers cut off, and two frightful cuts on the back of the head. The decks and bulwarks of the *Iron Prince* this morning likewise showed several bullet-marks from bad shots and sword cuts, the captain's and after cabins being a good deal covered with blood, not forgetting Mrs. Dunn's bonnet, the ribbons and trimmings of which were more red than any other colour.

One advantage in bringing the prisoners to Hong Kong is, that there the plot was laid, and there the opium shipped, and there, of course, if possible, an example should be made. Again, they might lead to ferret out other pirates, as evidently the police could have had no idea of this plot in time. One thing I am pretty confident of, which is, that all these piratical affairs are hatched originally at Hong Kong, and that piracy in these neighbouring waters will not be put down until first the Home and Imperialist Governments combine to do so; and secondly, until a better detective police force, to meet the Chinese character, is established in Hong Kong. Sending out gun-boats is well and laudable enough, and now and then may succeed, after the damage is done, as in the case of the schooner *Eagle*; but what chance, I may ask, is there of capturing the three junks which hovered about the *Iron Prince*, in concert with the eighteen pirates on board, and only sailed away when they heard the shots, and saw it was not a certainty? In this affair, the pirates, who were desperate enough, and evidently did not fear death, made three grand mistakes. They first thought the arms and ammunition were in the captain's cabin; they secondly had no ammunition with them, so after the first discharge of their pistols they had nothing but their daggers to resort to (nine of them now on board) against firearms; and thirdly, they forgot to drop the anchor. But for these pieces of good luck, and the gallantry of the captain, passengers, and that portion of the crew not Chinese, the *Iron Prince* would now be ashore, or burnt, the cargo gone and all on board killed, except the pirates themselves, and perhaps the two women. An odd circumstance is, that each of the four prisoners was found with two dollars in his pocket, being his passage-money to and fro.

It now only remains for me to say that my chief object in writing this hurried account is to draw attention to the valour displayed, in the hope that, first, either the colonial or Home Governments may take notice of such; secondly, that the mate's widow and eight children may be provided for by those who saved their property on the occasion, and by other charitable persons; and thirdly, that Mrs. Dunn's heroism may be properly appreciated by her own sex and others, in some tangible form. Before closing, I may add that the deceased mate was formerly mate of the *Spark*, and was highly respected and valued. The captain, from my own knowledge, and others' who accompanied me in the *Iron Prince* on its previous voyage to Macao, is as good a type of an Englishman as one would wish to see in these Chinese seas. And now one word for coast travellers and shippers of cargo: Always carry a revolver, and never send valuable cargo in coasting vessels where a Chinese crew only is shipped. Where would the *Iron Prince* have been but for the captain and passengers and that portion of the crew not Chinese?

I am, sir, yours obediently,
Frederic Brine

From *The China Mail*, reprinted in
The Argus, Melbourne, 12 July, 1862

CHAPTER TEN

ANGLICAN BISHOP AT WAR WITH WILD BORNEO PIRATES

THE RIGHT REVEREND FRANCIS MCDOUGALL, THE FIRST BISHOP OF LABUAN

The Bishop of Labuan has written to *The Times* an account of an affair with pirates, in which the Right Rev. Father took an active part. The Bishop writes:–

"Mr. Helms wrote word that there was a force of six Illanum vessels anchored off Muka, threatening the town at the mouth of the river, while their armed boats were plundering and picking up the people along the coast. This news effectually roused us all. The Rajah Mudah [Crown Prince] ordered steam to be got up, and hailed the little *Jolly Bachelor* (the gunboat anchored astern of us) to throw off her housing and prepare for fighting. We landed the Chinese carpenters and coolies brought from Sarawak to build the fort, and as soon as daylight and tide had made, we steamed out over the bar, took the *Jolly* and [Sir James] Brooke's gig in tow, and steered down the coast towards Muka.

"Meanwhile we made ready for action, as we felt that when we fell in with the pirates they would fight resolutely, and that our force was very small to cope with them. Their vessels are well armed, very fast, and carry at least 100 men each. The *Rainbow* is a small strongly built iron screw boat, of 80 tons register, 35-horse power engine, carrying two

9-pounders mounted on poop and forecastle. We had also a 12 and 4-pounder on board, with their ammunition (the 12-pounder was disabled after a few rounds), which we had brought up for the new fort; together with eighteen of the Sarawak Fort men, ten of whom we kept to strengthen our own crew, the other eight we turned over to the gunboat to reinforce her. She carried two brass sixes, and two small swivels on her taffrail. The steamer's crew had only six available muskets, and no other arms but their knives and handspikes; they were stationed at the forecastle and poop guns. The Fort men worked their own guns amidships, and were armed with Wilkinson's excellent rifle carbines and swords. There were eight Europeans in all including Captain Hewat, Mr. Moore, engineer; Mr. Jackson, mate; the Rajah Mudah, Mr. Hay, Mr. Stuart Johnson, Mr. Walters, a Borneo Company engineer, and myself, and with us we had the Datu Bandar of Sarawak, Pangeran Matusin of Muka, and Hadjee Mataim, good and true men.

"We all had our own rifles and smooth-bores, and were to do our best to silence the enemy's guns and prevent them boarding. Mr. Walters was to give his aid to the engineer's crew in handling the hot water hose. As there was no bulwark, Brooke had some planks hung over the iron poop rail, and lined them with the cabin mattresses to save our legs from shot and shears. The same was done on the bridge for the captain's protection, and turned out to be a very wise precaution, which saved many of us on the poop from ugly hits. We had not steamed on long before we saw some boats pulling along in shore of us – one had a tripod mast, and these we took to be the sampans of the private squadron prowling along by the mouth of the rivers. We made chase, and Brooke gave them a few shots ahead and astern with his long-ranged Whitworth to bring them to, upon which they beached their boats and bolted into the jungle. Then several of the boats, called 'barongs' pulled into shore, and found to their surprise that we had been chasing their own friends, with whom they had a good laugh, and warned them against the use of tripod masts in future. After this we steamed about all day and saw nothing more, and anchored off the Brintulu River about sunset."

Three large prahus were seen full of men, and Brooke asked two of his native followers whether it was certain that they were pirates, and receiving an answer in the affirmative, set to work to sink and destroy. The zest with which the Bishop recounts the slaughter is very remarkable.

"So we took our stations, loaded our guns, and prepared for action. The leading boat had already gained on the other two, and was going nearly as fast as the steamer herself. I never saw fellows pull so. We put on all steam, cast off the *Jolly*, and tried to get between her and the point, but she beat us, and passed inside of us into shallow water, where we could not follow. Then she opened her fire upon us, which we returned with interest. She, like the others, had no heavy guns, but they all carried three long brass swivels, called lelahs, and plenty of rifles and muskets. One of the captives told me afterwards that the long lelahs in the boat he was in took seven men to lift, and that she had forty muskets and rifles, and that none of the others had less, some more. Our plan of action was to silence the brass guns with our rifles, to shake them at their oars with grape and round shot, until we could run into them without their being strong enough to board us. The steamer was kept dodging about within range until the time came to run in; then we got into a good position to put on all steam and given them the stem, which was always admirably and coolly done by Captain Hewat whenever the order was given by the Rajah Mudah. The first boat having for the present escaped into shallow water, our attention was turned to the second, from which her consort had evidently tried to divert us. She was now fast nearing the shore, and the chase was most exciting. When the prahu was 200 yards from us she fired her lelahs, and then made a dash for the shore; we opened all the guns we got to bear, and kept on at full power until we ran into her, struck her midships, our stem running right over her, and then backed off again. We called out to the slaves and all who were not pirates, or who wished to surrender, to hold on by the wreck until we could take them off, and then steamed away after the remaining vessel. When we came up with her she was also fast slipping into shore, and we ran into less than two fathoms of water with a rocky bottom under us, before we could strike her, which we did too far forward to sink her, but she was disabled by the collision, and sheered round alongside of us, but did not fight at all. The unwounded pirates jumped overboard, leaving their own wounded, and slaves, and captives, whom we told to remain in the vessel until the boats came to take them off. The first vessel which had escaped, seeing the fate of the others, ran ashore among the rocks, just inside Tanjonz Ridorong, and the crew and captives all ran into the jungle. The *Jolly Bachelor*, with Messrs. Paul and Lucas on board, was ordered to stay to look after them, while we saved all we could of the former boats. Several of our crew recognised friends and acquaintances among those we saved, and the joyous, thankful look of the captives, when they came on board and found themselves among friends, was, indeed, a compensation for the awful work we had been engaged in. Many were wounded, some with our fire, others with the fearful cuts of the heavy Illanun swords and Sooloo knives of the pirates, who, when they found they could not get away, commenced murdering their captives, and only our running them down put a stop to their dire work of spite and despair."

Very few of the pirates who were not wounded surrendered.

"They are marvellous swimmers; they took their arms into the water with them, and fought with our men in the boats when they were trying to pick up the captives. My hands and those of Mr. Walters, who was a very kind and able assistant, were soon full of work with the wounded, friends and foes alike, arresting haemorrhage, extracting balls, and closing frightful sword or chopper wounds, such, perhaps, as are hardly ever seen in civilised warfare. One man was brought up with the top of his skull as cleanly lifted up by the blow of a Sooloo knife as if it had been done *secundem artem* by an adept at *post mortema*, who wished to have a peep at the dura mater *in situ*; it was like the lid of a box partly open, and required considerable force to shut it and get it into its right place again. He had also two heavy cuts on his back. The man is still alive, and seems likely to recover. Another poor fellow could not be got up the ladder, because a long-handled, three-pronged, barbed

Illanun spear was sticking in his back, which I had to cut out to liberate him. We soon learnt from the captives, among whom were two women and four Sarawak Chinese traders, that the other three pirate vessels had gone out to sea, and were to wait there until those we had just secured rejoined them; so when we had saved all the people we could, we steamed out to sea in search of them."

After an hour or so the look-out at the masthead reported three vessels in sight, right a-head.

"At this time it was quite a calm, and when we came near enough to see them from the deck we saw them sweep up to the central vessel and lay themselves side by side, with their bows at us, as if they meant to engage us in that position. However, as we went on towards them, the sea breeze sprang up, so they changed their tactics, hoisted sail, and opened out into the line with their broadsides towards us to rake us as we came up. Out plan was, as before, to shake them first, and run them down in detail. Brooke did not give the order to fire until we came within 250 yards of them, and they opened their lelahs upon us some time before we commenced firing. This was a different affair from the last, for in that the pirates bent all their energies to escape into shallow water in shore of us, and, therefore, made a bad fight of it. Here there was no chance of escape; and they coolly did their best to fight us, and to take us too, which they seem to have thought possible. Indeed, they told the captives they would soon take so small and low a craft as we were, for they would board us and 'amok' – kill – everybody. They fired briskly, and did not attempt to get away, even when we got all our guns to bear upon them; but as we steamed round to get our stem fairly at the sternmost vessel they seemed to think we were retreating, and pelted us with their shots more sharply than ever, directing their chief attention to us on the poop, where we had one man killed, and two severely wounded in no time, and we should have suffered more if the temporary bulwark of planks, &c., had not stopped their balls. After the first prahu was run down I had to go below to attend to our own wounded as they came in, but I plainly felt the concussion as we went into the others."

One of the vessels was cut right in two; the steamer went straight on without backing, and she sank the other, one-half on either side of us. She was the largest, and had a very valuable cargo, and much gold and bags of Dutch rupees. The pirates fought to the last, and then would not surrender, but jumped into the sea with their arms.

"The poor captives, who were all made fast below as we came up to engage them, were doubtless glad when our stem opened the sides of their ships, and thus let them out of prison. Few, comparatively, were drowned, being mostly all good swimmers. All those who were not lashed to the vessels, or killed by the Illanuns, escaped. Our decks were soon covered with those we picked up, men of every race and nation in the Archipelago, who had been captured by the pirates in their cruise, which had already lasted seven months. One poor Chinese came swimming alongside, waving his tail over his head, and the other captives held up the cords round their necks to show that they were slaves, lest they should be taken for Illanuns, and shot or left to their fate. We soon picked up the poor fellows, and the Chinaman came under my hands, being shot through the arm. Many of the pirates we took were badly wounded, some mortally; the greater part were killed or disabled by our fire before we closed. As I was dressing one man, with a shot in the wrist, he addressed me in English, and having expressed his gratitude for his wonderful deliverance from the pirates, he told me he was a Singapore policeman, and was going to see his friends in Java when he was captured. There were also several other Singaporeans – a mother and daughter, who had a child with her, and two men, British-born subjects, Bencoolen Malays, who were taken in their own boat, trading to Tringannu. The husband of the younger woman and owner of the boat was killed by the pirates, and she, like every woman who falls into their hands, had suffered every outrage, insult, and injury that could befall a woman.

"One poor creature, who was still suckling a child of two years old, as Malays do, was almost a living skeleton; she was shot through the thigh, and after I had dressed her my kind assistant quaintly said of her, 'Poor, poor thing! She has not meat enough on her bones to bait a rat-trap.' It is a marvel how these poor captives live at all under the terrible tortures and ill-treatment they endure, sometimes for months, before they reach their destination, and settle down as slaves to the worst of masters. I asked many of those I was dressing if their wounds hurt them much, and they said, 'Yes, they hurt; but nothing hurts so much as the salt-water the Illanuns have made us drink; they never gave us fresh, but mixed three parts of fresh water with four of salt.' If any of the rowers jump overboard, the pirates have a supply of three-pronged and barbed spears, with long bamboo handles, ready to throw at them. When hit by one of these, they can neither swim nor run, and are easily recaptured. They are made to row in relays night and day, and to keep them awake they put cayenne pepper in their eyes, or cut them with their knives and put pepper on their wounds ...

"Our weapons, though few, were good and well served, and, in justice to the maker, I must mention that my double-barrelled Terry's breech-loader, made by Reilly, New Oxford-street, proved itself a most deadly weapon from its true shooting, and certainty and rapidity of fire. It never missed fire once in eighty rounds, and was then so little fouled that I believe it would have fired eighty more with like effect without wanting to be cleaned. When we ran down the last pirate, all our ammunition for the nine-pounders was expended, and our own caps and cartridges for the small arms had nearly come to an end, so that if we had had more prahus to deal with we should have been in a sorry plight, and had to trust to our stem and hot-water hose to do the work. But the whole affair was most providentially ordered in our not meeting the six boats together, when their fire might have been too much for us; and then in their departing from their usual plan of rushing at us *en masse* to board, and by their separating and giving us the opportunity of running them down one after the other."

The unusual episcopal skirmish was reported in *The Times* in London and soon after an edited reprint appeared in *The China Mail* of Hong Kong and *The Brisbane Courier* on Wednesday 26th November 1862.

CHAPTER ELEVEN

CRUISING AFTER PIRATES IN CHINESE WATERS

CAPTAIN HENRY CRAVEN ST. JOHN OF THE ROYAL NAVY

In 1864 the coasts of China, and particularly the southern parts, were infested with pirates. I commanded a [steam] gunboat, whose particular duty was to keep them in check. The Gulf of Tonquin, the island of Hainan, and the coast from thence up to Macao was unknown and unvisited except by myself, or an occasional other gunboat. There was no commerce, neither port nor town existing of sufficient size to excite trade, excepting perhaps Hoihou, the chief town of Hainan. The anchorage there, however, is very bad, being merely a roadstead, and to get to it numerous dangerous shoals have to be passed. Islands and shoal water stretch a long way out from the main coast line, forming at all times innumerable safe retreats. Rough sketches of the coast have been taken at different times, but to this day it remains unsurveyed.

The island of Hainan is 300 miles round, and the length of the other coasts which I have mentioned would amount to, roundly, 400 miles. The whole of this considerable extent of coast was, in the days I am speaking of, entirely at the disposal of these lawless Chinamen.

I was lying at my anchorage in Hong-Kong harbour one day; a fine large opium junk, armed to the teeth with a dozen 12 to 18 pounder guns on board, and a crew of about forty-five men lay close to me.

In the afternoon a number of passengers went on board her. These people intended taking advantage of the security afforded by such a vessel – supposed security would perhaps be more applicable. At any rate, when an opium junk was about to proceed up the coast, owing to the strength of her crew and armament, applications for passages were sure to be made.

She was bound for Swatow, a port 180 miles to the northward, and towards dusk she got under weigh. As she reached the outer roads of Hong-Kong, or a few miles from the Lymoon Pass, it fell calm, and she anchored. This was about nine o'clock. A few hours afterwards, probably about midnight, a large junk quietly ran alongside, a number of men jumped on board, and before the passengers and crew could show any resistance, they were entirely in the power of a band of pirates. The crew and passengers were at once secured under hatches, and the junk got under weigh and steered for the back or south side of the island of Hong-Kong.

Soon after daylight, one by one of these unfortunate beings, men and women, as they came up from below, had their hands tied behind them, their feet tied together, and were then flung overboard, a single exception being made out of the eighty-three on board. This was a boy about twelve years old. He was spared, being small enough to make their tea and prepare their opium pipes, etc. The pirates then took the junk, which had a most valuable cargo of opium, a description of plunder these gentlemen particularly appreciate, being easily turned into money, and made for a favourite harbour a little to the north of Macao. Here they divided their spoil, burnt the junk, and dispersed. This plan was frequently adopted to elude pursuit. Seven went to Macao, and from thence took their passage by the usual passenger steamer to Hong-Kong. The poor little urchin whom they had spared, but whose father had been drowned, was allotted to one of these seven.

Before the steamer reached her destination, the captain noticed the boy, who appeared to be in much distress, and being a kind-hearted man (peace to his ashes!) asked what ailed him. On hearing the story I have just related, instead of running the steamer alongside the jetty at Hong-Kong, as was usual, he anchored in mid-stream, hailed the police-boat to come alongside, drew up the hundred odd Chinese passengers, and with the boy's assistance picked the seven men from amongst them. They were taken possession of by the police and locked up.

The previous evening, one of the eighty-two unfortunates who had been flung overboard arrived at Hong-Kong, and gave the same account as the boy did. This man's fate was evidently not drowning. It appeared when he found himself in the water, and going quickly to the bottom, he managed with a desperate effort to free his hands by slipping them through the lashing, and then bringing himself to the surface he soon got his feet free. Chinamen as a rule swim like fish, and fortunately for this one, he was no exception. He reached the nearest island safely, and from thence to Hong-Kong in a fishing-boat must have been a pleasant journey after the short but peculiar one he had just gone through. His account had been received previous to the boy's; both agreed, and in consequence I was sent out to examine, and, if possible, capture some of the other pirates. Of course it was useless;

no trace whatever could be obtained.

The seven men were tried and condemned at Hong-Kong, and one morning I had the satisfaction of seeing them all hanged. I think a more cold-blooded affair could hardly be imagined than the above wholesale drowning of eighty-two fellow-countrymen.

I was cruising up the coast one day, merely on the look-out, having no definite information to go on, when, on passing a small island, two fishermen paddled off in a sanpan.

"Have got pilong," one immediately said.

"Where?" I asked.

"Can makee see," he replied, and on looking in the direction he pointed, I saw two small junks making the best of their way to sea. There was no wind, so I steamed quietly on, knowing they could not escape. About a dozen other smaller junks now put off, and opened fire at the two larger ones. Guns, jingalls, and other explosive instruments were discharged indiscriminately. As I ran alongside the nearest of the two junks, this fusillade ceased, and I soon had both junks secured. The crews I took on board the gun-boat, and steamed in and anchored off the town. The Mandarin, the governor of the place, at once came off, when the following conversation took place between us. First thanking me for my opportune appearance and capture of the two pirate junks, with their crews intact, numbering, all told, to twenty-one, he said: –

"These two junks have given me a great deal of trouble for four days; they have blockaded the place; neither a fishing or trading junk has been able to get out."

"Do you mean to say," I answered, "that these two

miserable junks, with twenty-one men between them, and mounting one two-pounder gun, have actually shut your port up for that time?"

"Yes," he said. "We are, my people are, very frightened of pilings."

"Have you no troops?" I remarked; "your personal staff seems to consist of at least fifty."

"Oh yes," he replied; "I have 800 soldiers on shore!"

There were something like a hundred junks of all sizes, some large enough to have run over the pirates without feeling the shock.

"Why did you not put some of your brave men in the fishing-junks and capture these pirates?"

"Ah, you English are very brave", he replied; "my men are very easily frightened."

Well, I thought to myself, that seems pretty certain.

"How many inhabitants are there in the town?" I asked.

"More than 4,000," was the answer.

"I think," I said, "if I were a Chinaman, I would turn pirate at once. They must lead very jolly independent lives."

"Yes, they do," answered this blue-buttoned warrior; "the only things they fear are English gun-boats."

A score or so of fishing junks had assembled round. The crews, consisting of quite as many women as men, were making a fearful clamour, talking over the last four days, and their sleepless nights; and now their relief had come, and their dreaded enemies were captured.

"Give us the pirates," they cried; the women particularly bawled for their possession.

"What do they mean," I asked my Mandarin friend, "by demanding these pirates to be handed over to their tender mercies?"

"Oh, they only want to drown them," he replied.

Just at this moment the poor Mandarin, who had evidently for some time been longing to reach *terra firma* again, had to be seized by two of his officials, and hurried to the ship's side, when his head was held well over the water, much to the amusement of his surrounding countrymen. A splash and an immense uproar at the same moment took place. The unhappy Mandarin recovered as if he had been electrified, and roared out sundry orders, which increased the confusion tenfold. It was a most laughable sight. The crews belonging to the fishing-junks, and the two or three score of soldiers and other officials rushing about with sticks, oars, and anything they could grasp, all giving directions at the same moment. The Mandarin was nowhere; he might just as well have gone on feeding the fishes; his directions were utterly lost in the general uproar and confusion. Two of the pirates had managed to slip from their guard, and took a header overboard; but they had no chance of escape, there were too many small craft about, and they were soon retaken. But to bring this story to an end. I handed over junks and pirates to the Mandarin. In twos, well secured, they were then placed in different junks, under a strong guard, and taken on shore. I bade my friend good-bye, and went on my journey up the coast. These twenty pirates were sent to Canton, tried, condemned, and executed.

The Chinese mode of decapitation is simple and expeditious; a short account of it may not be amiss here. A dozen or more of the condemned are taken to the execution ground, which at Canton is a small open space within the city. They are made to kneel down, their hands are then secured behind them, and the executioner goes along the line and arranges their heads and necks. I remember one poor wretch who shrunk up whenever the executioner approached, drawing his head into his shoulders, as if the very touch or nearness of the man was too much for him. The executioner tried to explain how much easier it would be for him to take his head off cleanly and neatly if he kept it well out, and thereupon gave it a good pull, and bared the unfortunate wretch's neck once more. Going to one end of the line he walks along, at each step with one blow severing a head from the body. The implement used is a sort of heavy half-sword half-butcher's cleaver, and is used with both hands.

I had been a couple of days cruising along the eastern coast, anchoring at night, and examining during the day-time the numerous creeks, bays, and hiding-places, but without success of any kind. Towards evening of the second day I reached a favourite creek, which, bending back from the head of a deep bay, twenty miles from the open sea, expanded into an inland basin, with innumerable smaller creeks and passages, twisting and turning about amongst the hills in all directions. It was a grand place for pirates. By having men stationed on the peaks of the hills, signals were easily passed along very quickly to their junks inside, which warning generally was in time to allow them to escape by some of the interminable creeks.

Soon after anchoring I went on shore to see the missionary priest, a Roman Catholic and a Jesuit. I never met or heard of a Protestant missionary taking up his quarters in such situations as I am now speaking of, viz., amongst the poorer villages far away from the open or treaty ports, where half the people live by piracy and robbery, in petty ways as well as in a more wholesale manner. A few words about this little man. He was an Italian of very good family, and had received an excellent education. Chinese he spoke like a native, besides six other languages as perfectly. He was a botanist, and full of intelligence on most subjects. Although he resided at this particular spot, his district was extensive, running inland about fifty miles, and to a greater distance along the coast. He had built a small chapel and school; how he managed this out of a monthly pittance of eight dollars was always a mystery to me. I believe, however, he made pilgrimages to Hong-Kong, and there, by his energy and charm of manner, managed to raise occasional help by subscriptions. Fifteen native children he entirely supported. He was the doctor, the friend, the counsellor of the village, and on more occasions than one had he, by his influence and the respect in which he was held in the surrounding district, not only kept the peace, but made villagers who had turned out against each other on some petty quarrel return home in friendship. His influence for good was very great; considering the people he was amongst, it was marvellous. His small, thin, delicate figure looked as if his life hung on a very slender thread.

"I suppose you are looking after pirates?" he remarked, as we walked up from the beach to his house. "A few days ago I had to cross the bay, and I feel sure there was a large piratical craft at anchor under one of the rocky points;

they are a bad lot about here, I fear; but you won't, I know, ask me anything I do not voluntarily tell you about these things. Poor people, they have hard times of it."

"Why do you call them poor?" I asked.

"Because those who do not live by piracy are squeezed by those who do, and squeezed into the bargain by the Mandarins."

"No wonder they don't become rich", I said; "but I must tell you about a neighbour of yours, who now is rather a friend of mine, although he is an arrant rogue, and the head of a pirate gang. I find him, however, very useful sometimes; but I will tell you how I made his acquaintance. A fishing vessel belonging to Hong-Kong was attacked by a couple of pirate craft, and of course taken. I suppose they thought no ransom would be forthcoming for such poor people."

"Yes, I fear that is the way they work their mischief," answered my companion.

"The pirates quietly sailed away with his junk and all his property, having first landed the owner and his family. The fisherman reached Hong-Kong, gave information, and I, as usual, was sent out to recover, if possible, the junk, etc. Step by step I traced the pirates until I ran them to earth at Kato; here a good deal of the stolen property was found stowed away in the house belonging to the head man of the village, and it required a deal of perseverance before he would part with it; but after sending a twenty-four pound shot through the roof of his house, he thought better of his sins."

"It was time he did," laughingly rejoined Voluntari.

"He keeps fifteen junks employed robbing his own

countrymen chiefly, but foreigners as well when a good opportunity to do so occurs. Since my first little episode with this worthy I have frequently called on him, and although, of course, I gain no news about his own craft, he has no objection to give information relating to the movements of his neighbours, or rather one of his neighbours, who happens to be a fellow-piratical chief. It was only about three weeks ago I took two large junks which I should never have found except through this unneighbourly rascal."

"I have heard of him," answered the priest, "and I fear he is a great rogue. The most wealthy men in many of these out-of-the-way villages live chiefly by piracy and plunder."

I decided to remain about the locality for a day or two longer, and early next morning got the gun-boat into a small bay, so narrow, and so perfectly hidden, that she had only just room to swing round her anchor, and until you came over the low hills which surrounded the spot, nothing of the little craft could be seen.

About three miles off I knew pheasants and partridges were to be found, and crossing the piece of water which intervened, I beat all the likely cover along the edges of the millet and maize fields. Toward mid-day I had bagged a few brace of each, some quail, and half-a-dozen snipe, and the sun being by this time warm enough to make a drink refreshing, I made for the village at the foot of the highest range in the neighbourhood, hoping to get some good water, or perhaps tea. As I reached the place, to my surprise it appeared deserted; not a human being, neither pig nor yelping cur, being visible. But as soon as I got amongst the houses, a face, then a head appeared, at an open casement; then another, until any number of heads popped out.

"Lofu! Lofu!" (tiger! tiger) they cried.

"Where?" I said, thinking of the No. 6 shot with which my gun was loaded.

"He come down just now, and walk through the village; he is very hungry."

"I daresay he is," I answered, "but I don't see him; where did he go?" That, however, no one knew; probably picking up a pig, he had returned to the thick impenetrable cover, or the mountain-side.

Quietly walking down to the nearest village during the day-time certainly appeared a very cool proceeding, but I was assured this was by no means an unusual incident, and that generally a pig or calf disappeared. The inhabitants themselves, when it so happened, drove their animals into their houses, shut themselves in, and remained perfectly quiet until the tiger thought proper to walk away. Sometimes they send to Canton for professional huntsmen, who generally manage to bag one or two of these troublesome beasts in a year. Either finding the remains of the animal that has been carried off, or, if that cannot be done, setting a bait, they then fix a cross-bow some yards from the trail by which the tiger will probably come, a string being led from the trigger of the cross-bow across his path, and pressing against this string as he quietly passes along, he lets loose his own death-warrant, in the shape of a poisoned arrow, discharged with all the force that a bamboo bow twenty feet long is capable of giving. I have seen some very beautiful and fine skins taken from these tigers in the south.

Returning to the gun-boat, soon after leaving the village with its inhabitants in a happier state of mind that when I entered it, I found a couple of Chinamen on board, who had brought word that some large pirate junks were at anchor a few miles away, in quite a different creek, and entirely hidden and separated from where the gun-boat then was by a mass of mountains. We were under weigh in ten minutes, steaming for the spot indicated. The course, however, led past my pirate friend's residence, and as we reached the village, a sampan pulled vigorously off with a couple of men in her. On seeing them approach I stowed the first informers away, to ascertain, without their seeing each other, the news that these men evidently wished to give. They, too, had information in substance much the same as the first gentlemen.

I did not quite like this eagerness to show me where the said pirates were, but of course without disclosing my doubts, and keeping the informers out of sight of each other, on we went. The creek was reached; it was about half a mile wide, and very shallow at the extreme end – the gun-boat, in fact, could not get within a mile of the bottom of it – so I anchored, and started with my two boats, taking about twenty men with me. As we pulled along the south side, within fifty yards of the shore, I noticed several men running along amongst the trees, which here grew thickly up the hill-side, and as they were all making for the head of the creek, as we were, I conjectured that those I saw thus hurrying on were bent on picking up odds and ends of spoil from the junks, which I now felt sure we should very soon find. My boat had got a couple of hundred yards ahead of the other, fortunately, and had just opened out the mastheads of a fine large junk hidden behind a low point covered with thick bushes and trees. "I have you, my friend," I inwardly said. At that moment, a flash, a report, and a shower of grape passed over our heads, ploughing up the water like hail on the other side of the boat. It passed through my mind instantly that I had been caught napping in a cleverly devised trap. Pulling short round, three strokes landed the boat in front of the battery, not five yards from their guns; another discharge, which certainly ought to have sent us all into the middle of next week, and the next moment we were amongst the pirates. Every bush and tree appeared to have a rascal behind it blazing away with a jingall; one fellow's eye I caught sight of along his barrel, and feeling at the moment rather vicious, pulled the trigger of my short rifle at him, but a wretched snap was the only result. However, he missed his object as well. The scuffle was soon over, the pirates being driven from their battery and junk into the thick surrounding woods and cover, where I did not care to follow them. The battery and junk now took my attention. The former was armed with 18-pounder carronades, one of which had evidently been loaded to the muzzle, the discharge having capsized it backwards. By allowing us to approach so near before opening fire they had missed their mark; if we had only been a hundred yards instead of fifty, I don't think many would have escaped. As it was, our luck had been extraordinary: not a man was touched either by jingall or gun.

On one occasion a fine clipper tea-ship, when on her way down the China Sea, got becalmed near the south-east part of Hainan. In a very short time fifteen junks appeared on the scene, and with the assistance of large sculls were soon within range, and opened fire. Fortunately for the vessel a light breeze sprang up, and with her lofty spars and quantity of light canvas she soon drew ahead out of range, and escaped closer quarters.

On the information reaching Hong-Kong I was ordered out to see if anything could be done towards capturing some of these junks. It was a lovely evening when we left, moonless but starlit, and as we steamed quietly through the shipping, and reached the open water to the west of the island, one could not help feeling how peaceful and quiet everything was. Keeping on during the night, we passed through the labyrinth of islands that extends nearly thirty miles to the south-west, and at daylight had reached the first of those that stud the south coast, directly west of the Canton river. A single junk was in sight, well inshore, and some miles ahead; but as it was quite calm the course I was steering would bring me within half a mile of her. Her great batwing-like sails flapped as the long swell lifted and rolled her from side to side, and on looking through the telescope I saw several neat round holes through her mat sails. I thought it strange, moreover, for an honest junk to be alone in that locality, knowing well that they usually went in small fleets for self-protection.

Decided to have a better look at her, I altered course; but before the little gun-boat's head was round, a boat from the junk had been launched, a dozen men had jumped into her, and were pulling for the shore as hard as possible.

I first caught the sampan, and then towing the junk to a favourite anchorage, burnt her; we then proceeded down the coast with the twenty-four pirates on board, whom I handed over to the Governor of the nearest province. Three exceptions I made – one because the rogue had once actually belonged to the *Opossum*, the gun-boat I commanded; another, because he was quite a youth, and had been to England; and the third because he was only fourteen years old, and I thought at that age he might learn a new trade, although he had been seven years with the pirates. To shorten a long story, this junk had, about three months before, been taken by pirates, when in company with a small fleet of Hong-Kong trading junks. After killing the crew, the pirates had kept her. They had then been so fortunate in their depredations that their own companions had attacked them; but, being a good sailor, the junk outstripped her envious friends, and when we hove in sight was all but at her journey's end, Macao, where her crew would have divided 20,000 dollars, and dispersed.

As we steamed up to her I observed the rascals flinging things overboard, but little dreamed they were bags of dollars, which were thus reduced to something less than half the number mentioned when I got on board.

The prisoners were forwarded to Canton. Six or seven, however, managed to escape on the way. The remainder were tried, condemned, and executed. On their trial they swore that those who escaped bribed the Mandarin to allow them to do so; and that had they themselves only possessed, or been able to raise money, as their more fortunate companions had done, they also would have been allowed to take to their heels. The authorities, at any rate, believed these wretched men, and the Mandarin, a first-class, red-buttoned individual, was recalled from his station, degraded, and sent into retirement. Altogether it was a queer piece of justice. In time I managed to get the unfortunate man reinstated, so far as his rank went, but he was never again given the governorship of the province.

On leaving Quanghai I kept on to the west, intending to reach Tienpak, where I thought I might hear some news regarding the Hainan pirates.

Tienpak was a queer place to get to, situated five miles up a narrow creek, scarcely fifty yards wide, which at low water led through flat sands, but at high tide the whole immense extent of sand was covered with three or four feet of water. After the military Mandarin had been on board I returned his visit on shore, and found him comfortably settled in a temporary residence on the outskirts of the town. He had collected all the prettiest girls of the place to wait and attend upon him during his short stay at this rough village. None of these people had ever seen a European before, and their curiosity in consequence was greatly excited by my arrival.

One girl, as she handed me a cup of tea, begged to be allowed to touch my whiskers, – such articles being scarce, if not wholly wanting, amongst her own countrymen.

I jokingly asked them, "Who would like to live on board the gun-boat?" and next morning, rather to my consternation, half-a-dozen of these fair ones came off, got up in all their best robes and cosmetics. The rough but honest old Mandarin accompanied his harem. It was amusing to see these girls, who, I fear, really thought half of them might be chosen to remain on board, trying to make themselves useful at once, by dusting and arranging the different articles in my cabin.

But adieu we bade them, and started for Hainan, –Mandarin, two war-junks, and gun-boat. A hundred miles west of Tienpak, I found a narrow entrance leading through some low sandhills into a spacious basin, which, on steaming across it, proved to be ten miles in width. No signs of junks were to be seen; but finding the mouth of a large river emptying itself into the north-west corner of the basin, I followed its course seven or eight miles up, passing several earth-batteries on either bank in that distance. Here we came across a large junk loading with oil, and from the crew ascertained that a couple of days before a fleet of pirates had been in the bay. This was bad luck, but there was nothing for it except the chance of finding them about Nowchow, an island just to the north of Hainan. Thither therefore we went, but the birds had flown from here also, probably for the southern parts of Hainan. It was rather more than provoking, considering that ten to one these were some of the very fellows who had attacked the clipper ship. However, better luck next time, I thought, as I turned the gun-boat's head towards Hong-Kong. Our coal was getting very short, and we had only enough, and barely that, to take us back. We anchored for a couple of days *en route*, at a favourite snug bay, and landing early the following morning with my gun and setter, I soon picked up some snipe, a few teal, and several quail. In crossing a soft muddy patch in the marsh I came upon the print of a tiger's track, perfectly fresh. Probably the beast, after hunting about the skirts of the villages in the valley, had crossed the swamp on his way to the mountains. The four toes measured exactly seven inches across. Partridges, as the day advanced, began to utter their curious wild note, as they answered one another from almost every hillock along the lower ranges. Turning homewards, I soon added a brace or two to my bag, and felt well satisfied with my forenoon's sport and walk as I reached the beach. Almost as I stepped on the clear sand, a bullet whizzed past my head, and went with a thud into the bank a few feet off. The report had hardly done reverberating amongst the hills, before my telescope picked out the enemy, some 300 yards off on a grassy mound, and not a little to my astonishment, the enemy was one of my own marines. It appeared that during my absence a small pirate craft had turned up amongst the bushes which line the creek, and that I was taken for one of the crew by those who were hunting them up. During the night the quartermaster on watch believed he heard the tiger. I slept, however, too soundly after my week's work to be easily disturbed, and I don't know whether the man was dreaming or not. I have no doubt, if I had time, I might have got him, by watching at night with a calf or pig for a bait; as it was, I returned next day to Hong-Kong to find another piratical report waiting for me.

From Henry Craven St. John, *Notes and Sketches from the Wild Coasts of Nipon*, 1880, Edinburgh.

CHAPTER TWELVE

A DARING ATTACK ON A BRITISH BARQUE

THE CAPTAIN'S REPORT

One of the most audacious outrages committed for some time by Chinese pirates took place on Sunday last. The British barque *Elizabeth Childs*, Captain Lindbergh, left this port on Saturday afternoon with a general cargo for Newchwang. She carried 12 hands all told, and as is usual with British merchantmen, was unarmed. On Sunday evening, when about 10 miles from Mendoza Island, a suspicious-looking junk hovered in the vicinity of the barque, and although warned off by Captain Lindbergh, subsequently grappled her. After hurling stinkpots on deck, some 40 pirates, all carrying firearms, which they used in a random and reckless manner, boarded the *Elizabeth Childs*, drove the crew forward, where they were kept at bay by one band of pirates, while the rest looted the ship of all the portable valuables they could find. The approach of a steamer alarmed the pirates, who then hastily left their prize, taking with them, however, the ship's sidelights and the booty they had collected in the cabins.

The following statement has been kindly supplied to us by Captain Lindberg:–

"We left Hong Kong on Saturday afternoon (29th March) for Newchwang, with about 280 tons of general cargo. The vessel was towed by a steam-launch through the Ly-ee-moon Pass, and at half-past 7 p.m. she left us off the Nine Pins. There was little wind, but it was very dark, and inclined to be foggy. About 10 o'clock I anchored, on account of a strong current running to the northward, and remained at anchor until 2 o'clock on the following afternoon, when a southerly breeze set in. I then got under weigh. During the afternoon I saw a number of junks cruising about, but I noticed two more particularly, between which there was constant communication, kept up by means of small boats. At 7 p.m. we were about 40 miles from Hong Kong. It was very dark and hazy. I observed one of the two junks before-mentioned drawing up very close to the starboard quarter of my vessel. This rather surprised me, as we can sail a great deal faster than a junk. The night was very still, and listening attentively I caught the sound of oars, and at the same time the second officer, with a night-glass, saw two men going aloft on the junk's mainmast. I then took the glass, and looked in the same direction, when I saw the junk under sail with some men sitting up aloft. The junk came up within close quarters a minute or two later, and I hailed them, saying, 'What do you want? If you come so near as to foul us I will fire into you.' I had no intention of carrying this threat into execution, but said it in order to intimidate them, as I began to suspect that they were not lawful traders. No reply was returned from the junk, but those on board ceased rowing, and thinking that all was right, shortly before 8 o'clock I went below into the cabin, and marked the position of the barque upon the chart. At a few minutes after 8, whilst I was still below, I heard the chief officer say to the man at the wheel, 'Starboard your helm.' Upon hearing this order shouted out, I hastened on deck, and found the junk about a hundred yards off on our starboard beam. As I did not approve of the mate's orders,

I called out to the man at the wheel, 'Hard down; luff all you can; if he doesn't luff up we'll be into him.' As soon as we commenced to luff, the junk bore off into our starboard forerigging, and threw a boarding grapnel on board. I was at this time standing on the quarter-deck with my first and second officers, and noticed a light at the junk's mainmast-head, which appeared to me like a fuse, as there were some sparks issuing from it. The grapnel was followed by a shower of burning fire-pots from the junk's mainmast on our deck, where they exploded with a loud report. Having a seven-barrelled revolver below, I went to my cabin to obtain it, and rushed up on deck again with it. I fired at the pirates three times, but without effect. I then fired two or three more rounds, but do not know whether any of the shots told. The pirates replied with a volley, from about 40 or 50 rifles and revolvers, but fortunately all fell wide of the mark, and no one was injured. I went below, where I found the second officer with my Chassepot rifle. He asked me for some cartridges, which I gave him, but unfortunately, when he attempted to load it, he found it so rusty that it could not be cocked. Whilst this was going on, I observed a lurid light through my cabin window, and this was followed instantly by a terrific report. The ship trembled, the skylight over the cabin flew off, and our lamps were extinguished. We rushed up on deck, the second mate first, and he ran forward. When I got on deck I found about 40 men boarding my vessel on the starboard quarter, firing their weapons at random as they advanced. Seeing none but a swarm of armed pirates around me, and being unarmed myself, I beat a hasty retreat below, but not so hasty as to be unobserved, for as I was descending the companion a pistol shot was fired at me, and the bullet grazed the store-room door and finally lodged in the cabin floor. Recognising the hopelessness of offering resistance to the miscreants, I concealed myself in a small closet in my berth, and was scarcely ensconced there when more than a dozen men came rushing down with lights, loudly calling out, in very good English, 'Captain, captain, come out: we know you are down here.' Thinking myself more secure in my hiding place, I concluded to remain there, and did not reply. Through a chink in the door I could hear and see everything that transpired. Amongst the pirates I specially remarked a man dressed in Chinese clothes, but wearing a thick and long moustache, whom from his appearance I strongly suspected to be a European. That man pulled out the drawers in my cabin, and emptied the contents on the floor in front of the closet wherein I was concealed. He took my ship's documents, chronometer, my watch and chain, and some other valuables, but rejected the clothes. Whilst this fellow was thus engaged, I heard the afterhatch being lifted, and a gang of pirates troop below. I heard good English repeatedly spoken during my imprisonment. After being below a period which appeared to me at least half an hour I heard a loud call in Chinese from the pirates on deck, and those below thereupon rushed up on deck. After waiting about five minutes and hearing no further sound I cautiously crept out of my hiding-place and made my way stealthily up on deck, where I met the officers and crew, who had been kept forward by a body of armed pirates. From what I could ascertain, it appears that the lights of a steamer were observed by the pirates on deck, who gave the alarm to their comrades below, who promptly came up and left the barque, taking the ship's side-lights with them. Upon making inquiries I found that no person on board had been seriously hurt, notwithstanding the storm of bullets under which the pirates effected the boarding of the vessel. One of the seamen had a very narrow escape, a bullet cutting his waistband and grazing the skin. Heaps of fire were burning on the deck, fore and aft, which we of course cleared off as soon as possible. Notwithstanding the loss of my chronometer, I made up my mind to proceed on my voyage, but was compelled to abandon this intention upon discovering the loss of the side-lights. Under these circumstances I could not safely go on, and accordingly put the ship about to return to Hong Kong, where I arrived today (April 1) at 1 o'clock, anchored in the Sulphur Channel, and was towed by a steam-launch belonging to the Patent-slip to moorings off West Point.

"The pirates, when below, ransacked the officers' berths as thoroughly as they did my own, and amongst other things took the chief officer's gold watch and chain. I cannot say whether any or what cargo has been abstracted from the hold, but the total value of the articles I know to have been taken is about 500 dollars. I could not identify any of the pirates, as I did not get a good view of them, but two of my crew say they could recognise a couple of the robbers. The quarter-deck is literally covered with bullet holes, also the fore-house."

We understand that some time last week a Chinese junk was pirated in the same neighbourhood, and it is probable that the two piracies were committed by the same persons. It is evident that they are led by men who have had much intercourse with foreigners – if, indeed, they do not carry a European adventurer with them. It is probable that they expected a much larger booty than they acquired from the *Elizabeth Childs*.

From *The Hong Kong Daily Press*, Wednesday, 2nd April, 1879

CHAPTER THIRTEEN

STEAMER *NAMOA* ATTACKED; CHINESE PIRATES ARRESTED AND EXECUTED

THE HONG KONG DAILY PRESS AND *THE CHINA MAIL*

CAPTAIN AND TWO OTHERS MURDERED

December 11.

Hongkong was startled this morning by the news of a tragedy such as one might think was impossible in these days. The annals of the colony furnish many instances of murderous attacks on British vessels by Chinese pirates, but it has long been thought that the steps taken to suppress piracy had rendered steamers safe from anything of this kind. The feeling of security may have led to an injudicious relaxation of vigilance, but whether such is the case or not the event which has sent a thrill of horror and indignation through Hongkong this morning shows that powerful and bloodthirsty bands of pirates capable of attacking large and well-equipped British steamers still exist, and that they are ready to take advantage of any opportunity to prosecute their deadly work. This latest instance of piracy on a British vessel has resulted, we are sorry to say, in the death of the well-known and much respected commander of one of the [famous Douglas Line of] steamers, Captain [Thomas Guy] Pocock, of the *Namoa*. His fate was shared by a European passenger and one of the native [Chinese] quartermasters of the vessel. The details of the tragedy are as follow:–

The *Namoa* left Hongkong for Swatow at 8 a.m. yesterday morning, with five saloon and 220 Chinese deck passengers on board. The Chinese were chiefly returned emigrants from San Francisco and the Straits who were going home with the savings they had accumulated in their absences from their native country.

All went well till 1.15, at which time the vessel was passing the Island of Ping Hoi. Suddenly, from among the Chinese passengers a band of between forty and fifty men made their appearance on deck. They had changed the dress in which they came on board for a kind of uniform, not unlike that worn by Chinese soldiers. All were armed with revolvers and cutlasses. Before any of the crew could realise what this demonstration meant, the pirates, evidently following a carefully laid plan, had divided themselves into four gangs and commenced a simultaneous attack on the saloon – where the captain and passengers were at tiffin – the engineers' and [deck] officers' quarters, the bridge, and the engine-room.

The attack was so sudden and so determined that resistance was impossible, and apart from that the pirates had taken steps to prevent anything of the kind by first taking possession of the arms and ammunition belonging to the ship.

The engineers' and officers' quarters were first opened fire on. The second engineer and second officer were sitting at tiffin when several shots were fired and stinkpots thrown in upon them. The second engineer, Ramsay, was shot through the arm, but wounded as he was, he made his escape to the engine-room. The second officer was made a prisoner and ordered under threats of instant death to show where the treasure and valuables were. Another gang had attacked the third officer, Eddy, on the bridge. He jumped from the bridge and made his escape to the engine-room, where he was followed by the pirates. He also received a shot in the arm. The third engineer, who was in the engine-room when the attack commenced, was joined by the second engineer and the second officer, both seeking refuge in the same place. The three men concealed themselves under the boilers, and for some time eluded the search of the pirates.

In the meantime another gang had attacked the saloon, some of them at pointing their revolvers through the skylight, called on the captain to come on deck. One man spoke in pidgin English. He said: "We are going to rob the passengers, and we want to settle with you." Captain Pocock, after some parley left the table and walked towards the door of the saloon. He had hardly reached the deck when one of the pirates, who was standing at the door deliberately fired at him, the bullet taking effect in the right breast. Captain Pocock did not fall at once, but managed to stagger into his stateroom, and sank dying on his bed, blood flowing profusely from his fatal wound. He expired there about half-an-hour afterwards.

Meanwhile the pirates were pursuing their fiendish work. The saloon passengers had rushed from the tiffin table and concealed themselves in their rooms [Passenger cabins on China Coastal ships often opened into the main saloon], into which shots were fired and stinkpots thrown. The second officer, surrounded by a party of pirates with revolvers and drawn cutlasses, was compelled to go into the saloon and tell the passengers to come out of the rooms and go into the captain's stateroom and stay there if they did not want to be killed. The passengers thereupon came out of their rooms and went into the stateroom where Captain Pocock lay dying. Here they were locked in, and a watch of four men put over them. The chief engineer, who was at tiffin in his own room, ran aft to the saloon, several shots being fired at him on the way. He got into the captain's stateroom, and was kept a prisoner there with the others. The chief officer had hid himself in the pantry, where shots were fired at him and stinkpots thrown in. It being impossible to stay there, he came out, and was imprisoned in the captain's stateroom, the object of the pirates evidently being to get all the officers and Europeans into this place and keep them there. The second and third engineers and third officer were still concealed in the engine-room. The pirates took the second mate there and ordered him to tell the concealed men that if they came out no harm would be done to them. They then came out, and were imprisoned in the captain's stateroom. All the officers, engineers, and European passengers having been put into this place the door was nailed up and the windows closed, and the guard of four pirates continued to keep watch over the place, occasionally intimidating the prisoners by thrusting their cutlasses and the muzzles of their revolvers in through the opening of the jalousies [shutters].

Miserable as was the condition of the imprisoned passengers, one of their number had been still more unfortunate. This passenger, a lighthouse-keeper in the Chinese Custom service, named Peterson, was not in the saloon with the others when the attack commenced. Feeling unwell he sat down on deck aft, and was taking a glass of claret and a biscuit there. When the first rush was made aft by the pirates they began their bloody work by shooting this man, who fell with four bullet wounds in his head.

The systematic way in which the attack was carried out is shown by the fact that the pirates at once took charge of the ship. They made the firemen take charge of the engines and compelled the crew to carry on such work as they wished done. Three native [Chinese] quartermasters were fired at, all of whom were hit. One of them was thrown overboard and the other two fell, seriously wounded. The ship was taken out to sea for some distance, and at 4 o'clock she was turned towards Hongkong again. Meanwhile a portion of the band had been devoting themselves to the work of looting. It happened that there was no treasure on board, but the pirates tried to make amends for this disappointment by taking everything of value that could easily be carried. The crew were compelled to turn out and ransack all the luggage of the passengers, European and Chinese, and all the money and valuables that could be found anywhere on the ship were taken.

At 7.30 p.m. [on Friday, 12th December] the ship had been brought back to the place where the attack was commenced, where six junks were waiting. The ship's lights were all extinguished and the whistle was blown as a signal to the junks, the crews of which responded by throwing blue lights on the water. The steamer was then anchored, and the work of transferring the loot to the junks was commenced. When this had been accomplished with the assistance of the *Namoa*'s native crew the pirates regaled themselves with a feast on deck, and then made preparations for taking leave of the vessel. The ship's sidelights were thrown overboard, the firemen were ordered to draw the fires and open the safety valve so as to blow off the steam, the windlass was disabled, and generally everything done that could be thought of to delay the ship from getting away. Before leaving, the pirates threw a bag containing about $200 into the engine-room as a cumshaw [gratuity or baksheesh] to the firemen. They quitted the ship about 9 o'clock, and a quarter of an hour afterwards the officers, engineers, and passengers broke out of their stifling prison, where the dead body of Captain Pocock lay. The ship was then got in readiness as quickly as possible for returning to Hongkong, where she arrived at 8 o'clock this morning. The wounded were at once removed to the hospital. The body of the Captain Pocock lay in his stateroom, and on the deck was that of the passenger Peterson. The deck of the ship was strewn with such portions of the passengers' luggage as had been rejected by the pirates, while all over the ship could be seen the marks made by bullets and stinkpots.

The pirates did not take any of the cargo, although there were forty chests of opium on board, their desire evidently being not to carry away anything by which they could be traced.

H.M.S. *Linnet* with Captain Stewart, of the Chinese cruiser *Kaipan*, on board, will be sent to Ping Hoi to-morrow to prosecute inquiries. It is surmised that the pirates (or the junkmen, at least), are Shaukiwan men.

Friday, 20th February 1891.
Three of the men concerned in the recent notorious piracy on board the British steamer *Namoa* have been arrested by the Chinese authorities at Canton. The men have confessed their guilt, and state that they were hired in Hongkong to co-operate in the work by two ringleaders, one named Li Chant and the other Fung.

The Hong Kong Daily Press, Thursday, 11th December, 1890.

EXECUTION OF NOTORIOUS *NAMOA* PIRATES AT HONG KONG

On the afternoon of the 11th May, says the *China Mail* of June 3rd, 15 prisoners were beheaded at Kowloon City. Amongst the number were six *Namoa* pirates, including the three leaders of the gang – namely, Fung San Yau, Lai A Tsat and Chan A Yu. The other three were Wan A Fat, Cheung Sui Chang and Ho Fat To. The last named was the captain of one of the junks on board which the pirates put their plunder. The remainder of the fifteen were men sentenced for various crimes, but they appear to have been all unknown in Hong Kong. The execution attracted an unusually large crowd, and the interest of the spectators seemed to centre in the *Namoa* men. This was particularly the case as regards the large contingent of visitors from Hong Kong.

It is just five months and a day since the piracy of the *Namoa* [a Douglas & Company coastal steamer] and the murder of [her] Captain [Thomas Guy] Pocock and Mr. Peterson [of the Imperial Maritime Customs Service] took place. For a long time it seemed that the leaders in that diabolical business were to escape with the fruits of their crime. They got, thanks to the apathy of the naval authorities here, a very favourable start. The police of the colony, if they were to depend on their own efforts, were utterly powerless. But the Chinese authorities bestirred themselves in the matter in a way that showed they were very much in earnest. General Fung Yu, an officer of untiring energy and unwavering determination, undertook the task of tracking and bringing to justice those of the pirates who were known to have sought refuge in Chinese territory. The result has exceeded in a very large measure the expectations of this colony; for not only have 15 of the miscreants now paid for their crime with their lives, but among these three men who were undoubtedly the leaders of the gang have suffered. One of them, Lai A Tsat – a man whose boldness and cunning in carrying out such exploits have made him a legend both at sea and on shore for a long time – was the person who had charge of that portion of the gang of pirates whose duty it was to seize and keep guard over the European officers, engineers and passengers of the *Namoa*. He was referred to by the witnesses in the inquiry here as the pirate chief. The real chief, however, was Fung San Yau. He was the man who directed the whole of the operations, a man far superior to Lai A Tsat in intelligence, though not his equal in daring. Mr. Wodehouse's almost complimentary reference to Lai A Tsat's lack of brutality and bloodthirstiness was misplaced, for it is well known now that this ruffian insisted on the necessity of setting fire to the ship before leaving it, and Fung San Yau had great difficulty in overruling him. The other leader, Chan

A Yu, did not specially distinguish himself in the piracy. He was under police supervision, and on the eve of the piracy sought permission from the inspector of police at Shankiwan to go and "collect some rents in the country." Of the three remaining pirates, whose bodies are now lying on Kowloon beach nothing particular is known here.

The short but impressive ceremony at the execution was of the kind usual on such occasions. The prisoners were brought down from Canton in a gunboat, and amid the usual firing of guns from war vessels and fort, they were put into a couple of small boats to be taken ashore to the execution ground, where a crowd of Chinese and Europeans ranged themselves around an oblong square formed by armed [Chinese] "braves." The tide being out, the boats stuck in the mud when within about 50 yards of the shore, and had to be shoved off and rowed to the pier. A few minutes later the prisoners, with their arms corded tightly behind them and their ankles loaded with chains, came slowly along the pier to the place of execution guarded by a squad of "braves." Meanwhile the chief executioner and his two apprentices, having cleared a space sufficiently large, and stuck four of their heavy swords into the ground, whiled away the time in chaff with some of the officers present. The *Namoa* men were among the first lot of prisoners who arrived, and a howl of execration from the crowd greeted their appearance. "You're Ko Lo Chai (Lai A Tsat)," said the chief executioner laying his hand on the shoulder of a tall, thin man with a "chop dollar face" and keen piercing eyes, "We'll begin with you,". "All right," responded the pirate leader, "I'm number One." He had been swearing in English and Chinese, one of the Chinese officers said, all the way to the execution ground. He was placed at one end of the square, and all the others knelt in a line with him. A few seconds sufficed to put them in order, and then the slaughter began. Lai A Tsat kept looking round at the executioner while that worthy examined the sword which he had selected; and while he held his long thin neck outstretched he continued to speak as if he wished the spectators to know he was not afraid. "You may kill me now." he said, "but I shall revive again", on which Fung San Yau, who was the fourth man in the row, muttered some comment. "Now don't you move," said the executioner as he pulled the pirate's pigtail out of the way of the sword. The kneeling man said something about each having his own luck, and as he said it the sword came down, and "Ko Lo Chai" was no more.

The others, most of them very miserable looking wretches, shuddered, and gave what seemed to be an unwilling look round. They had not long to wait, for the brawny butcher was getting through his work with great celerity, prefacing each stroke with the warning "Don't move," and accompanying each blow with a vigorous utterance of a Chinese expression which might be rendered into English as "Done for!" When he came to Fung San Yau it was apparent to his experienced eye that that distinguished villain had already, in a figurative sense, "lost his head." The man of blood and steel swore at him roundly, and told him that if he did not keep steady it would be worse for him. It was the worse for him, for the blade struck him almost in a line with the shoulders, and the head did not come off, which was no doubt the reason why there was a rapid convulsive movement of the legs for a few seconds afterwards. The chief executioner, who found the others easier to deal with, handed over the sword to his son, a promising youth of 15, at the twelfth man, and he had no reason to find fault with the youngster's work. When the end of the line was reached, the executioner in chief returned and completed the decapitation of Fung San Yau. The whole affair only occupied a few minutes.

The China Mail, Hong Kong. Wednesday, 3rd June 1891, copied by *The West Australian,* Perth, Thursday, 16th July, 1891.

CHAPTER FOURTEEN

A EUROPEAN SMUGGLER BESET BY PIRATES

THOMAS W. KNOX

A friend of the writer had a narrow escape from death at the hands of Chinese pirates. He was engaged in smuggling at the time of his adventure, and was therefore not in a position to invoke the full protection of the authorities. The ship to which he was attached was anchored off the coast, not far from Macao and under the shelter of the Sun Chow Islands. In the daytime operations were suspended, and nearly everybody slept; but at night there was activity from one end of the ship to the other, and many chests of opium were transported to the shore. The officials in the neighborhood had been properly bribed, and everything went along smoothly. My friend was second mate of the ship, and accompanied half the boat loads to the point where the opium was delivered to the comprador of the Chinese house to which it was consigned, while the first mate attended to the other half. The captain, third mate and supercargo looked after matters on shipboard during the absence of the first and second officers. The rest of the incident is best told in his own words.

"It was about five miles from the ship," said he, "to a place where we landed the opium and turned it over to the comprador. Each of the boats had a Chinese crew of rowers under charge of a Malay tyndal or boatswain, and the only white man of the party was the mate in charge. Between sunset and sunrise each boat made two round trips, and for the first two nights there was no trouble of any kind. On the third night each of us had made one trip; the first mate's boat went ahead of mine, and it was our rule to get one party clear off from the ship before beginning to load up for the other. You see we were liable to a visit any time from some of the customs officials who hadn't been 'squared,' or more especially from the foreign employees of the government who were on the lookout for a capture out of which they could bag a good reward. Only one chest of opium was brought on deck at a time, and not until it was safe in the boat was another one hoisted up. In case of a sudden visit the boat had orders to pull off at once into the darkness, and at the same time the hatch would be closed and everything made shipshape. By the time the officers could get on the deck there wouldn't be a chance for suspicion that we were doing anything else than lying at anchor. Of course it would require lying of another sort to convince them that our presence there was entirely innocent, but we were ready with an abundance of that kind of the article.

"Just as the first mate was ready to pull off on his second trip for that night, one of our sharp-eared fellows detected the sound of oars in the water. Everybody was ordered to keep still and listen, and sure enough we could distinctly hear the splash that indicated the movement of a boat. It was a slow and cautious sound, and indicated very plainly that the men who were making it wanted to get as near as possible before they were discovered. There was no time to unload the opium from the mate's boat; he dropped astern with the slight current that was running and was soon out of sight. The tackle was passed down to my boat, and in half a minute we had her swinging by the davits where she belonged and everybody out of her. The Chinamen were ordered below, and as they went down the hatch one of them said to me, waving his hand in the direction of the approaching boat: 'Plenty piecee la-li-loong blongy this side'; ('good many thieves around here'.) I caught his suggestion on the instant and immediately told the captain what the man had said.

"The captain was at first inclined to laugh at the idea, as no pirates had been heard of there for a long time, but a moment after said it was just as well to be on the watch for mischief. To confirm the suggestion that there might be something wrong, the approaching boat stopped rowing, which it would not have been likely to do if its mission was an honest one. Everything was still on the ship, and we had hoisted in the boat so quietly that the little noise we made was drowned to their ears by the sound of their own rowing.

"The half dozen European sailors of our crew were on deck with us. The captain sent two of them below with me to bring up some rifles which were kept ready in the cabin, and also a box of hand grenades that were intended for the kind of fighting which might be going on in the next quarter of an hour, I carried a revolver at my waist, and so did the captain. I buckled on an extra one and brought up another for the captain, and in less than three minutes from the time I went below I was on deck again, and everybody was armed and at his post. Of course you understand that the Chinese part of the crew is of no use. Chinamen make good soldiers when properly drilled and disciplined, but in their civilian condition they cannot be relied upon. The best thing to do with them was to keep them below where they had been sent.

"After resting a few minutes, and hearing no sound from the ship the rowers bent to their work again, and very soon the boat was at our side. It was a long and low craft of the kind called a 'snake boat,' partly from its shape and partly because of its superior speed. We hailed her, and the only reply we received was 'Flin,' ('Friend'.) A moment later a stinkpot was flung upon the deck.

"The missile was well aimed in one respect, but badly in another. Instead of striking the deck and breaking to pieces, as was intended, it fell into a tub of boiled rice which the cook had set out for the breakfast of our Chinese boatmen. The soft rice received it tenderly, and the odoriferous weapon was harmlessly embedded where it could do no great injury to those for whom it was intended.

"The pirates endeavored to follow their opening shot and take advantage of the confusion it might have created. They sprang at the sides of the ship under her fore chains; we saw what they were up to, and as fast as a head showed above the rail in the dim light it received a bullet from rifle or revolver at very close quarters. While several grenades were flung at the boat two of the sailors dropped their rifles and armed themselves with handspikes; one of them said afterward that he could shoot much faster with a handspike than with a gun as he lost no time in stopping to reload. Two of the scoundrels got over the rail, and one of them had me by the throat when a sailor laid him out with a blow across the back, and finished the job by flinging the fellow overboard. He struck just in time, as the man was unusually powerful, and had me pinned in such a way that

I could not use my revolver.

"In five minutes the fight was over. The pirates, as many as were left of them, paddled off as fast as their snake boat could carry them, and in a direction opposite to that whence they came. Hardly were they gone before the mate came rowing through the darkness. He had found it no easy matter to get his crew to return to the ship, as they knew very well that we had been attacked by pirates, and they had no liking for the company of those fellows. All the mate's threats to shoot them unless they bent to the oars were of no avail; they would not pull a stroke until they heard our shout of victory and the sound of the oars as our assailants pulled away.

"We hadn't a man hurt, although we had a very narrow escape from capture and consequent death. And the unhappiest man of all our party was the first mate, because he didn't have a hand in the fight.".

From Thomas W. Knox, *The Talking Handkerchief and Other Stories*, 1900, Akron, Ohio.

CHAPTER FIFTEEN

WORLD NEWSPAPERS DENOUNCE RENEWED PIRACY

SOUTH CHINESE PIRATES AND THE BIAS BAY GANG

The Island of Hong Kong is one of a large group of islands which extend north and south of the mouth of the Pearl, or Canton, River. The Portuguese, who were among the first navigators to brave the dangers of the South China seas, christened the group in the 18th century by the significant name of "Ladrones", and it is a fact no less true than regrettable that after a quarter of the 20th century has elapsed the name is as appropriate to-day as when it was first bestowed on this piratical locality.

The pirates have, however, altered their methods. They no longer, as of old, operate from piratical junks, running alongside their victims and carrying them by boarding. Their methods are simple, more business-like, and safer. They now mark down a vessel which their excellent system of intelligence leads them to suppose will be the most valuable prey. On it they embark in the guise of Chinese passengers, largely as deck passengers, though some travel by the superior classes. Their arms, almost invariably revolvers, are concealed in the nondescript dunnage with which every Chinese passenger, honest or not, is laden.

Detection – though occasionally they are detected – is exceedingly difficult. When at sea on a given signal the engine-room, officers, and, where it exists, the wireless-room are held up. And it almost invariably happens that in a few minutes the ship is in their hands, as often as not without a shot being fired or a life sacrificed. Next the officers are compelled at the pistol's point to navigate the ship to a remote bay or creek where the pirates have their base; the vessel is looted, and the loot and pirates are landed either in the ship's boats or more usually in local craft which are waiting for this purpose. It often occurs that Chinese passengers who appear well-to-do are carried off for ransom. It may appear strange that so much success attends them, but they have the enormous advantage of absolutely safe bases from which to work, while it must be admitted that considerable ingenuity is displayed in planning the *coupe*.

There is, however, another side to the question, which complicates matters enormously and adds to the great difficulty which ships' officers experience in combating the pirates afloat. While during the process of piracy all goes smoothly and no resistance is offered the pirates behave in a reasonable manner apart from their plundering. They do not murder or insult the passengers. One occasion is on record where a pirate had removed the captain's shot gun in its case from the cabinet, and, failing to put it together, he petulantly threw it overboard. The captain complained to the chief of the pirates, who at once handed him $200 to get a new gun. If, on the other hand, resistance is shown the pirates are not alone prepared to kill their opponents, but if successfully opposed they are prepared to sacrifice the ship with every soul on board, including themselves. This happened in the case of the steamship *Tai On*, and more recently in that of the steamship *Sunning*.

On November 15, at about midnight, while the *Sunning*, of the China Navigation Company, was on a voyage from Amoy to Hong Kong, she was suddenly seized by pirates. The surprise was complete. The second officer, who was on watch at the time, was peering over the canvas dodgers of the bridge in the attempt to pick up a navigation mark, when he was seized by the ankles and thrown on to his head by pirates who had climbed on to the bridge unobserved, it is thought from forward by means of the grilles. All other officers were held up at the point of the revolver, and in a short time the ship was entirely under the pirates' control. They gave orders to make for Bias Bay, and appeared so well satisfied that the officers had accepted the situation that they allowed them a good deal of personal liberty.

The second officer, however, was a man of great courage and strong personality. He was also hurt, both in dignity and person, by the "up-ending" episode on the bridge, and he determined to retake the ship. He managed unobserved to obtain a revolver and some cartridges from his cabin, and communicated his plan to the chief officer. Shortly after, he and the chief officer and the captain were on the bridge with some pirates, endeavouring to pick up an important navigation light. The second officer drew a pirate's attention by pointing outboard as if to a light, and, as the pirate peered over, struck him a violent blow on the back of the head with the lead, which stunned him. The chief officer joined the *mélée* and, snatching a rifle from one of the pirates on the bridge, stunned a man running up to help.

In a few seconds the bridge was cleared. Other officers

managed to make their way there *via* a skylight, while a brisk fight went on in which several pirates were shot. Soon after dawn the pirates realized that they could not hope to carry the bridge, and set fire to the vessel. A few then embarked in one of the ship's boats with some members of the crew, and one or two Chinese passengers; the others apparently remained on board, of whom at least two are known to have perished in the flames. The boat was afterwards picked up by H.M.S. *Bluebell.* Her arrival, aided by the skilful seamanship of the captain and officers of the *Sunning*, enabled the fire to be got under, but not until most of the ship was gutted; and she was towed back to Hong Kong a complete wreck. The case in point well illustrates the utter disregard for consequences, even to themselves, shown by the pirates in face of opposition.

It is only within the last seven years or so, a period corresponding with the utter chaos in China, that the situation has become so intolerable. During the last half of the 19th century piracies of big ships were not very numerous. In 1868, 1874, 1879, and 1885 there were bad cases. In December, 1890, occurred the well-known piracy of the *Namoa*, which aroused so much indignation. She was pirated in the now approved manner and is one of the first ships which are definitely known to have been taken into Bias Bay after capture. The efforts of the British Navy, however, and the exertions of the Chinese authorities – for then there was a reasonably stable administration at Canton – put a period to piratical outrage, and cases were few and far between until comparatively recently.

But by 1921 the administration of the two Kwang Provinces had fallen into chaos. Inland brigands were rampant, while upon the waterways of the delta of the West River and in the remoter bays of the coast the pirates, in apparently absolute security, plied their nefarious sailing unchecked. Between January, 1921, and March, 1927, inquiry shows that no fewer than 14 sea-going ships and five large steam launches are known to have been pirated and taken into Bias Bay; while, as for piracies within the knowledge of the Hong Kong police which cannot be attributed to the Bias Bay gang, the figures between January, 1926, and January, 1927, inclusive, show piracies of 19 trading junks, eight fishing boats (large), five cargo boats, and one customs launch. The pirates in all these cases, except that of the customs launch, operated from launches and boarded their defenceless prey.

The authorities in Hong Kong had all this time been piecing together the available information with reference to known gangs or individuals, who, it must be remembered, all resided within Chinese territory. The most important and systematic gang of pirates was found to be those who invariably took the captured ships into Bias Bay, and finally it was possible to know definitely that members of these gangs lived at the north-east end of the bay in the township of Fan lo Kong (Fan Wo Kong in Chinese, but the spelling on the Admiralty charts has been adopted) and the neighbouring villages of Kwai Chau, Hoi Chau, and Cheung Pai.

Bias Bay is the name given by cartographers to a large inlet situated some 45 miles east-north-east of Hong Kong. Its hills are visible on a clear day from the Peak at Hong Kong. It extends inland for some 20 miles from the island of Tuni Ang, which lies on the west side of the mouth of the bay. The coast line of the interior of the bay is very irregular, and on the west side there are innumerable small islands. At the extreme north-east corner is a creek, known as the Fan lo Kong creek (or harbour), which extends for about five miles farther in a north-east direction. In the middle of the bay itself, for 12 miles or more deep water exists.

Beyond this the water shoals rapidly, and in the mouth of the creek there is little more than 9 ft, for about a mile. Thereafter it can be navigated only by small craft and sampans. At the mouth of this creek, one on each side, lie the villages of Hoi Chau and Kwai Chau. Cheung Pai is close at hand, while in a well cultivated plain some mile or two away lies Fan Lo Kong town, where there are 10,000 inhabitants. It is in these towns that the gang live. The Hong Kong police, indeed, actually know the very houses of some of the individuals. Yet to outward appearance the district is inhabited by prosperous cultivators. And there lies one of the great difficulties of the position. Given time to get ashore and to conceal their booty, the pirates are at once peaceful farmers. "Even such farmers as cut up the Madras troops at Hlinedatalone in Burma. Even such farmers as slew Cavagnari Sahib and the Guides at Kabul".

The problem is a most difficult one. In the nineties things were easier, for, as has been said, there was a stable Government in Canton. After the *Namoa* piracy in 1890 the [Chinese] Viceroy gave orders for intensive action, and 15 pirates were publicly executed by the Chinese authorities at Kowloon City on the old frontier. When Li Hung-chang was Viceroy he employed the most severe methods, and well-nigh succeeded in rooting out all piracy. But chaos now has fallen on the unfortunate provinces. Chan Kwing Ming [Chan-Chiung-ming] during his administration at Canton in 1922–1923 was never secure; yet he did his best, and, in friendly co-operation with the Hong Kong authorities after the piracy of the *Hydrangea* on December 27, 1923, he sent an expedition, which resulted in the collection of much information, while seven pirates were shot. A short time later another expedition led to the shooting of five more. But there the matter has ended.

In 1925 the so-called Nationalist Government came into power in Canton. It so happened, however, that the tract of country lying behind Bias Bay and Mirs Bay (the bay between Bias Bay and Hong Kong) in the direction of Waienow has never actually come under the direct control of this Government, for the adherents of Chan Kwing Ming still held some sort of foothold there. It is possible that this factor has influenced the Government at Canton. It is also possible that they view with equanimity the pirating of ships owned for the most part by that nation which is described by their Bolshevist advisers as "the Imperialists" and even as "the enemy". However that may be, protest after protest has been made, and nothing whatever has been done.

It is true that early in 1927, when the Government of Hong Kong offered co-operation with the Canton Government a flat refusal of foreign aid was tempered by an intimation that Canton was taking action. It proved, however, as empty a promise as the usual run of those which emanate from this *soi-disant* Nationalist Government. An expedition was dispatched, and spent its time in sporadic and aimless attacks in the district of a political enemy, one of Chan Kwing Ming's adherents, whose territory lay between Mirs Bay and Bias Bay, full 20 miles as the crow flies from the pirate settlement.

Such has been the history of piracy in these waters in the past. For two years piracy on piracy has been committed. Protest upon protest has been lodged with the Minister for Foreign Affairs at Canton. But nothing has been done; not a single step has been taken to ameliorate the intolerable position. Not long ego in a conversation with Mr. Teichman [later Sir Eric, a British Consular official], Mr. Eugene Chen [Chinese Minister for Foreign Affairs] acting had the cool audacity to suggest that if the natives of the villages at Bias Bay were in the habit of pirating British ships it was the duty of His Majesty's Government to station a warship there permanently. The calm effrontery of the suggestion that in cases of piracy it is only for the Government of the victims, and not for the Government of the guilty parties, to take action is typical of Mr. Eugene Chen's political methods. It does, however, convey a direct invitation to His Majesty's Government to take action in Bias Bay, and it is difficult to understand his loudly protested horror when, its patience finally broken down by the piracy of the *Hop Sang* on March 22, 1927, His Majesty's Government took direct action, in despair of any reasonable co-operation from the local Government.

On the morning of March 23, at daybreak, a British force landed at the village of Kuei Chei and Hoi Chaun. The inhabitants fled before them. Not a soul was hurt. The animals and even the poultry of the villagers were not harmed. The houses alone suffered damage, as they were destroyed either by fire or explosives. Such was the lesson meted out to the pirates. At last they have learned that the arm of the British Government is as long as its patience. But it is a curious commentary on the Nationalist Government that, for all the singular restraint and humanity shown in dealing out this salutary lesson, for all that the action taken by the British was one which a responsible Government should itself have taken, the action of the British authorities has been seized upon merely as a source of lying propaganda. Not content with stigmatising our expedition as a breach of Chinese sovereign rights, we have been accused of looting and of the slaughter of a thousand innocent Chinese.

From a Hong Kong Correspondent, *The Times*, Printing House Square, London, Leader for Tuesday, 31st May, 1927.

CHINESE PIRATES – HOW TO CHECK THEM.
POWERS CANNOT AGREE

British Official Wireless Agency News, London, Thursday 26th April.

Questioned in the House of Commons regarding piracy in Chinese waters, The Secretary of State for Foreign Affairs (Sir Austen Chamberlain) said he was aware that piracy continued, but the activities of the pirates had been considerably reduced during the past six months, during which period there had been only three instances in which their operations met with any measure of success. In none of these instances were British ships involved. The attempt to secure action by the Powers had met with no success, only Japan being prepared to co-operate with the British.

The waters in which piracy occurred were now regularly patrolled by Japanese and British warships.

A policy against the pirates, continued Sir Austen, was discussed by the British Minister in Peking with General Li Chun during the former's visit to Peking. Li Chun was emphatic in his protest against piracy, and expressed the hope that he would clear up the Bias Bay area within three months.

From *The Argus*, Melbourne, Friday, 27th April, 1928.

CONTINUING PIRACY IN THE CHINA SEAS

Shipowners and their officers take what precautions they can, but piracy in the China seas goes on. The attempt to seize the British ship *Haiching,* while she was on a voyage from Swatow to Hong Kong, was defeated, but only because of the great gallantry of her officers and guards and the chance that two British destroyers happened to be near enough to answer the master's wireless appeal for help. As the ship was bearing Bias Bay, the notorious pirates' lair, in the early morning, a number of ruffians, who had come on board at Swatow in the traditional guise of peaceable passengers, stole through a coal bunker in the boiler room and, thus avoiding the iron grille which is one of the defences of ships in those seas, got into the main part of the vessel. The pirates shot the sleeping stand-off engine guards and then attempted to rush the bridge. Three times they tried to take it; but the defence was too determined for them. Only one man reached the bridge, and he was shot down. But this successful resistance had its tragic price. Mr Woodward, the third officer, was shot dead by one of the pirates before the miscreant could be killed by Mr. Perry, the first officer, who was himself wounded. The pirates suffered heavily under the bullets of the defenders, and when they found themselves baffled they set fire to the ship. For three hours the attackers were kept at bay, and then, with the bridge burning under the heroic officers, the destroyers came up in the dawn. That was the end of this particular attempt at piracy. The fire was extinguished, the pirates were put under arrest, and the ship was brought into Hong Kong. The matter-of-fact heroism of that handful of sailors on the bridge of the *Haiching* will quicken the blood of the landsman whose life follows a less adventurous course.

The pirates preying on shipping along the Chinese coast all come from the Bias Bay district, which is not far from the Hong Kong border. The Hong Kong Government has struggled against them for years. Repeated protests have been made to the Chinese authorities, but, in a China torn with almost incessant civil war, Governments have not the will or the strength to do more than give soothing assurances and promises - never fulfilled - that serious action will be taken. An occasional expedition against the pirates has inflicted some punishment, but no sustained effort to drive them from their lair has ever been made. After many warnings that continued failure to put an end to an intolerable danger to shipping would force the British authorities to deal with the matter themselves, His Majesty's Government took independent action in the spring of 1927, and again in the autumn. A number of villages were visited and the houses of notorious pirates were burned. But these isolated efforts, unsupported by the vigorous co-operation of the Chinese, could not avail to stop what is in effect an industry, long established, well organized, and richly endowed with capital, brains, and daring. A Hong Kong Correspondent, in an article on another page, shows how efficiently the business is conducted. There is a solemn humour in the discreet negotiations of the promoters and the drawing up of prospectuses and lists of directors, which, though not publicly circulated, are there for the enticement of those on the look-out for a good speculative investment. The stratagems by which arms and men are blandly put on board the ship that is to be rifled also have their humorous side. It is when the murders begin – and at the least sign of resistance Chinese pirates murder promptly – that the humour goes out of the business. Then the old sea spirit of the mercantile marine has to do all that can be done against odds. But more often than not the able and courageous pirate chiefs have so planned their enterprise that the ship is seized before resistance is possible. Then the successful company promoters have only to share the spoil. For a while a few years ago the thieves fell out and their internecine strife roused the hope that honest seamen might come into their own; but that hope did not linger long, for the superior advantages of plundering others, rather than fighting among themselves, soon brought the various gangs into profitable co-operation again. The patrol of Bias Bay by British submarines had an effect that was more discouraging to them. When destroyers and submarines interfere with their business, pirates begin to think. The profits are not what they were, and once an industry ceases to pay it begins to dwindle.

From *The Times*, Printing House Square, London,
Editorial for Thursday, 12th December, 1929.

EXTRACTS FROM EDITORIALS

Unanimous condemnation of the *Tungchow* piracy, with several suggestions for remedying the situation, is the feature of comment upon the outrage in the foreign press of Shanghai to-day. Appeals are made to the Government to take action to stamp out this menace to coastal shipping. Extracts from the editorials appear below:–

Piracy on the China coast is like a malignant disease, which courses through the veins of shipping and is extraordinarily hard to thrust out. But this latest case is so shocking in its implications that it may well prove the signal for the start of a curative drive by all the shipping companies, which will once and for all sound the doom of pirates from Bias Bay or anywhere else.

Shanghai Evening Post and Mercury

Piracy in our era is an anachronism ... China has become its last refuge and what makes that the more astonishing is that, on the rivers and along the coasts of this country, there are a considerable number of warships of all nationalities who could put an end rapidly to maritime banditry if it were decided to take measures which commonsense indicates and international law justified. One of the chief causes of Chinese piracy is the negligence of the authorities if it is not their impotence. Certain bays in Kuangtung have become inviolable refuges for the bandits. These lairs are known. It should not be difficult to purge them if the effort were properly made. But nothing serious has been done ... If the Kuangtung authorities agreed to co-operate with the Chinese and foreign gunboats to clean out Bias Bay and other creeks which are so freely used by the pirates, the latter would be soon eliminated ... If they persist in divesting themselves of that duty others should act in their place.

Le Journal de Shanghai

The growth of banditry and piracy in China cannot be effectively checked by separate retaliation when the gangsters attack. It can be done only by adopting a general plan of combating the bandits. For this purpose many former Russian soldiers would prove extremely useful. At the same time the sacrifices made by Russian émigrés in performing their duty of maintaining law and order should impress the authorities with the need for reconsidering their relations with Russian émigrés, with the view of paying better attention and care to the interests of that community.

The Slovo

The boldness of the marauders is significant of the weakness of the authorities in dealing with them ... The proper co-ordination of the country's police activities is one of China's greatest needs and demands the attention of the Government. If the land areas were properly policed the day of the pirate would soon be ended ... We feel however, that the reorganization of the whole police system of China is what must come about before criminal activities are fundamentally curbed. That reorganization is not going to be an easy task and in Provinces where civil disorder still reigns it may not be possible to make immediate changes of importance. But the foundations of a better system should be laid and national police co-ordination work started in Nanking where the Department of Police Administration might perhaps be profitably separated from the Ministry of the Interior and constituted a separate Ministry.

The *Shanghai Times.*

From *The North-China Herald,* Shanghai, 6th February, 1936.

CHAPTER SIXTEEN

THE *TUNGCHOW* PIRACY

HENRY G.W. WOODHEAD
EDITOR, *PEKING & TIENTSIN TIMES*
AND *ORIENTAL AFFAIRS*

I was due back in Tientsin at the end of 1925, and reached Shanghai, via Canada, on December 15. Two days later, on the morning of Thursday, December 17, I embarked upon the British coasting steamer *Tungchow* [China Navigation Company] for the four days' trip to the Northern port.

I was feeling very seedy when I got on board, and finding that I had a cabin to myself, I lay down. When, a few hours after sailing, we reached the ocean, we ran into a northerly gale, with very rough sea, so I did not emerge from my cabin that day ...

About 5 p.m. on the 18th, however, feeling the need of exercise and fresh air, I took a walk round the deck. It was almost impossible to stand, much less to walk, as the vessel was doing almost every imaginable antic except somersaulting, and was also shipping quantities of water. I gave it up after a few turns, returned to my cabin, lay down on my bunk, and resumed reading. About 6.15 I heard some scampering overhead, but thought that the crew had been summoned to make fast one of the boats. A few minutes later my Chinese steward sidled into my cabin, locked the door, pulled up the shutter over the porthole, and then turned out the light and crept under the opposite berth. In the dim light I could just see him peering through the grating which opened into the corridor. I asked him what was the matter, but could only obtain some incoherent reply about "Jen Tao" or "bad men" being on deck. I decided to go out and see what had happened. The steward reluctantly unlocked the cabin door to let me out, and I heard him relock it immediately afterwards.

I proceeded to the dining saloon, where I found four of the passengers – none of whom I had met up to this time – sitting in a corner. When I inquired what had happened they told me that the ship had been captured by pirates. I believe I replied "Rats," or a word to that effect. One of the men then told me that when he had tried to reach his cabin – an outer one – he had been met by two Chinese, armed with pistols, who had driven him back into the saloon. We knew nothing further for several minutes, when two or three Chinese, brandishing revolvers and knives, rushed into the saloon and took this passenger – a Mr. Sharp – outside. We feared that he was about to be shot, but a few minutes later he returned to say that he had been assured that the foreign passengers would not be molested; as the occupant of an outside cabin he had been mistaken for a ship's officer, and the pirates had taken him out to search for the weapons he was supposed to possess.

He had hardly rejoined us when Chief Officer Nisbet was brought in by a couple of pirates who had their weapons pointed at his back. He sat down looking rather dazed, and told us that the ship had been captured, the captain had been shot, and we had turned about and were now proceeding in the direction of Hongkong. He was then led off to the bridge. Next Second Officer Scott who had been on watch at the time, was led out of the pantry by another group of pirates. These men explained by signs, and in broken English, that they did not intend to rob us, but that we must give up any firearms we possessed. A French passenger who had just joined us was the only member of the group who had a pistol, and as he had his wife and children on board, and the consequences might have been serious if it were found in his cabin, he decided to surrender it.

It was not, of course, until later, when I had talked with all the officers, that I discovered what had happened. A party of some twenty-five Hakkas (Southern Chinese) who had shipped as passengers, made simultaneous attacks upon the bridge, the engine-room, and the officers' quarters. The officer on watch was tripped up and overpowered; the helmsman fled; and the captain, who had come out to see what was happening and grabbed at one of the pirates, was shot through the groin and collapsed on the chart-house floor.

It was Third Engineer Bickford's watch. His attention was attracted by shouts and a stampede down the ladders of several Chinese, brandishing knives and pistols. He fled through the stokehold and up an iron ladder to the boat-deck, making for the chart-room, where he knew there were some arms. He was tripped up as he entered, sat upon by armed pirates, and then, to his intense indignation, put on duty at the wheel.

Chief Engineer Johnston and Second Engineer Knowles and the chief mate were in the officers' quarters aft. They were surprised by armed pirates, who drove them into the mess-room, and then searched their cabins for weapons. Guards were then placed over the foreign and Chinese passengers, and the capture of the vessel was completed without any serious resistance.

A few minutes after I had reached the saloon one of the passengers asked to be allowed to see the captain. He returned in a few minutes to say that he appeared to be badly wounded, and to inquire whether there was anyone with a knowledge of first-aid. A missionary lady, who had been married only the day before sailing, stated that she had done some nursing, and volunteered to dress the captain's wound. This she did, though the ship's medicine chest contained no lysol or other disinfectant, and, as we afterwards discovered, no aspirin, and no narcotic except the dregs of a bottle of laudanum of unknown strength. Captain McIntosh, who was an old acquaintance of mine, was lifted on to a mattress on his cabin floor, where he lay for the next forty-eight hours.

About 8 p.m., that is, an hour after the usual time, the pirates were graciously pleased to allow us to have dinner. One of the three tables in the saloon was reserved for the passengers' meals, the others being occupied by pirates, who either sat around or lay upon them day and night. Of the sixteen foreign passengers, all but three put in an appearance at dinner, as well as the one Chinese who was travelling first-class, foreign style, and it was at this meal that I met most of them for the first time. I occupied the wounded captain's seat. The assembled company was naturally somewhat crestfallen, and the ladies whose husbands had not accompanied them were very apprehensive. I ordered a bottle of champagne, and it proved to be a really valuable stimulant, for the two women who sat next to me both reported next morning that they had had a fairly good night. We drank to our speedy release from the pirates, who could not understand sufficient English to glean what we were up to.

The ladies, with the exception of the missionary bride, retired immediately after dinner, and the male passengers, after discussing the outlook for some time, decided that they would take two-hour watches, in pairs, with the captain. My turn was between 3 a.m. and 5 a.m., and I shared the watch with an American Roman Catholic priest. The missionary and her husband stayed in the captain's cabin all night, resting on his bunk, and settee, as they had volunteered for day duty also. The captain was delirious when I went up, and only appeared to recognize the third engineer, of whom he was especially fond. It was pathetic to hear this strong and experienced master groaning with pain, and constantly reproaching himself with the fact that he had been "thirty-one years with the company, and never lost a ship before."

That night did little to relieve our depression. The *Tungchow*, when captured and turned about, was about six hours out from Wei-hai-wei, where she was due about midnight on December 18, and we assumed that as soon as she was overdue inquiries would be made regarding her, and possibly a British warship would be sent out from Wei-hai-wei or Shanghai to search for her. It seemed possible, also, that the same company's vessel, *Linan*, which was in sight when we were captured, might have observed and reported upon our sudden change of course. When, however, the pirates notified us of their intention of shooting every foreign passenger – men, women, and children – in the event of any interference, on the ground that as they were certain to be hanged they would make sure of us first, we were not so anxious for the appearance of a British or other warship.

The first morning the pirates were very suspicious of our going on deck. In fact, they drove us back into the saloon when another steamer came into sight. Some of us tried playing bridge, but we found it impossible to concentrate. There were three revokes in one hand when the pirates, alarmed at the proximity of a Dutch steamer, ostentatiously loaded and cocked their weapons and took up "action stations".

The pirates informed the chief officer on the morning of December 19 that Swatow was to be our destination. It was doubtful, however, whether there was sufficient coal in the bunkers to reach that port. Moreover, the captain had high fever, and it was feared that complications had set in. A deputation of passengers and one of the officers explained to the pirates the urgency of getting the captain ashore for proper treatment, the coal shortage, and the risks of interference from a warship if the *Tungchow* went so far south. Their reply was that the officers and engineers would be shot if we did not reach their destination, and a repetition of the threat to murder all the passengers if any vessel attempted to approach us.

During the day the ship's name was painted out, and systematic looting of the Chinese passengers and the cargo holds began. In the latter some hundreds of tons of beans were discovered, and these the pirates ordered to be used to supplement the coal. We saw no more of our Chinese fellow-passenger this day. Having been told that he would be taken ashore and held for ransom, he went into hiding in a cabin occupied by two Roman Catholic priests, and was apparently forgotten by the pirates as well as by most of us.

The second night after our capture found the *Tungchow* rolling and pitching heavily in a strong monsoon. I had again been assigned the watch between 3 a.m. and 5 a.m. with the captain – this time alone. When called just before three I gingerly picked my way past or over the pirates who were lying about all over the saloon floor, and climbed up to the bridge. In the rain and the pitch darkness, however, I could not find the entrance to the captain's cabin, and after tripping over several obstacles, one of which was a recumbent pirate near the wheel-house, I had to ask the assistance of the young American I was relieving to pilot me to the scene of my duties.

The bridge of the *Tungchow* is, I believe, notorious as a bad place to be on during a gale along the whole China coast. I could not stand without hanging on to some support, nor sit without feeling dreadfully sick. The captain, who by this time was conscious, recognized me, and I had to ask him whether he would mind my lying on the floor beside him while I was in attendance. The old man was very distressed at the idea of any passenger being on the bridge in such weather, but was satisfied when I lay beside him and held his hand. I should have called my relief at 5 a.m., but it was still pitch dark, and I was too frightened to wander about on the bridge again, so I remained with the captain until about 6.30.

The weather abated on the morning of the 20th. A shot was fired on deck while we were having breakfast, but we found that it was only a pirate trying out one of the ship's rifles. At lunch-time that day the saloon presented an extraordinary spectacle. While we were eating, pirates were grouped round one of the other tables counting up and sharing out the notes, cash, and jewellery which they had looted from the Chinese passengers. After the bank-notes had been counted they restored to the chief officer a sum of ninety dollars that had disappeared from his cabin when it was searched for arms.

The general attitude of all the foreign passengers towards the pirates had, up to this time, been one of aloofness. There were among them two particularly murderous-looking ruffians, who always went round with finger on trigger, and appeared to be looking for an opportunity of shooting someone. During the sharing out of the loot one of the passengers, a newcomer to China, went over to the pirates' table, sat down on the settee beside one of these men, and began joking with him. He carried his foolery to the extent of exchanging hats. The pirate did not look too pleased, but made no protest. At the suggestion of the American priest, who came from the Hakka district, I went over and warned the passenger against too much familiarity. He returned to his own seat, and there argued in favour of "palling up" to the worst of the pirates. The more experienced of us stuck to the view that it was unwise. And we proved to be right. That night, under the pretence that they suspected this passenger of having stolen the chief officer's certificate, which was missing, half a dozen of the pirates took him down to his cabin, where they ransacked his baggage, ostensibly in search of the missing document. Behind his back they winked at the chief officer, who was ordered to attend the search, making it clear that this was *their* idea of a practical joke, but the poor little victim got such a fright that he did not occupy his cabin for the rest of the trip, but begged to be allowed to share one on the main deck.

The same night the pirates began to bring up portmanteaux, baskets and boxes taken from the Chinese passengers, to stow away their loot. It soon became almost impossible to move round the saloon owing to the litter of bags and trunks, with pirates lying on or between them. They also brought up all the ship's supplies of kerosene, and ostentatiously stacked the tins near one of the saloon doors, remarking that they would use it to set the ship on fire in the event of any interference. Various plans for attempting to recover possession of the ship, which it was now obvious was heading for Bias Bay, were discussed between the officers and passengers, but without arms and with no possibility of concentrating all of the officers and passengers on one deck, they had to be abandoned. Three or four pirates were always on watch in the engine-room, in the first-class saloon, in the Chinese passenger quarters, and on the bridge.

I did not take a watch with the captain during the night of December 20–21, and for the first time since our capture undressed and got a few hours' sleep. The next night the chief officer, who, who was feeling the strain of constant duty at the pistol's point, asked me to join him on the bridge to keep him company, and to keep an eye on things when he had to go into the chart-room to check the course, or to come down to the saloon for a cup of coffee. It was a lovely starlit night. About midnight we were somewhere in the vicinity of Swatow, where we passed through a fleet of fishing junks, and also saw, at no great distance, a large Hongkong-bound liner, which overtook us. Several times I was left on the bridge alone, with only pirates for company, while the chief officer checked off the position of lighthouses, etc., on the charts.

When I came down to the saloon early on the morning of the 22nd I noticed that the pirates had brought up the cases of sycee (silver) from the strong-room, and had opened them up. They were arraying themselves in new clothes which they had stolen from the Chinese passengers.

At breakfast time we were close to the coast. We had, in fact, entered Hong Hai Bay, and there appeared to be some difference of opinion between our captors as to whether we should make for Bias Bay or San Chau Inlet. Taking us into Hong Hai Bay added twenty miles to our course, and used up more of our scanty supply of fuel.

About 9.30 a.m. the chief officer came down and told me that the pirates had taken over the navigation of the vessel, professing to be familiar with the locality. He went back a few minutes later, glanced at the chart, and found to his horror that the *Tungchow* was heading straight for some submerged rocks. He managed, just in time, to convince the pirates of the danger, and made a change of course that cleared these obstacles.

It must have been about 11 a.m. when he reappeared, took me aside, and after warning me not to alarm the women, confessed that he feared it was "all up." We were being taken to Bias Bay by a route that would keep us out of sight of other steamers, and should be completely lost to sight when we rounded the next promontory. He could not predict what would happen, but said that the pirates had lied to him so continuously that he placed no reliance on their promise to free the vessel without molesting the foreign passengers.

I went to my cabin to think things over. It seemed to me that there were three possibilities. We might be released after the pirates had got ashore with their loot. We might be taken ashore and held for ransom; or we might be sent down with the ship, in order to destroy all trace of our fate. I wrote what I feared might be a last home letter, and left it on a shelf in my cabin. It then occurred to me that the light shoes I was wearing would not be very serviceable if we were carried off into the mountains, so I put on a pair of stout boots, leaving the laces loose so that I could kick them off in an emergency. I found the unattached women, suggested that they should meet in one cabin, and there joined them, with Mr. Sharp, after sending in a bottle of champagne. Their cabin was forward, on the starboard side, just by the ladder leading up to the bridge, so we had a very limited view from the porthole.

After sitting there for about half an hour I went up to the bridge to find out what was happening. To my amazement I saw a steamer coming towards us, inshore, and about a mile distant, and the smoke of another on the horizon. The pirates on the bridge were lying down with their rifles pointed at the chief and second officers. The latter, when he caught sight of me, called out, "For God's sake get down below!" From the cabin port I watched the first steamer, which proved to be the *Sinkiang*, and owned by the same company as the *Tungchow*, pass us at a distance of not more than half a mile. As she came abreast she hoisted and dipped the Red Ensign. I waited with bated breath to see what would happen. It seemed incredible that she would not recognize us, even if our name had been obliterated from the bows. (As a matter of fact, one of her officers who had served on the *Tungchow* did recognize the ship, and reported to the captain, who, when we returned the salute, assumed that we were on the way to Hongkong to dock). I saw a Chinese quartermaster tear down from our bridge with a Red ensign under his arm, and a few minutes later the *Sinkiang* hauled down her flag and went on her way. This was the narrowest squeak of recognition that we had while the pirates were in charge. It was quite unusual for the company's steamers to come so far inshore, and I heard afterwards that the captain of the *Sinkiang* (which carried an anti-pirate armed guard, and was fitted with grilles) at first thought we were pirated, and only decided not to change course after his salute had been reciprocated.

We turned into Bias Bay, and I again went out to explore. I had just reached the deck when I received a message from the chief officer requesting passengers to remain in their cabins with locked doors when the pirates disembarked, and asking me to sit with the women. I returned to the cabin, pulled up the porthole shutter and locked the door, and then we all sat down in the semi-darkness to wait. From the bridge we could hear the leadsman singing out, "Mark Five," "Mark Four," "Quarter less Four," etc., and about 1.30 we heard the anchor go and the engines reverse.

It seemed ages, but can only have been a few minutes, before there was a tap on the porthole shutter, and the chief officer called out: "Tell the ladies not to be alarmed if they hear some shots. They will probably only be fired to signal to the shore." A long wait and another knock on the shutter, followed by the chief officer's voice telling us that "at the moment everything in the garden seems lovely". Still the seconds ticked slowly by, and then we heard the anchor winch start up, and felt the vibration of the engine. A moment or two later the chief officer asked Mr. Sharp to come outside. He returned to tell us that he had duly recovered the four hundred gold dollars in notes that he had hidden under the saloon settee, on which the pirates sat the first night. There was an interval of about ten minutes, and then the steward knocked at the cabin door to tell us that lunch was ready. It was a thankful but very shaken lot of passengers that poured out on deck to see the pirates' boats well astern, and to realize that at last we were free.

As soon as we had anchored the pirates on the bridge attracted the attention of their friends ashore, and within a few minutes fifteen or twenty sampans (small boats) were alongside. The loot was quickly loaded into them, with the aid of the ship's crew. Some of the shore accomplices tried to come aboard with a view to doing a little looting on their own, but were angrily threatened by the pirate chief, and driven back to the sampans. We anchored at 1.25 and weighed anchor at 2.10 p.m. Before leaving, the pirates are believed to have distributed some $400 in cash among the crew, stokers and stewards, the latter each receiving $3 (so mine told me) "in small money." The chief officer was presented with $30, and the chief engineer with $25, "for services rendered," of "overtime." The pirates got away with about $30,000 in specie and some $10,000 in cash, which they stole from the Chinese passengers. They also looted everything of value that the latter possessed, and broached some of the more valuable cargo. They must have been disappointed in their venture, for they had (quite correctly) learnt that it had been intended to ship several lakhs of taels in the treasure-room. At the last moment, for some unknown reason, the native banks concerned cancelled the consignment.

None of the foreign passengers was molested, nor did any of them report the loss of anything except one cap.

The *Tungchow* made for Hongkong at full speed, and was off Waglan Lighthouse about 5.45 p.m. Attempts to induce the staff to transmit a message to Hongkong stating that the *Tungchow* had been pirated, the captain wounded, and that medical assistance would be required immediately on arrival, given first by flag signals and later by lamp-Morse, were received with incredulity. The word "pirated" had to be repeated seven or eight times.

Entering Hongkong Harbour through Lyeemun Pass, the *Tungchow* dropped anchor opposite the Taikoo Dockyard about 6.45 p.m. A police launch soon came alongside, and was sent off to fetch a naval doctor, who, after examining the captain, reported that he had seriously crushed his ankle when he collapsed after being shot, and that his removal to a shore hospital must be postponed until next morning.

The police were at first inclined to be very unreasonable to the foreign passengers. They flatly refused to let any of us land that night. I had a somewhat acrimonious interview with the inspector, pointing out that the *Tungchow* must have been reported missing some four days previously, that our families at home or in China must have been in a frantic state of anxiety regarding our safety, and that it was ridiculous not to let us ashore to send off cables reporting our safety. He was still obstinate, and I then demanded that an appeal be taken to the Governor, as to the right of the police in a British port to detain a British subject who was under no suspicion of any crime, overnight. Finally he agreed to allow two of us (British subjects) to proceed to the steamship company's offices some miles up the harbour. We were entrusted with a score or more of messages to despatch to passengers' relatives. I reached the office about 10 p.m. and the staff very kindly took over the responsibility of despatching the cables. With considerable difficulty I got into touch with Reuter's agent, and handed him a cable and a mail story of the piracy, which I had prepared between Bias Bay and Hongkong. We arrived in Hongkong with only one ton of coal on board, just sufficient to keep the electricity plant going until we were towed up harbour and coaled.

The *Tungchow* started back for Shanghai and Tientsin, in the teeth of a strong monsoon, on the afternoon of December 24. At Shanghai there was a Naval Court of Inquiry at which I was called as the first witness. I was allowed to swear to my *Peking Leader* story of the episode, thus saving considerable time.

I heard in Shanghai that owing to the fact that a civil war was raging in North China, and the cables had been interrupted, no anxiety had been felt regarding the *Tungchow* until the day of our arrival in Hongkong, when her owners applied to the British Admiral for a search to be made.

An episode of this kind may be amusing to look back upon, but is by no means amusing when it is in progress and one cannot foresee the outcome. Two of the *Tungchow*'s passengers had to be sent home, nervous wrecks, within a few months.

My part in the adventure aroused more amusement than sympathy. My directors cabled to me at Hongkong asking why I had overstayed my leave and proceeded thither without their permission! And when I reached Tientsin on January 4 a large number of friends welcomed me at the wharf, under the pretence that they understood that I would present each of them with a gold watch – part of my share of the pirates' loot!

From H.G.W. Woodhead CBE, *Adventures in Far Eastern Journalism: A record of thirty-three years' experience*, Far Eastern Edition, Tokyo, 1935.

CHAPTER SEVENTEEN

THE CASE OF THE S.S. *SUNNING*

DEREK CRANE

On the afternoon of Monday, November 15th, 1926, the *Sunning*, coasting steamer of two thousand five hundred gross tons, was ploughing her way through the China Sea. Two days before she had sailed from Shanghai with general cargo and some sixty passengers. Of these, only a Russian lady and an Eurasian gentleman occupied first-class cabins on the upper deck; a dozen Chinese were second-class passengers with accommodation on the main-deck amidships; and the remainder were "deck passengers" of the poorer class.

The ship was manned by a Chinese crew of sixty-five, and six British officers, Captain Pringle, a veteran of the China Coast; Mr. Beatty, chief officer; Mr. Hurst, second officer; Mr. Cormack, chief engineer, another old-timer; Mr. Orr, second engineer; and Mr. Duncan, third engineer.

Early that morning the ship had called at Amoy to embark a further contingent of forty or fifty "deck passengers" and, as she sped upon the last stage of her voyage to Hong Kong, that somnolent atmosphere, peculiar to an afternoon at sea, pervaded her. Seven bells had just struck, disturbing the reverie of the second officer, who was leaning from the bridge and gazing straight ahead at the grey sky and the wind-lashed water. Suddenly, without warning, he felt his legs twisted from beneath him and fell heavily to the deck. Next moment he was staring into the muzzles of two revolvers. Powerless to resist, he staggered to his feet and, backing step by step from the threatening revolvers, made his way down the companion leading to the lower bridge and entered the captain's room, his assailants close behind him.

Captain Pringle, just roused from his afternoon sleep, was idly stirring a cup of tea. Resistance would have been suicide. He threw his arms above his head in surrender. Next moment the Chinese wireless operator was ushered in by another armed escort, presumably to act as interpreter. He, however, could not speak the dialect of the attackers, but the Eurasian passenger, who was summoned could, it was found, speak fluently many Chinese dialects.

He ascertained that the *Sunning* was under the complete control of a pirate gang, the Amoy contingent of "passengers." The engine-room, the bridge and the wireless-room were in the hands of the marauders, and all the officers had been overcome and disarmed. The pirate chief, a man of superior type, clad in a long blue robe, and wearing horn-rimmed glasses, now joined the group in the captain's room, and dictated his terms. No further violence, he declared, would be committed if the ship was steered to his instructions, and the activities of his men were not interfered with. Six unarmed men cannot argue with forty desperate and bloodthirsty ruffians, brandishing firearms with reckless abandon. After some discussion on points of navigation, it was agreed to set the course for Chelang Point, some hundred miles to the south, and eighty miles from Hong Kong. Once there final directions would be given. So satisfied were the pirates with the complete success of their coup and the apparent acquiescence of the officers that, as the afternoon gave way to evening, the officers, although under the constant scrutiny of armed guards, were permitted a certain amount of freedom and were able to converse.

Second Officer Hurst, as he paced the bridge, remembered a .32 Colt and fifty rounds of ammunition stowed away among his clothing in his cabin. If only the pirates had overlooked it! Sauntering towards his cabin with well-assumed indifference, he found it guarded. Just as his hopes fell, his eye caught a passing ship framed in the port-hole of his cabin, and he directed the attention of the guard to it. The pirate ran out to get a better view over the rail. Like lightning Hurst was in his cabin – a tense, anxious moment – the gun and ammunition whipped into his pocket – a careless stroll back to the bridge – a casual opening and shutting of the chart drawer – and so was forged the first link in a chain of amazing adventure.

At 6.30 the six officers sat down to a gloomy meal. The second officer found an opportunity to divulge a vague, half-formed plan, the success of which depended upon securing further arms. Patience and stealth brought a .45 Colt and fifty rounds from the cabin of Duncan, the third engineer, and this was placed beside the smaller gun in the chart drawer. To this small armoury the chief officer added two chain shackles to serve as knuckle-dusters if it came to a hand-to-hand fight later on.

Just before midnight there were together on the bridge, the captain, the chief officer and the second officer, the pirate chief and his second in command. The chief engineer was in the engine-room and the second and third engineers were under guard in the captain's room, together with the Russian lady and the wireless operator. The Eurasian passenger was still being compelled to act as interpreter for the pirates among the other passengers. At 11.55 p.m. Hurst picked up the Chelang Point light, and called out to Beatty. The chief officer looked out for a few moments, then handed his binoculars to the pirate chief. As the pirate leaned forward, focussing the glasses, his colleague peered over his shoulder to see what he could with the naked eye, while Beatty indicated the direction of the light. This was Hurst's moment! Stooping quickly, he grasped a twenty-eight pound sounding lead, fortunately there for the purpose of weighting down the matting on the bridge, and swung it twice with deadly accuracy. The two pirates fell to the deck, their skulls cracked like egg-shells.

The old captain, pacing his conquered bridge dejectedly, turned in amazement. "What in the name of God are you doing?" he exclaimed. In answer the second officer seized a revolver from one of the fallen pirates, and thrust it into the captain's hand. "There's a gun for you," he said, "we're going to fight for it." The mate seized the Winchester rifle carried by the second pirate, but he was not to keep it long. The guard who had been watching over the other officers in the captain's room had heard the disturbance on the bridge and came flying up the companion with levelled revolver. Not an instant too soon Beatty's newly acquired weapon crashed on his skull, with such force that the rifle split in pieces.

This third dead pirate, however, provided a revolver for the chief officer, and Hurst, rushing to the chart drawer, got out the two he had concealed earlier. With one in either hand he lay down in a position where he could command the companion-way leading to the bridge on the starboard side, while the captain and the chief officer covered the port side. By this time the alarm had been raised among the other pirates, and it was certain that an attack would come at any moment. The three men waited. Then there came a scrambling of feet and a clamour of voices, as a howling mob rushed for the companion. The second officer waited in the darkness until the leaders were within six yards range, then he fired twice with each hand. Four men toppled over, and the rest scurried away. In the brief respite that followed thoughts turned to their colleagues in the captain's room. How could they be brought to the citadel on the bridge?

Meanwhile, the two junior engineers had heard the fighting without being able to discover what was happening. At the first shots they locked the cabin door and shuttered the windows, and now sat waiting. To the credit of these two gallant young men, in this moment of peril they thought not of themselves, but of the lady whose lot had been cast with theirs. If massacre there was to be, then she must be the last to die. And so they concealed her in the captain's private bathroom and locked the door.

Just then the glass in the skylight of the room was smashed and a revolver butt appeared through. Duncan and Orr prepared to fight, but through the broken glass appeared the face of the chief officer; he had crawled from the bridge to this skylight, on a slightly lower level, to bring aid to his fellow-officers. Quickly he told Orr and Duncan to pile chairs upon the cabin table, and with another chair to smash the skylight and its fittings sufficiently to permit them to climb through. With speed born of their danger this was quickly done and once more the lady was their first thought. After her, they scrambled through, and running round the funnel and ventilators aft of the bridge, climbed to comparative safety. At this moment Beatty had repelled the latest onslaught on the bridge, emptying his revolver into the fleeing mob. Turning quickly round, he was just in time to see the head and arms of a man climbing on to the bridge from the port side. Rushing over, he aimed a vicious blow at the head – then to his horror he saw that it was Duncan! Had not the third engineer swung his head to take the blow on the shoulder, or had the chief officer had but one bullet left – well, neither Beatty nor Duncan like to think of that to-day!

Once on the bridge, the lady passenger was ensconced in a sheltered corner of the wheel-house, and the wireless operator set to guard her. Hurst, meanwhile, handed a revolver to Duncan, and of the five officers only Orr remained unarmed. Nothing daunted, he crept cautiously down the companion and secured a revolver and ammunition from the body of the nearest dead pirate.

It was now about 1 a.m., and the officers' position, although by no means impregnable, was greatly improved. From their position on the after well deck and on the poop the pirates could not bring direct fire to bear on the bridge, and the officers were able to take up positions commanding the only access to the bridge without unduly exposing themselves. Even so, their store of ammunition was rapidly diminishing, and they could ill afford to waste a single shot. Attack after attack had been repelled, and now, soon after one o'clock, there came a suspicious lull.

Gradually a ruddy glow illumined the inky darkness

of the night, and the crackling of burning wood broke the silence. With horror they discovered that the cabins beneath the bridge had been set on fire. The pirates then scrambled to the lower bridge, where four of the ship's six lifeboats were stowed. Pouring kerosene into the two after boats, they set them alight, trusting the flames to spread to the other two. Nearer and nearer to the superstructure of the bridge came the flames, fanned forward by the following wind. And then, just as hope was fading fast, the seamanship of an old sailor came to the fore.

By this time the vessel had practically lost all way, for the stokehold and engine-room crew had fled from their posts soon after midnight, and were huddling with their panic-stricken shipmates in the fo'c'sle. Leaning from the bridge, Captain Pringle hailed the boatswain and ordered the anchors to be let go. A few minutes later the cables rattled out, almost at once the ship swung round head to wind, and the threatening flames swept away from the bridge and aft towards the pirates.

About this time a figure staggered to the bottom of the companion, and by the light of the flames the officers recognized their chief engineer. Rushing down, they picked him up and carried him to the wheel-house, wounded in two places – by his comrades' bullets! It transpired that in one of the earlier attacks on the bridge, the pirates had compelled him to walk in front of them, thinking to restrain the officers from shooting. In the darkness he had not been recognized, and he fell amongst his enemies. Fortunately, his wounds were comparatively slight.

Anxious hours passed, a raging inferno separated the pirates from the bridge, and their shooting was intermittent. About half-past three, in order to obtain a clear view of what the pirates were doing, the third engineer climbed down to the lower bridge, crept aft through almost unbearable heat, and took up a position on top of the wireless-room. From here he saw the pirates scurrying to and fro on the poop deck, busily preparing to lower the two boats stowed there. In his revolver there was one last round. Picking the best target, he fired, and another pirate fell dead. The flash of his gun, however, had given away his position, and two shots rang out almost at once. Quickly, he retreated to the bridge.

His little expedition, however, caused the pirates to appeal for a truce – shouted in English, probably by an interpreter from among the second-class passengers. If the pirates took to the boats, would the officers agree to stop firing? The promise was readily given! At that moment there was not another round of ammunition on the bridge!

By about half-past four both boats had been lowered, and the officers had regained the control of their ship. Their peril, however, was by no means past. The fire beneath was still blazing furiously, and before long the bridge upon which they were standing would be in flames. Of the four boats on the lower bridge, three were already completely destroyed, and the bow of the fourth was scorched and smoking. Captain Pringle ordered this boat to be lowered and, in accordance with the rule that the first boat lowered shall be commanded by the junior officers, the second officer and the third engineer took charge. With Hurst and Duncan, the Russian lady, still bravely enduring her ordeal, the wireless operator and two Chinese quartermasters, the boat was lowered. She was still held to the ship by her painter, as it was the intention of the captain to have her hauled forward to take off the Chinese women passengers. Scorched by the fire, however, the painter parted, and the boat was carried away by the heavy sea.

For more than twelve hours that life-boat was buffeted before the strong north-east monsoon. On the evening of November 16th she was sighted by the Norwegian freighter, s.s. *Radensfjell*, when, not without considerable difficulty, a line thrown from the steamer was picked up and the boat hauled alongside. A lowered rope was tied around the lady's waist, and she was hoisted on board like a sack of coal. The officers and the seamen scrambled up a rope ladder.

Dawn found their comrades on board the *Sunning* manfully striving to prevent the flames from spreading along the deck to envelop the whole ship. But help was already on the way. With the pirates clear of the ship, Captain Pringle had been able to send out an S.O.S. H.M.S. *Bluebell*, a sloop from Hong Kong, arrived at 7 a.m. and a boarding party took charge of the stricken *Sunning*. The whole of the centre superstructure was by now burnt out. The bodies of eleven dead pirates strewed the after-deck, the incinerated remains of others being found later. Six of the Chinese remaining on board were immediately placed under arrest on suspicion of complicity in the piracy, and the sloop then left to scour the surrounding seas in search of the boats. A few hours later she returned and transferred to the *Sunning* a further thirteen prisoners, the occupants of one of the boats, picked up several miles away. Of the second boatload of pirates no trace was ever found. A naval aeroplane reconnoitring in the vicinity a few days later sighted an empty boat far out at sea, and this gave rise to the belief that disaster had overtaken them. It is thought, also, that the Eurasian passenger must have been carried off in this boat, for he was never seen or heard of again.

By this time the news of the piracy was known along the China Coast, and two ships of her own company had raced to the scene and were now standing by the *Sunning*. One of these ships, the s.s. *Suiyang*, also bound for Hong Kong, made several efforts to take the *Sunning* in tow, but time after time, the tow-rope parted, and the attempt had to be abandoned. After nightfall, however, the salvage tug of a Hong Kong dockyard arrived. By midnight the tow to Hong Kong, a slow and difficult task in the prevailing weather, began. It was not until the afternoon of the 17th, having taken sixteen hours to cover some eighty miles, that the little tug steamed through Lyeemun Pass into Hong Kong harbour with her helpless charge. Immediately on arrival the Hong Kong police took charge, and the nineteen prisoners were removed to safe custody.

Meanwhile, the *Radensfjell* having wirelessed the rescue of Duncan and Hurst, H.M.S. *Verity*, a destroyer, sped northwards, overtook the Norwegian ship, and brought the two officers, the lady passenger and the Chinese back to Hong Kong. Of the nineteen prisoners brought to trial, the scrupulous fairness of British justice set thirteen free, while on the morning of January 27th, 1927, the remaining six went to the scaffold.

From Derek Crane, *The Blue Peter*, London,
Volume XV, November 1935.

DIPLOMATIC EXCHANGES BETWEEN THE CROWN COLONY OF HONG KONG AND THE CHINESE GOVERNMENT IN CANTON

From H.E. the Governor of Hong Kong
To H.M. Consul-General, Canton
20th November 1926.

Sir,– I have the honour to enclose for your information copy of a report, dated the 20th November, by the Captain Superintendent of Police on the piracy of the China Navigation Company's *Sunning*, which took place off Chilang Point, south of Swatow, on the afternoon of the 15th November.

From this report you will observe that Mr. H. Lapsley, a British subject, in the employ of the Eastern Extension Australasia and China Telegraph Company Limited, is missing and may have been abducted by the pirates. I shall be glad if you will request the proper Chinese Authorities to make prompt and careful inquiry as to his whereabouts with a view to obtaining his speedy return to Hong Kong.

I have the honour also to request you to be good enough to draw the attention of the Canton Government to this further outrage by the Bias Bay pirates and to request that immediate steps may be taken for the extermination of these pirates whose immunity for so long a period is a standing disgrace to the Canton Government. The Hong Kong Government will gladly co-operate in such measures as the Canton Government may take for the suppression of the Bias Bay pirates.

I have, etc.
C. Clementi, Governor, &c.

From H.M. Consul-General, Canton
To H.E. the Governor of Hong Kong
3rd December 1926.

Sir,– Your Excellency's despatch No. 292 of November 20th regarding the piracy of the *Sunning* was received on the eve of my departure for Hong Kong where I had been instructed to meet His Majesty's Minister on his way to Peking.

I arranged however for Mr. Vice-Consul Fitzmaurice to address a letter to the Canton Minister for Foreign Affairs demanding the immediate suppression of the Bias Bay pirates and offering the co-operation of the Hong Kong Government in accordance with your suggestions.

I have the honour to enclose a copy of the above letter, which Mr. Fitzmaurice delivered in person to Mr. Wai Yuk, the secretary left in charge of the Ministry for Foreign Affairs, at the same time making verbal representation regarding the urgent necessity for dealing with the pirate menace.

This interview is doubtless responsible for the article in the *Canton Gazette* of November 27th stating that if co-operation in the suppression of piracy is offered by the British authorities the Nationalist Government will consider it most seriously.

On my return from Hong Kong I called on General

Tan Yen-Kai, the Chairman of the Political Council, and pressed strongly for immediate joint action to be taken as regards Bias Bay and I followed this up with a visit to the Foreign Office where I make similar representations to Mr. Wai Yuk.

I explained to both officials that the British forces were prepared to do all that was necessary and that if the Nationalist government were unable to spare troops for the expedition, the presence of a few Cantonese officers or officials would be sufficient to constitute a nominal co-operation.

I could not elicit a satisfactory answer from either General Tan or Mr. Wai Yuk. They promised to consult the government and let me have a reply shortly, but I gathered that they foresaw difficulty in overcoming the anti-British prejudices of the government supporters sufficiently to enter into an operation which would imply a resumption of more friendly relations with the British authorities. They both referred to the recent arrest of Kuomintang members by the British police in Tientsin and stated that the resentment aroused thereby would make co-operation difficult at the present time.

I finally warned them that if they rejected our offers of assistance in dealing with Bias Bay and would do nothing themselves, the British authorities might be forced to take independent action as the constant threat to shipping was becoming insupportable. They both raised strong objections to such a course, however, saying that it would be resented by the Chinese as an infringement of China's sovereign rights.

To this I replied that if the Canton Government

attempted to make propaganda out of the matter, we should publish the facts showing that we had first urged the Chinese authorities to take action themselves and had then offered them every facility for a joint operation, and if in spite of all this they still allowed such a gross scandal as the Bias Bay piracy base to continue in existence, they would be condemned in public as a dangerously incompetent administration.

I have the honour to be, Sir,
Your Excellency's most obedient humble servant,
J. F. Brenan, Acting Consul-General.

From Acting Minister for Foreign Affairs, Canton
To H.M. Consul-General, Canton
6th December 1926.

Sir,– I have the honour to acknowledge receipt of your letter dated the 25th November, proposing to co-operate with us in suppression of pirates. I duly forwarded it to our Government for consideration, and as is on record, a letter was already sent to you in reply.

Now I have received a despatch from the Headquarters of the Generalissimo [Chiang Kai-shek], which reads as follows:–

"The case has been entrusted to us by order of Government. The pirates in the eastern regions have been holding out in their dangerous positions among mountains and near the sea. Our national troops have made repeated attacks on them, but when they could not escape by land, they would flee to sea, especially to the islands in British

Territory at Mirs Bay, such as Ping Chau, Wong Nai Chau &c. When the troops left, they would come to land again from the islands at sea and cause trouble. It is for this that piracy has not been successfully suppressed. If the Hong Kong Government can agree to render us assistance and instruct their police and soldiers to stop the pirates at Kowloon and New Territory, or give us facility of access to British Territory in pursuit of the pirates, good result will be achieved and piracy stopped without difficulty. As to co-operation in the undertaking, it would be better for the Governor of Hong Kong to send a deputy to Canton to discuss with us."

On receipt of this, I find it necessary to send you this despatch for your information, and I hope you will communicate it to the Governor Hong Kong.

With regards,

Eugene Chan [Ch'en Yu-Jen].*

*Using his western name when exchanging pleasantries, and his official name when matters became more serious (Ed.).

From Acting Minister for Foreign Affairs, Canton
To H.M. Consul-General, Canton
2nd December 1926.

Sir,– I have the honour to inform you that I have just received a letter from the Commander-in-Chief to the effect that it has been reported to him that on November 17th four or five British warships suddenly appeared and went to and fro in the Hsin Hsia Ch'ung and Hsin Chiang district, while several aeroplanes also patrolled there. The warships have not yet left, and the aeroplanes pay frequent visits. I was requested to take the matter up strongly with you.

I would observe that foreign warships should on no account pay visits to, or patrol in, the interior of China. For several warships and aeroplanes now suddenly to travel to and fro in the Hsin Hsia Ch'ung district is a serious infringement of China's sovereign rights and is most liable to create a feeling of apprehension among the people. I therefore lodge a protest and request you to be so good as to instruct the warships and aeroplanes to withdraw as soon as possible. Otherwise, if any misunderstanding should arise and lead to any disturbance, this Government will accept no responsibility. I take the opportunity of mentioning this point, and request the favour of a reply in the interests of friendly relations.

I have, etc.,
Ch'en Yu-Jen.

CHAPTER EIGHTEEN

A TRYING TIME UNDER BANDITS' PISTOLS

AN INTERVIEW WITH CAPTAIN G.H. HODGSON AND HIS OFFICERS

Hongkong, 1st September.
The Jardine coaster *Yatshing,* while on her way to Shanghai from Swatow, was pirated by a gang of "passengers", August 30. The vessel was ordered to make for Bias Bay, where the gang decamped with loot valued at $10,000 and seven Chinese passengers as hostages. The *Yatshing,* on being released, came to Hongkong.

Shanghai, 2nd September.
A private telegram received here yesterday from Hongkong by Messrs. Jardine Matheson & Co. Ltd., agents for the owners of the vessel, the Indo-China S. N. Co. Ltd., confirms the report and adds that the ship was pirated two hours out from Swatow and that there were no casualties. The *Yatshing* is commanded by Capt. G.H. Hodgson and is on the Tsingtao, Shanghai, Swatow, Canton run.

Pineapples and tinned chicken are not conducive to one's wellbeing whilst in the act of pirating a ship at sea during dirty weather caused by a typhoon in the vicinity, so say the pirates who pirated the *Yatshing* on August 30, two hours out from Swatow.

The good ship *Yatshing* duly arrived at buoys opposite Hunt's Wharf on Sunday evening showing no outward signs of her terrible experience, but in an interview with Capt. G.H. Hodgson and his officers a representative of the *North China Herald* was able to realize the harrowing and nerve-racking experience which these men "who go down to the sea in ships" experienced during the 24 hours in which their ship was in the hands of these sea fiends.

The vessel left Swatow at 7 a.m. on Tuesday the 30th, and all went well until 9 a.m. when the captain was conversing with the chief engineer and a passenger on the starboard side. Without warning, several pirates appeared from nowhere and flourishing pistols, indicated that their victims were to put up their hands and submit to a search. This being carried out, the captain, together with others who had been rounded up by other members of the gang, were pushed into the officers' mess room. Several shots were fired in different parts of the ship and resistance by any of the foreigners would have been the equivalent of suicide. The second officer was on the bridge at the time and a mob of six, rushed the bridge and pressing pistols to the officer's body instructed him to alter the course of the ship towards Hongkong.

The captain was kept in the mess room under armed guard until noon, when the pirate leader entered and finding that the temperature was unbearable, instructed his underlings to conduct the occupants to a cabin. It was at this time that the pirate leader, ascertaining that the captain was one of this party, gave instructions that the captain was to be brought to the bridge. This being done, the pirates ransacked the ship from stem to stern. They locked the chief officer in his cabin with two passengers, Mr. and Mrs. Brown of Hongkong, together with the first and second engineers and later entered this apartment and thoroughly ransacked the chief officer's room. Their ideas of the value of the contents were somewhat amusing. For instance: the chief officer had an expensive pair of binoculars and a camera. The pirates left these valuables but annexed such personal adjuncts as sleeve armlets, garters, studs, cuff links, silk shirts, and pyjamas, these pretty necessaries especially catching the eye of the raiders. During this unwelcome intrusion, the chief officer mentioned to the pirate leader that he would like to keep a gold wristlet watch and a silver cigarette case, both of which were presents which in addition to their intrinsic value had a great sentimental value. The pirate leader waved his underlings aside and taking up the two articles, pressed them upon the lucky chief officer saying in Chinese "have them by all means; we will not hurt you if you do our bidding."

While this little episode was being enacted, one of the pirates fired off a revolver from a position just outside the door, the leader cautiously looked out and saw that the report was from one of his own men's weapons. Calling the man inside the cabin, he roundly cursed him and told him that a repetition of the incident would result in one dead pirate being thrown overboard. The search was then continued and after silk socks, and a brand new Stetson hat had been annexed, the pirates left to carry out a search of the other cabins. Before leaving, however, they courteously asked the chief officer to hand over any money which he had and eventually left with $130 in notes. The second officer was on the bridge during this little interview and was not present in his cabin when the pirates took a fancy to his silk shirts and personal accoutrements, but was busy looking down the business end of a pistol whenever he scratched his head or did anything not directly connected with navigating the ship. It was apparently the desire of the two pirate leaders not unduly to molest or rob the officers and engineers and their ideas in this connection were conveyed to their subordinates. In the leaders' absence, however, these orders were not rigidly adhered to and little unauthorized raids were a feature of the proceedings, during which, brightly coloured articles found their way into the pirates' capacious pockets, or rather into the despatch bag belonging to the chief officer, which early in the proceedings had been annexed as being an ideal repository for articles of this nature.

The itinerary for the passengers and those officers and engineers not actively engaged in the navigating and propelling of the vessel was as follows:– 9 a.m. until 1 p.m., cooped in the mess room until the pirate leader thought that the room was too hot: 1 p.m. to 6 p.m., in cabins which became unbearable because of the heat and 6 p.m. to 9 a.m. (at which time the pirates left the ship) in the saloon. During this last sojourn, a little matter of 15 hours, all were compelled to sit round the saloon table and place their arms on the table. Some fell asleep from sheer exhaustion but the others remained awake watching the pirate guard as they brandished their pistols at the slightest movement. It must here be stated that the third engineer, who was on watch at the time of the piracy, was confined to the engine room during the whole 24 hours. He was not molested but was told to carry on and obey orders from the bridge. No pirates stood over him but two of them guarded the two approaches to the engine room.

The captain, in deference to the pirates' wishes, backed up with an occasional prod in the ribs with a pistol, kept the usual Hongkong course and at 9 p.m. rain made visibility difficult and after explaining the situation to the pirate leader, the anchor was dropped and the ship remained in that position, some ten miles from the shore, until 5.30 a.m. on August 31, when the ship was got under way and proceeded to the Tam Chau inlet, arriving at a position about half a mile from the shore. Three boats were lowered and the pirates left with eight Chinese hostages and the captain, the captain being in the second boat to leave. On arriving at the shore, some difficulty was experienced in landing with the loot and it was at this time that the pirate leader noticed a gramophone amongst the loot. He asked the captain to whom it belonged and on receiving the reply that the gramophone was the captain's property ordered that it be returned to the boat. The loot being landed to the leader's satisfaction, the captain was ordered to return to his ship and, for some unaccountable reason, one of the hostages, a Chinese student named Chang bound for Shanghai College, was instructed to accompany the captain.

A further difficulty was encountered in getting the captain's boat off the beach and, on the request of the captain, the leader instructed several of his men to assist in pushing the boat off. This being accomplished, the captain left and after watching him reach his ship, the pirates proceeded on their way uphill. It is a significant fact that during the approach of the *Yatshing* to this locality, the pirates continually asked the captain and the second officer the situation of Chilang Point, Ping Hai, Sha Mun, Tam Shui and Tak Sha Mei which interrogation would seem to indicate that the pirates had no definite idea of where they wanted to land. As it was, their landing place was not at Bias Bay but was in the Tam Chau Inlet near Hong Hai Bay which is about 12 miles overland from Bias Bay. The actual place where they landed was not inhabited and no village was in sight.

In connection with the pirates' procedure while on board the steamer, it is peculiar that they only allowed the officers two buns each, but instructed the saloon boy to give their prisoners all they wanted to drink, at the same warning them that any resistance would result in their immediate death.

Whilst the second officer was on the bridge, one of the pirates attempted to take the officer's watch and finger ring: the leader saw this incident and attempted to strike his subordinate. Later, however, in the absence of the leader, the same pirate forcibly took the ring and watch from the officer, the while brandishing a revolver and intimating that any resistance or recourse to the leader's protection would mean that the officer would be shot.

Amongst the ship's cargo was a quantity of tinned fruits and meat and the cases were opened by the underlings who gorged themselves on the contents. Just before the ship anchored, dirty weather was encountered, and the result was that some of the pirates were forced to disgorge pineapple and tinned chicken through the exigencies of *mal de mer*. It was not a pleasant experience and it is thought that in future, the pirates will stick to their usual fodder of rice and what goes with it.

While the ship anchored and the pirates were convinced that the captain had no ulterior motives in so doing, the leaders became most considerate. They had camp beds brought on the bridge and the captain and the chief officer were ordered to sleep, the while guards stood over them with loaded revolvers watching every movement. The pirates also had a camp bed taken down to the engine room for the third engineer and he was also instructed to go to sleep, and if he required a drink, he had only to say the word and anything in the shape of liquor would be immediately forthcoming. During the enforced anchorage of the ship, two ships were sighted at about 4 a.m. and the guard was immediately doubled. The inmates of the saloon being told that any signalling would result in immediate death. Indeed, a pirate was told off to guard each prisoner with the instructions to shoot if any motion was made.

The compradore of the ship considers himself very lucky: he said yesterday that out of the three ships pirated at that time, he was the only compradore who had escaped from being held as a hostage. He was threatened throughout the night and told to indicate where the ship's money was kept. The pirates told him that they had information that $5,000 in cash was in his care and they either had to have it or the compradore would die. He was able to convince them that there was no such amount on the ship, explaining that his company had no need to carry such a large sum of money as they had offices in every port on the coast.

He told our representative that a Chinese passenger in the next cabin to his own was a wealthy Tientsin merchant and this poor unfortunate is one of the seven who are held by the pirates. The compradore thought that this man was carrying a large sum of money in cash, an amount probably in the region of $6,000, and that this was obtained by the pirates. An estimate of the total loot was given as being in the region of $22,000 but, of course, such an estimate is purely problematical, although well-to-do Chinese are known to carry large sums of cash and jewellery when travelling, especially as in the case of the Tientsin merchant it was thought that he had journeyed to Swatow to collect a large sum of money due to him.

There were three passengers, a Mr. and Mrs. Brown of Hongkong and a Japanese lady. The former were journeying to Tsingtao for a holiday and on reaching Hongkong (after the ship had been pirated) gave up the idea and remained in Hongkong. Mrs. Brown is reported as having borne the terrible strain remarkably well and the Japanese lady was allowed to remain in her cabin during the whole time the pirates were on board. The chief officer's loss is in the region of $400 and the second officer's near $500.

A somewhat amusing incident occurred whilst the pirates were ransacking the chief officer's room. He is an Australian and his sister recently presented him with an Australian boomerang. This article was hanging on the wall and was taken down by the pirates and examined. After a brief consultation amongst themselves, they decided that the purloining of this unknown instrument would bring them bad luck and casting it away as a devil, they hurriedly left the cabin. Another matter which might be mentioned is that the pirates took every fountain pen on the ship, but finding that one would not write, requested the chief officer to fix it: he was unable to do so, and the pirates threw it away in disdain. It now reposes in the captain's cabin as a momento of an extremely unhappy and dangerous experience. The pirates also left behind a Chinese snuff bottle which contains some kind of narcotic: the chief officer is keeping this but is keeping it out of sight as he does not wish to have anything which will remind him of his terrible experience. They also left behind their hats and were seen entering the boats with two and three hats on top of each other and on their heads, one of which was undoubtedly the chief's new Stetson.

Whilst our representative was on board on Monday morning, the chief steward brought to the chief officer a list of articles taken by the pirates: they included egg spoons, serviette rings, carving knifes, bath towels, tea cups and wine glasses. A pearl handled tin opener was used by one of the pirate guards on the bridge to pick his teeth, after opening tins of pineapple and chicken which he consumed in the form of a sandwich.

Another article, which the chief officer found in his shoe, is what is thought to be a polished elephant's tooth and a talisman of the pirates. This is in the hands of the Hongkong police.

On Monday morning Capt. Hodgson lodged a protest at the British Consulate and the following is his report of the piracy as detailed to the Hongkong police on his arrival at that port:–

"I am master of the steamer *Yatshing*. The ship is of 1424 registered tonnage and is registered at Hongkong and flies the British flag. The crew comprises six European deck and engine room staff and a native crew of 78 hands as follows:– 20 deck hands, 19 engine room staff, 10 stewards and 29 compradore staff. The ship is not equipped with wireless and carries no guards. She is not fitted with grilles or piracy protection devices. The total firearms provided by the company consists of four Winchester rifles and three revolvers with ammunition in addition to which, I and the Chief Officer each had a private revolver. The ship sailed from Hongkong at 12 noon on Sunday, August 28, with a general cargo of about 600 tons of Canton and local cargo. There were no through passengers from Canton but we took on five Chinese deck and three European 1st class passengers from Hongkong, the latter being bound for Tsingtao. We arrived at Swatow at 7 o'clock, Monday, August 27. About 900 tons of cargo was loaded there and about 80 Chinese deck passengers, also a European lady and two children were taken on for Shanghai. The ship was not searched at Swatow by the authorities but a search was made by myself and the officers. I had been warned by letter that private gangs may operate and I took all precautions consistent with the circumstances. We left Swatow at 7 o'clock, on Tuesday, August 30 and all went well until 9 o'clock same date at which time I was on the aft part of the bridge deck on the starboard side, conversing with the chief engineer and a passenger.

Without warning a rush was made up the ladder by several men. They were armed with revolvers and immediately covered us and we put up our hands. There was a general simultaneous rush by the gang to all important points of the ship. The 2nd Officer was on watch on the bridge at the time. I was bundled into the mess room as were also the remainder of the European males on board. I heard several shots fired at the time of attack and owing to the suddenness of the attack it was impossible to offer resistance. The position of the ship at the time was Lat. 23°.20'00" Long. 110°.58'00" the nearest land being West Peak on Namoa Island bearing north 6¼ miles, the nearest port being Swatow. The ship was turned round and put towards Hongkong. I was kept in the mess room under armed guard until about noon when we were all moved to a passenger cabin. One of the pirates asked for the Captain and I was taken to the bridge by two pirates. I was told to navigate under their orders. None of the pirates spoke English but the No. 2 Compradore was on the bridge to act as interpreter. Mr. Harris the 2nd Officer was also there with five pirates. The usual track for Hongkong was steered.

The pirates consistently asked questions about various places including Ping Hoi, Sha Mun, Tam Shui and Tai Sha Mei. I was at first told to go to Ping Hoi and to steer close inshore. I told the pirates that the unusual route would cause other ships to become suspicious. The steering was then left to me and I then had orders to steer for Tam Chau Inlet. I kept my usual Hongkong course until after dark and at about 20 o'clock I headed for the Inlet but at 21.10 o'clock owing to rain I decided to anchor, as visibility was poor. At 21.10 o'clock I anchored in Lat. 22°.36'00" N. and Long. 115°.03'40" and remained there until 05.39 o'clock on August 31 at which time I got under way and proceeded to the Inlet, arriving at a position about half a mile from shore in Lat. 22°.40'15" N. and Long. 115°.00'00". I was ordered to lower three boats. I complied and the pirates loaded them up with loot taken from passengers and crew. They also took off seven Chinese passengers and ordered me to go with them. The three boats left the ship and made to a position on the fore shore of the mainland where we landed. There was no village in sight but I saw men on the hills who might have been acting as sentries for the pirates. The crew rowed the boats ashore and after all the pirates had landed with their loot and hostages, they ordered us back to the ship. There were about 18 pirates, mostly armed with revolvers; some had knives and choppers. I got the ship under way at 10.45 o'clock on August 31 and steamed for Shanghai but shortly after getting under way, I saw a steam launch heading towards us.

I also saw several junks and sampans heading in our direction from shore and as I had been warned by the pirates that other pirates might attack us if we did not get away quickly, I turned so as to keep the launch astern and I decided to steam for Hongkong. We arrived there at 17.15 o'clock on August 31 and I reported the matter. There were no casualties except that a European, Mr. Meikle was cut slightly on the hand. I was robbed of clothing, money and jewellery, etc., but I am at present unable to state the value. We carried no bullion and there was nothing on board to attract the attention of pirates. The cargo was not touched. The pirates told me that they had only got $3,000 and were disappointed at their haul. All the firearms on board were taken by the pirates. I cannot describe the pirates in detail but the man who appeared to be the leader was as follows. Age unknown, medium height and build, shoes and socks, black clothing. I cannot describe any others as all Chinese appear alike to me. The pirates took our food for their own use and left us with very little."

From *The North China Herald*, Shanghai,
Saturday, 10th September, 1927.

CHAPTER NINETEEN

A SUBMARINE PATROL IN PIRATE WATERS

GILBERT HACKFORTH-JONES
OF THE ROYAL NAVY

The lights of the Peak were beginning to twinkle in the dusk of a November afternoon as H.M. Submarines *L4* and *L5* slipped unobtrusively out of Hong Kong Harbour. To the outside world this exodus was but one of those routine movements which regularly occur in a naval port. The local Press were informed that two submarines had sailed for exercises and no one thought any more of it. Three days later the world rang with their exploits – the successful capture of pirates on the threshold of their own base, Bias Bay. And this is the story of how it occurred.

My part in the adventure was necessarily that of an eyewitness, for I was, at that time, spare Commanding Officer of the flotilla, an unenviable task entailing weeks of idleness waiting for one of the twelve submarine captains to go sick. And I may say, in parenthesis, that they were a singularly healthy lot. It is not difficult to imagine with what joy I heard that submarines were to be used for pirate-hunting. I volunteered to go as additional watchkeeper and was detailed to join *L5*.

Our much maligned Hong Kong government had for years been the target of caustic comments in the Far Eastern Press on account of its apparent inability to put a stop to the depredations of the pirates of Bias Bay. This latter place is only twenty-odd miles from Hong Kong with its large naval forces, and yet ship after ship had been captured and looted by pirates with impunity. True, an expeditionary force had been landed some months before the events here related and had burned the pirates' village to the ground as a warning that the British Lion was getting restive, but this had not acted as a deterrent.

Chinese piracies are carried out in this manner. The pirates pay their fares and board their victim at a port of call in company with dozens of genuine passengers. Then, when the vessel is within a short distance of the pirates' base, they attack and overpower the ship's officers and men and force them at the pistol muzzle to obey orders. On arrival at the base the ship is looted, certain wealthy passengers are kidnapped for ransom and the pirates depart, leaving their victim free to continue her voyage. Very simple to perform and equally difficult to prevent without the expenditure of vast sums of money on armed guards. The idea of using submarines instead of surface vessels for the trap was that the former could watch Bias Bay during daylight hours without betraying their own presence, and it was thereby hoped that the pirates would not be warned, as they had been on previous occasions by patrolling junks, of the presence of foreign warships.

The day before our stealthy departure the local Intelligence Service received word that a gang of notorious pirates had set out for Swatow with the avowed intention of boarding a vessel which was believed to be carrying specie. Our orders were to "catch the pirates red-handed," and we were told that any steps taken to achieve that result would receive the Admiral's fullest support. These instructions were the nearest approach to a *carte blanche* that are or were ever issued in peace-time and were a source of great satisfaction to the two submarine commanding officers.

As we steered clear of the narrow waters of the Limun Pass we found that a moderate North-Easterly monsoon was blowing. Banks of clouds and occasional patches of driving mist were not in favour of a night patrol, but we were confident that we should be able to intercept any vessel which tried to enter the bay by night. We arrived off Mendoza Island, a rocky sentinel off the mouth of the bay, after dark, and by previous arrangement *L5* took the inner patrol whilst *L4* scouted in the offing. It was a difficult and dangerous task patrolling at night this rock-bound bay which was completely unlighted; the charts were none too accurate and the presence of a large fleet of fishing junks constantly cruising about made the problem of remaining undetected an interesting one.

It was, of course, useless to dive during dark hours, for it is impossible to see through a periscope at night. I had the first watch from eight till midnight, and by the time my relief clattered up the conning-tower ladder my eyes were sticking out like hat pegs. The captain remained on the bridge almost continually and great was the keenness of the sailors on look-out duty. The 4-inch gun was loaded, the searchlight ready for switching on and the gun's crew, sleeping in their clothes, handy at the foot of the conning-tower ladder. After leaving the bridge I turned in "all standing" and determined to stay awake all night in order to be on the top line for anything that might occur, but, needless to say, I soon dropped off and did not wake until the cry of "diving stations" brought me out of my bunk in a brace of shakes. I looked at the clock and saw it was 6 a.m.

The night had passed, no pirate had been sighted, and now it was getting light enough for us to dive and resume the vigil by periscope observation.

In a few minutes the crew, shivering and yawning in the damp cold of the submarine atmosphere, assembled at their stations. The searchlight and ammunition were passed down from the bridge, the captain closed and clipped the conning-tower hatch and pressed the diving hooter push. As the alarm hooters sounded through the submarine the tanks were flooded and soon we were slowly moving through the waters, a depth of thirty feet showing on the gauge, and with our periscope protruding a few inches above the surface of the water. When all was settled down satisfactorily the captain ordered the Port watch to remain at their stations and fell the remainder out to breakfast and daily routine, whilst the officers took turns at the periscope.

It was a long day whose tedium was relieved by the necessity of dodging the patrolling junks, which constantly obliged us to lower our periscope and descend to a greater depth to avoid collision. That we were successful in avoiding detection by them goes without saying in the light of subsequent results. At 5 p.m., in accordance with previous orders, we altered course and steered out of the bay towards the open sea, knowing as we did so that *L4* was diving towards the position we had just vacated. By the time it was dark we had gained the outer patrol line and came to the surface.

No one who has not spent fourteen hours in a submerged submarine can realize the pleasure and relief in tasting once more the fresh air of heaven, coupled with the satisfaction of smoking the first cigarette. This latter luxury was denied us, for smoking on the bridge was out of the question owing to the danger of betraying our presence with glowing cigarette ends, whilst down below the necessity of charging the electric batteries after our long dive ruled out any form of naked flame whilst the batteries were gassing. It had been my watch at the periscope when we had surfaced, and I continued to keep the last dog watch as we patrolled slowly on one engine. At 8 p.m. I was relieved and went down to enjoy an evening repast such as only a submarine sailor can devise. A gargantuan helping of overdone roast beef, baked potatoes and the inevitable beans was placed before me, and I lost no time in removing all traces.

As I was gazing rather breathlessly at a larger plate of stewed gooseberries and wondering if it were wise further to afflict my interior, I heard certain sounds of activity in the control room. There was no doubt from the looks of excitement on the watchkeepers' faces that something was afoot, and so I went on the bridge without wasting any time. It seemed very dark as I reached the outer air, and the monsoon seemed to have freshened considerably. The captain was gazing intently inshore, and as I peered into the darkness trying to accustom my eyes to it, he spoke.

"There!" he said. "And again. He's opened fire! Starboard twenty!" This to the helmsman.

"Stop the charge ahead on both engines!" This down the voice-pipe.

"What is it, man?" This to a breathless telegraphist, who waved a flimsy signal form in the darkness. The rating repeated the message from memory. "From *L4*,

*S*ir – 'Darkened ship refuses to stop, have opened fire'." "Steady as you go!" ordered the captain as the bows of the submarine swung on to the flashes of light which stabbed the darkness away inshore. Together we stood and peered ahead, counting eight flashes and no more. A quarter of an hour elapsed and I for one began to feel fidgety. Running towards an unlighted shore at full speed in pitch darkness is an unpleasant experience. I began to think of the last time we had obtained a fix by land bearings and of certain rocks which were likely to bestrew our path. Then, as our imperturbable captain began to move restlessly, a faint red glow began to show inshore, whilst in confirmation came the message: "Steamer is on fire, am proceeding alongside." The faint glow became a rosy blaze and showed to us the corner of Cake Island in silhouette. This island guards the right-hand corner of the bay and a hasty bearing showed us that we were on a safe course.

The captain ordered the engine room to increase to the maximum possible revolutions. As we banged our way across the troughs and crests of the monsoon seas the gun's crew was ordered to close up. In the pit of my stomach, meanwhile, was an unpleasant feeling that we had missed the killing. All we could now do was to render what help was necessary. And it was even as I had foreseen.

L4 arrived in the inner patrol position at the appointed hour, and, as it was by now completely dark, she surfaced and commenced the patrol which, on the previous night, we had performed without success. She had not long to wait for events. At the moment that I, some eight miles distant, was spearing the first baked potato with practised hand, the Officer of the Watch in *L4* saw a faint glimmer of light to seaward and called his captain up to look at it. As the minutes passed it became apparent that the light emanated from a steam vessel approaching the bay, and the fact that she was not showing the regulation steaming lights betrayed that she was trying to make an entrance secretly.

The gun's crew was already closed up, the gun loaded with blank. Then, manoeuvring on his electric motors, the captain of *L4* got into a position where he could intercept the stranger without the risk of being rammed by her. No light was shown and no action taken until the stranger was well inside the confines of the bay. Then, at a word of command, the gun banged and a message was flashed in international code, "Stop engines." Immediately lights flashed on board the stranger, who, whoever, continued on her course at the same speed. "Stop engines or I will fire" received no more attention than did the earlier message. Two rounds of practice shell were fired close across her bows, and at the same time the 10-inch searchlight showed to the submarine for the first time her quarry. She was an old coasting steamer *Irene* [China Merchants Steam Navigation Company] with a high funnel and bridge at her after-end. Her fore decks were crowded with deck passengers, whose many voices could already be heard raised in terror-stricken cries.

As the *Irene* steamed close across the submarine's bows two common shells were fired into her engine room, for, unless her engines were disabled, the pirates would run her into shallow water and escape into the darkness. These shots did not appear to have any immediate effect, but as a matter of fact they caused the pirates to abandon the engine room and allowed the white engineer to shut off steam. Then, as the gun fired again, a party of men gathered on the extreme after-end of the *Irene* and opened fire with automatic pistols.

Bullets flew wide overhead, but the flashing of the pistols provided an excellent target for the gunlayer. Substituting a high explosive shell for the armour-piercing variety, which passed apparently harmlessly through the vessel, the gunlayer aimed and fired. There was a blinding flash on the stern of the *Irene* and the firing ceased. At the same time the steamer began to lose way and swing off her course. Smoke and flames sprang up from the fragments of her poop, whilst other fires which could not have been started by shell-fire became visible further forward. Shots and cries could be heard aboard the vessel and a life-boat was seen to plunge from the davit-head into the water, followed by men jumping frantically into it.

The situation was now desperate. The resistance of the pirates was broken and they could no doubt be captured, but this was now of little importance as compared to the lives of the deck passengers, who were in dire danger of being burnt alive. As soon as the *Irene* lost her way *L4* was taken alongside her.

These few words do not do justice to the difficulty of such a manoeuvre. A pitch-dark night, a heavy ground swell, a blazing ship, two hundred odd screaming passengers and no one on board with sufficient presence of mind to take the submarine's mooring ropes gives a fairer idea of the situation. After several unsuccessful attempts, during which many a bump was given and received as the two vessels ground their sides together, lines were passed inboard and were secured by the ship's European officers. [Of these, three were British and the captain was Norwegian. Her Chinese crew numbered 84.]

Then began the task of embarking the passengers. There was only one way in which to get them into the submarine and that was through the gun tower hatch. By training the gun on the beam the projecting rear edge of the shield just reached the upper deck of the burning vessel. Over this precarious gangway, dubiously at first, then rapidly and finally in panic-stricken hordes, poured the deck passengers, clutching what they could of their possessions. On reaching the upper casing of the submarine they were driven down the tiny gun tower hatch by the expedient of bodily violence when persuasion failed.

Some of the passengers were not so fortunate. In their terror of approaching flames they jumped into the water and heroic work by the sailors saved dozens of lives. Others, misjudging their height above the submarine's saddle tanks, jumped and, stunning themselves against the iron projections of the upper deck casing, were crushed as the two vessels worked alongside each other. Down below in the submarine the passengers were packed standing closer than any Coronation crowd. From the fore-end doors to the control room bulkhead there were stowed no less than one hundred and twenty-eight [the editor believes this number to be exaggerated].

Chinese, a solid mass of stinking, terrified humanity. Some of the women had babies in arms with them, and these of course had to be passed down after the parents. In the confusion families became separated and the first lieutenant of the *L4* still has to live down the story of what happened to him while he held the baby. A young lady of doubtful virtue showed her gratitude in the only way that she knew, by embracing a sailor. On being reproved by an officer the lady, thinking that he was jealous, turned her attentions on him and had to be forcibly removed. And so it went on.

When all the refugees had been stowed below, a small party, consisting of an officer from each vessel and a sailor, boarded the burning ship and went on to the fo'c'sle to let go an anchor. Then they were suddenly assailed by two enormous dancing bears that had been abandoned by their owner and were frantic with terror. There was nothing for it but to shoot the poor brutes, and this being done an anchor was let go and the party abandoned ship.

By this time the whole of the afterpart of the *Irene* was burning fiercely and radiating considerable heat. As the securing ropes were cast off and *L4* moved slowly away from her uncomfortable neighbour, *L5* successfully negotiated the entrance to the bay and steered close to the scene of operations.

The first thing we saw in the glare of the conflagration was a waterlogged ship's life-boat with some ten naked Chinamen seated on the gunwales and wailing as only distressed Orientals can. We steered up close alongside and hauled them on to the upper deck. I went down to assist and was greatly surprised to find that each man, as he gained the safety of the submarine, prostrated himself before me in all his nakedness and grasped my feet. One nude Chinaman looks very like another, and they all were very miserable, so we sent them below and wrapped them in blankets generously provided by the sailors. It was not for some days that we discovered that they were all pirates. Then we cruised round and picked up several more swimmers, what time *L4,* after laconically informing us of her intentions, set out for Hong Kong at her best speed. With complete disregard of the dangers and difficulties of a night passage through the islands which skirted the rocky coast, *L4* made a swift journey and arrived at her destination in the early hours of the morning, where her unwelcome cargo was unloaded.

Meanwhile the dramatic messages by which *L4* had informed the outside world of the course of events were creating a sensation at Hong Kong. Every ship in the immediate neighbourhood was ordered to proceed to Bias Bay at her best speed. The emergency destroyer, H.M.S. *Storm Cloud,* embarked the Senior Naval Officer and suitable entourage and dashed out of harbour, making the passage at twenty-five knots. H.M.S. *Delhi* and *Magnolia* joined the rush and soon Bias Bay was the scene of great activity.

As *Storm Cloud* raced towards her goal the Senior Naval Officer, a distinguished Irishman, began to take command of the situation and ordered *L4* to remain in the bay until further orders. But he had reckoned without the captain of the submarine who, being a compatriot, had equally certain views on the proper conduct of the situation and asserted himself by firmly announcing his expected time of arrival at Hong Kong and thereafter kept a strict wireless silence.

H.M.S. *Delhi* on arrival communicated with *L5,* and on learning that we had several survivors on board despatched a cutter to take them off. As the boat drew alongside us a very imposing sight met our eyes. A dozen Royal Marines, clad in tin helmets and full equipment and armed to the teeth, disembarked and stood on the upper casing ferociously jingling their handcuffs. The shivering refugees were hauled up from down below and handed over to their custody. It was such a cold night that we hadn't the heart to ask for the blankets and that was the last we saw of those valuable articles. When I left the flotilla a year later the correspondence on this subject had not then reached its zenith.

Meanwhile, *Delhi* and *Magnolia* set themselves to the task of extinguishing the flames. The *Irene* by now was a beautiful sight, her hull plating glowed red down to the waterline and the whole of her upper works were ablaze. It was a hopeless task to fight the fire, but the British Navy will tackle anything. They set to with such a will that in a short space of time tons of water were falling upon the hapless vessel, and after several hours they were successful to the extent of extinguishing the blaze, for the *Irene*, unable to compete with such a vast additional weight of water, heeled over and sank at her moorings.

And there she lies to this day, her masts projecting above the surface of the water, a warning to merchant shipping against the depredations of the pirates and the dangers of being rescued therefrom, and a lasting reminder to widows and orphans of the miscreants of the awful consequences which will befall those who take up piracy as a means of livelihood [the *Irene* wreck was later salvaged].

The sequel lasted as many months as the night's activities had hours. The identification of the surviving pirates was a difficult matter, for many of the passengers were afraid to inform against them, fearing the vengeance of their confederates still at liberty. When eventually seventeen pirates had been identified without any doubt whatsoever they were tried with all the usual pomp and circumstance of British law and, in the fullness of time, they were sentenced to death and duly hanged.

Meanwhile, the owners of the steamer, who had for years regarded the actions of pirates as one of those troubles which must passively be borne, were very incensed by the total loss of the *Irene* and clamoured loudly for compensation. In spite of advice to the contrary they issued a writ for fifty thousand pounds against the Commanding Officer of *L4*, who received it with great equanimity and is reputed to have offered the whole of his property, his bicycle, in full settlement of the claim. His amusement was, however, soon changed to annoyance when the claimants' case took more than six months to get into Court, and he was obliged to remain on the station long after the day when he should have sailed for home. The claim, of course, failed, for according to international law any vessel in the hands of pirates is liable to be sunk on sight, and the captain of *L4* was at last free to depart, but before he left there was a happier sequel to the incident.

Several of the crew received awards for their gallantry in saving some of the passengers from drowning, whilst the captain was rewarded with the Distinguished Service Cross for the successful manner in which he handled a very difficult situation.

As for the deck passengers of the *Irene*, history does not relate what happened to them. No doubt those who lost their life savings went back to start all over again. The

Chinese peasant is used to adversity and has learned to take his troubles philosophically.

The pirates of Bias Bay were quiescent for many months afterwards, but they also took the loss of their colleagues with commendable resignation, and within the year they were at it again, making use of shallow inlets further up and down the coast where the foreign devils were not likely to send patrols. Nowadays, of course, the activities of a mere pirate have paled into insignificance before the exploits of the more civilized gentlemen from other parts. The submarine is a handy weapon, however it is used.

From Gilbert Hackforth-Jones, 'Out of the Frying Pan'
The Blue Peter, London, Volume XVIII, 1938.

CHAPTER TWENTY

ON BOARD A PIRATE JUNK WITH THE QUEEN OF THE MACAO PIRATES

ALEKO E. LILIUS
AN AMERICAN ADVENTURER AND JOURNALIST

... I expected to find many strange, and perhaps also some gruesome things in Southern China. I found there displayed the naked passions of elemental humanity. And the savageness – and splendour – of it almost stunned me.

I have also met men and women who seemed to be in their natural surroundings only when they were moving in an atmosphere saturated with the nauseating, bodywarm smell of blood and the pungent reek of opium. I have heard the clinking of the shiny *fan-tan* "cash" and also of heavy gold coins, real Spanish doubloons from uncovered hoards. I have heard the groaning of tortured prisoners, too.

Parts of this book have been agony to write. It has meant the living over of scenes I prefer to forget. In my search for the unusual, I found more of it than I had bargained for. It may seem strange to the casual reader that one whose profession is journalism should feel reluctant to write his "story" after having gone through adventures such as it is the lot of few men to experience, with the sole object of obtaining "copy." But I can assure them that the agony of re-living such experiences is far greater than that of the actuality that is past ...

The Hong-Kong Governor's Private Secretary, Captain

Whyte, had a very frank opinion about journalists, especially journalists interested in the pirates of Bias Bay.

I had been assigned by a group of American and European periodicals to gather all possible information regarding these pirates and their activities. The Colonial Secretary very kindly opened his files for my inspection, and after several days of painstaking scrutiny of documents, telegrams, police reports and photographs I emerged from this stack of official blood-and-fire stories with a conviction that the bandits of Bias Bay certainly must know their job. On the other hand, I had got the impression that the pirates of Bias Bay were only tools of somebody higher up – somebody in Canton, Amoy, Swatow, or perhaps even in Hong-Kong ... Many facts seem to bear out the existence of an entrenched central organization ...

Having discovered so much, my next step seemed to be to go to Bias Bay. Everybody, from the American Consul-General to the room-boy in my hotel, told me that I was mad even to think of such a thing. It is simply not done.

Therefore, when I approached the good Captain Whyte, he plainly told me that I and all other journalists were nuisances, and I received the impression that it is not *comme il faut* to speak of pirates and piracies to any high official in Hong-Kong. I had hoped that the Captain would arrange for me to go with one of the customs or police boats that occasionally travel in those districts, but I was told that this would be out of the question. But to Bias Bay I was determined to go ...

On this morning a Portuguese and I were the only passengers on board the *Sui An* on the way over to Macao. He was a sea captain, born and reared in Macao.

Naturally, he knew all the ins and outs of the charming little Portuguese Colony. I ventured to ask him what he knew about pirates ...

"I'd like to meet some pirates," I said. "Would it be possible for you to introduce me?"

He assured me that it would be the simplest matter in the world. He would simply call on a man he knew, the captain of a junk which sailed up and down the coast. My Portuguese friend was certain that this Chinaman was in Macao, and that I would have a chance to speak to him. We made an appointment for a meeting the same afternoon in a gambling-house ...

I had engaged Moon, a young Chinese, as an interpreter, house-boy, and cook, and together we went to Macao to have a chat with "this Chinaman" ...

"This Chinaman" greeted me with a smile.

"Velly good you come to-day. Number One Master *she* here."

Then I noticed the presence of a Chinese woman in the room. I bowed. Hardly acknowledging my greeting, she began a severe cross-examination with Moon translating her rapid questions. Judging from her questions, *she* was the Number One Master "this Chinaman" had spoken of, and he himself was only a subordinate. She mentioned casually that she had been away on "business" and regretted if I had been delayed thereby. Her captain, she assured me, making a graceful gesture with one of her small, well-shaped hands towards "this Chinaman," could not do anything without her permission. She was going to sail the next morning at five. I could go along. The price would be forty-three dollars a day. Why just forty-three I never had a chance to ask.

It happened that she was going in the direction of Bias Bay, she said, and she was willing to take me there and bring me back. But there would be some delay, for she had business to transact on the way – very serious business. The delay, however, would be insignificant, she explained. Then as an afterthought, did I know that the trip would be rather dangerous?

"Dangerous? Why?"

She smiled, but did not answer.

Here was I, an American journalist, getting the chance of a lifetime, to sail with Chinese pirates to the central nest of the most merciless gang of high-seas robbers in the world, in an armoured junk commanded by a female pirate. Small wonder that I could hardly believe in my luck.

What a woman she was! Rather slender and short, her hair jet black, with jade pins gleaming in the knot at the neck, her ear-rings and bracelets of the same precious apple-green stone. She was exquisitely dressed in a white satin robe fastened with green jade buttons, and green silk slippers. She wore a few plain gold rings on her left hand; her right hand was unadorned. Her face and dark eyes were intelligent – not too Chinese, although purely Mongolian, of course – and rather hard. She was probably not yet forty. Every move she made and every word she spoke told plainly that she expected to be obeyed, and as I had occasion to learn later, she *was* obeyed. What a character she must be! What a wealth of material for a novelist or journalist! Merely to write her biography would be to produce a tale of adventure such as few people dream of.

That evening I heard from an American who had sailed the waters around Macao for fifteen years the following story about this remarkable woman:–

"Her name is Lai Choi San. So many stories centre about her that it is almost impossible to tell where truth ends and legend begins. As a matter of fact, she might be described as a female Chinese version of Robin Hood. They have much in common. Undoubtedly she is the Queen of the Macao pirates. I have never seen her. I have almost doubted her existence until you told me of meeting her. She is said to have inherited the business and the ships from her father, after the old man had gone to his ancestors 'with his slippers on' during a glorious fight between his men and a rival gang. The authorities had given him some sort of refuge here in Macao, with the secret understanding that he and his gang should protect the colony's enormous fishing fleets and do general police duty on the high seas. He even obtained the title of *Inspector* from somebody in authority, and that, of course, placed him morally far above the other pirate gangs.

"He owned seven fully-armoured junks when he died. To-day Lai Choi San owns twelve junks; nobody seems to know how or when she acquired the additional five, but it is certain that she has them. She has barrels of money, and her will is law.

"You may ask," he continued, "why I call them pirates, since their job is only to 'guard' the numerous fishing craft. However, the other gangs want the same privileges as the present 'inspectors' have, therefore they harass and plunder any ship or village they can lay their hands upon. They kidnap men, women and children, hold them for ransom, ransack their homes, and burn their junks and sampans. It is up to the protectors to undo the work of these others and to avenge any wrong done them. Naturally, there is bitter and continuous warfare between these gangs.

"This avenging business is where the piratical characteristics of the 'protectors' come in. There is frequent and profitable avenging going on wherever the various gangs meet. Lai Choi San is supposed to be the worst of them all; she is said to be both ruthless and cruel. When her ships are merely doing patrol duty she does not bother to accompany them, but when she goes out 'on business' she attends to it personally. When she climbs aboard any of her ships there is an ill-wind blowing for someone."

An orange-coloured haze hung over the hills of Lappa. Slowly the brown sails of our ship crept up, while the barefooted crew scurried back and forth upon the decks. Finally the junk was clear to heave away. On a nearby junk a Taoist priest in demon-red robes kowtowed and burned fire crackers to his special deity in order to drive away the evil spirits – all this for a few cents silver.

I was dazed! It was difficult to believe my luck. At last I was actually tramping the deck of an honest-to-goodness pirate ship! ...

I took a look at the crew. Here in South China I had been used to small, narrow-chested, almost effeminate men; but these fellows were almost giants – muscular, heavy-chested, half-naked, hard-looking – real bandit types. Some of them wore the wide-brimmed hat such as one sees all over Southern China. Some had tied red kerchiefs around their heads and necks.

There was nothing for me to do but climb up on the poop and make myself as inconspicuous as possible. I felt in the mood to do just that too – a white man, an intruder, searching for unusual "copy." What right, after all, had I to pry into their secrets? I was not a Secret Service man, nor a Government employee, whose business it was to find out all about these pirate clans; yet that was slight assurance that I should return unharmed.

My boy, Moon, did not venture any comments. I believe he was fully as dazed as his master. Still, he was loyal enough to hang on at the rate of $1.00 Mexican per day. No European servant would have done it.

There were twelve smooth-bore, medieval-looking cannons on board, and two rather modern ones. Along the bulwarks of the junk were bolted rows of heavy iron plates. The ammunition, both powder and shot, was kept amidships, the heavier shot being stored in a magazine just abaft the foremast. Rifles and pistols were kept in a separate cabin on the poop, next to the captain's quarters.

We glided out into midstream. The rays of the sun had begun to penetrate the haze, and a slight breeze filled the sails. In a few minutes we were outside Macao Harbour, and the heavy camouflaging plates were lifted away from the sides of the ship and placed along the deck. The crew pushed the guns forward, and we became a pirate ship, with rows of ugly, grinning cannons along her sides and a crew which – so help me, gods! – I should not have liked to command.

We hailed a boat, or rather a boat hailed us. The junk hove to and we came almost to a standstill; then the boat approached us and three women boarded the ship.

One of them I recognized as Lai Choi San. But what a different Lai Choi San! Yesterday I had seen her in a white satin robe, with green jade ornaments; to-day she was entirely transformed. Now she wore a jacket-like blouse and black trousers made of the strong, glossy material commonly used by coolies for garments. Her two *amahs* were dressed in similar fashion.

As soon as she stepped on board she kicked off her slippers, and for the rest of the voyage padded about bare-footed. No greetings were exchanged. After a few curt words to the captain, Lai Choi San, with a gesture of her hand, dismissed the boat which had brought her to the ship, and the junk swung out into the wind.

Lai Choi San went straight up to her cabin on the poop. This cabin was about as large as an ordinary grand piano box. One could not have stood upright in it; even when squatting there was scarcely head-room. However, the interior was lavishly decorated with intricate hardwood carvings, embellished here and there with dashes of bright colour. A tiny image of the Goddess A-Ma, the patroness of all seafaring people, hung against the wall next to a small ancestral tablet bearing the name of Lai Choi San's father.

Through the open door I saw her take an incense stick, light it, and thrust it into a pewter vase in front of the tablet. Then she emerged, her two *amahs* following her. As a matter of fact, those two *amahs* never left her presence.

Lai Choi San's favourite observation post was an empty packing-case on the top deck of the two-story poop; the two *amahs* squatted behind her. Her orders to the captain were given directly or, if he was too far away to hear, to one of the *amahs*, who immediately jumped down from her monkey-like position and ran to fetch him. She never spoke to any of the crew, nor did the *amahs*. Occasionally the captain asked her something, and she always replied very curtly and almost haughtily.

After all, she *did* rule supreme. She was the owner of eleven other junks, all bristling with cannons, rifles and pistols. There were no machine-guns. Though some of Lai Choi San's ships carried this deadly weapon, some of the other pirate clans along the West River do have war canoes equipped with machine-guns both fore and aft. These weapons are doubtless property stolen from the Chinese army.

The haze had now disappeared altogether, but dark clouds were piling up on the horizon. It probably meant rain squalls and strong winds. The captain gazed in the direction of the approaching clouds, and, turning to me, said in pidgin-English: "Much lain, much wind come byebye, maybe go way."

In the meantime, right above us, the sun was shining brightly, and the air was very clear. Ideal weather for a photographer, and what a subject to photograph. The moment Lai Choi San saw my magic box she rebelled. She gave an order to the captain, who approached and told me to put away the Kodak.

That was where I rebelled. I told him to go back to this pirate woman and tell her that since I was paying a good deal of money for the privilege of sailing with her I proposed to take as many pictures as I liked. If I was not to be allowed to do so, the whole trip would be a failure so far as I was concerned, and they might just as well put me ashore.

A hot half an hour of parleying followed, but finally she smiled graciously at me and I smiled back at her. I told Moon to go to her and ask if I might take her picture. I expected an outburst of indignation, but nothing like that happened. On the contrary, she agreed to pose. Oh, you inconsistent women!

Then the captain came, and with Moon interpreting we thoroughly discussed the problem of future photography on board the junk. In short, we agreed that I should not take pictures of anything of an incriminating nature. Incriminating nature! Could anything sound more unpromising to the ears of a journalist?

That same afternoon our adventures began. The horizon was dotted with the black sails of myriads of junks composing the fishing-fleets. Behind and above them hovered those dark rain clouds which blew ever eastward but never reached us. We sailed to the leeward of an island and out of sight of the on-coming junks. Within an hour the first ships were in line with our island; then we emerged from our hiding-place.

Madame gave a sharp order. She had singled out a large black junk with three yellow sails gleaming brightly in the sunshine. We sailed towards this ship, which was apparently heavily laden with fish. As soon as the junk recognized us it turned and fled, but we rapidly overtook it. Our crew had brought out the rifles and had put on cartridge belts, and so had Madame and both of her *amahs*. When we were within hearing distance of the fleeing junk one of our men fired a rifle shot. I was certain that the junk would fight, and was already wondering where I might hide myself from bullets or other missiles which would soon be flying about our deck, but nothing occurred.

A second shot was fired, and the junk's mainsail came down. We sailed up and hove to a short distance from her.

Forgetting Madame's request that I refrain from taking photographs of an "incriminating nature," I was ready to "shoot" a real battle scene. Here again I was disappointed, because nothing really exciting happened. A man on the poop of the other junk shouted something through a megaphone. Our skipper yelled back at him in a volley of rapid Chinese which I could not understand. Then a dinghy was lowered from the other ship, and the "enemy" captain came over.

Long before he reached our ship we could see him gesticulating wildly, and as soon as he was within hearing distance he began to jabber away excitedly. He was highly nervous, and as soon as he came aboard us he was taken below to the captain's quarters. Quite a while afterwards he again appeared, smiling broadly, and soon he was returning to his ship. Apparently the business had been settled to the satisfaction of everyone concerned.

While all these incidents were taking place Madame had continued to sit with her two *amahs* at her observation post, silent and unmoved as though she was utterly oblivious of what was going on. Whether she did this deliberately in order to deceive the onlookers on board the other ship, or whether such an attitude was her "second nature," I am unable to say. However, judging from my later experiences while "adventuring" with her, I believe the latter to be the case.

The captain seemed highly pleased with the enemy's visit, and I wondered how much money it had netted him.

These formalities completed, we sailed away in search of new victims. Two more junks were chased in a like manner, but they struck sail immediately after the first signal shot was fired. Their captains paid similar visits to our ship, and each time the captain's smile became broader and broader. He was highly elated and even jocular.

Anxious to know what the profits of the day had been, I shouted; "Hey, captain, feeling top-side? Makee plentee money"? And he replied: "Sure! Plentee money makee heart light." ...

Shortly before daylight we weighed anchor and sailed off again. To the east and northward high mountains were turning blue, and a few scattered sails could be seen along the horizon to the south.

The captain invited me to have breakfast with him, and the crew gathered round, roaring at my ridiculous manoeuvres with the chopsticks. I should have remained hungry had not Madame ordered Moon to bring me my fork and spoon. The women always dined separately from the men. The captain ate with the crew, and all fared alike.

About eleven o'clock we struck a calm. There was nothing for the crew to do but sit around and chatter, and so the captain and I had time to become friendly. He told me a great deal about Madame's business and her methods of procedure.

As an "inspector" it was her duty to sail from one fishing fleet to another and see that no harm should come to them from pirates. If a hostile junk was accosted it was the inspector's business to chase the pirate away, and if necessary fight him, sink the ship, and capture the crew.

Consequently, in order to be successful, she must be strong enough to hold her own with any kind of antagonists. This meant that the larger the ship and the more cannons it carried the better chance the inspector had to sit on the top of the piratical world.

Every junk had to pay tribute to the inspector. If it did not pay – why, occasionally accidents happened, and not infrequently did non-payers disappear. There were also other "inspector" junks hanging about and levying taxes on the fishing fleet when Madame was not around, and thus the helpless fisherfolk usually paid tribute to several inspectors in order to prevent trouble. Lately, however, a few of these smaller fry had decided to consolidate themselves into a stronger fleet and drive Madame out of business. This, at least, was rumoured, according to the captain.

Lai Choi San, being a good general, decided to stop all of these plans of her competitors while the stopping was easy. With a fair wind and barring accident, she hoped to reach an island that day where she knew several competing junks were harboured, and there talk matters over with their captains. Surely enough, within a few hours I had a wonderful occasion to witness Madame's rather unscrupulous methods of "talking matters over."

About noon a breeze sprang up, our sails filled, the mat creaked, the junk heeled over under the bellying canvas, and we sailed along steadily until we reached a hilly island heavily covered with vegetation. There, in a small bay, three junks rode at anchor. As soon as they sighted us two of them hoisted their sails and started to move away.

The captain rushed over to me. "You go down!" It was

an order to go below. I refused; but a few husky, slant-eyed gentlemen closed in upon me and pushed me, not too gently, in the direction of the open hatch, by way of emphasizing the captain's unquestionable authority. So below I went, and a moment later Moon rolled down to keep me company. The pirates most assuredly meant business.

The cabin was dark. A few rays of light found their way through a crack in the closed hatch. We could hear the crew running up and down the deck and shouting. I wondered what was going to happen, and if there was going to be a battle. Suppose there should be an old-fashioned hand-to-hand encounter; in that case my position would not be enviable. I had the uncomfortable feeling that in the event of the ship foundering I should find myself trapped.

"Moon, what do you think is going to happen?" I asked, more to hear his voice than in the hope of getting any reassuring information.

"No savee, master." As he spoke the whole junk shook from a salvo from our guns. The noise was deafening.

Boom! There went another! And a third, a fourth, a fifth and a sixth! A regular bombardment – but there were no reply shots. The enemy probably never got a chance to fire back. It was indeed a one-sided affair.

The nauseous smell of burnt black powder reached us down below. Then I heard more shouting and many rifle shots, apparently fired by our own people. I realized that if the other junk should return our fire my prison would not be particularly safe. I lay down flat upon the deck, hiding my head behind the base of the mast. But there were no return shots from the attacked party. After a while I sat up and tried, as calmly as possible, to talk Moon into believing that there was really no danger at all, and that our whole trip was a wonderful picnic. I was grateful for the fact that the cabin was too dark for him to see the expression on my face. Still, we sat there for at least an hour, during which time we had an opportunity for some thinking, perhaps a bit of praying, and much swearing, all of which resulted in a sufficiency of resolutions to be good in the future. Then the hatch was opened and I was allowed to come up on deck. The first thing I saw was two men bound hand and foot. Some distance away to starboard I saw the sinking hull of the junk. Without asking permission I put my camera into vigorous action.

I saw on the poop the Queen of Pirates, sitting on her throne-like box with her attendants behind her. They wore cartridge belts around their waists and held rifles in their hands, but, curiously enough, they offered no objection to posing for me in this piratical uniform.

I asked the captain who the two prisoners were. He replied with a snarl that they were the two captains with whom Madame had "talked matters over." Quite a forceful way of parleying, I thought; still, this was South China – and the Kingdom of the Pirates. I asked the captain if I might photograph the prisoners, and attend the execution in the event of their being shot. Of course, I could take as many pictures as I liked, but those men would probably not be shot, he whispered. Most likely they would be exchanged for heavy cash. If you shoot an enemy there is always a lot of explaining to do, and all sorts of authorities and relatives to pacify; but if you keep him for a certain period bound hand and foot, and occasionally let him go hungry for a few days, cash is almost certain to be forthcoming. And there is practically no danger.

I asked him how he knew that the relatives would pay up. He smiled. In this case it was an easy matter; he would simply deliver the prisoners to their villages, and the townsmen would pay cold cash to the amount of several hundred dollars per head. Yes, this was a rather easy matter to handle. It was hardly a case of kidnapping. Sometimes when a messenger was sent to the relatives they did not believe that a prisoner was really being held for ransom; and sometimes, again, relatives did not care to ransom the prisoners, hoping against hope that the captive would be killed, and that they would inherit all his wealth. But those cases were rare. It was after the third or fourth demand for ransom money that the prisoner's ear, or a finger, or a hand was chopped off and delivered with a message that next time some other part of his body would accompany the chit. Finally, if the money was definitely refused – well – it was just bad luck for the poor victim.

A dinghy was lowered, the prisoners were helped to their feet, carried on board the dinghy, and then rowed away. I wanted to go with them, just to see what their fate would be, and to witness the actual bargaining over the ransom, but I was not allowed to do so. The captain himself was in command of the dinghy. When they returned a couple of hours later he wore a satisfied expression, and so did the crew. Later I actually saw the captain show Lai Choi San a fat roll of bills.

It was on this second day that Madame first permitted me to ask her a few questions. I believe that she had a hard time trying to overcome her distrust of me. Occasionally she had deigned to smile somewhere in my direction, but I had not once heard her laugh loudly until, quite unexpectedly, one of the large muzzle-loading cannons was accidentally discharged close behind me, and I jumped a few feet in the air, almost scared out of my wits. That was the only time that I saw her really merry ...

Presently she told me a little more about her early life. Her father had had four sons, but they were all dead. She had been his only daughter, and being a frail and delicate child had not been expected to live. Her father used to take her with him on his trips along the coast, regarding her more as a servant than as a child of his own. And now she loved the sea.

The old man had started his life penniless, as a mere coolie, but he had had a remarkable career for all that. He had been a brave lad, and probably ruthless. He got into the good graces of a brigand chief, whose haunts were somewhere along the West River. This chieftain made him his Number One man, and when a few years later the old bandit died "unexpectedly" the Number One man proclaimed himself chief. And so he took possession of a few junks and went on the warpath against the neighbouring pirates, whom he drove out of their strongholds. Thus he became respected and feared among the seafaring merchantmen along the South China coast, made a goodly amount of money, and collected junks as one collects stamps or Chinese porcelain. He acquired a large fleet, but some of the ships foundered and some were burned by treacherous crews; but the fishing junks – several hundreds of them – each paid him a certain amount of money as long as he guaranteed that no other pirate would harass them in their lawful pursuit of livelihood.

When he died, with "his slippers on," from wounds received during the encounter which my friend, the American in Macao, had told me about, he left Lai Choi San seven ships, the strongest and largest on the waters of the West and Pearl Rivers. She also attested that she had "acquired" a few more, and that to-day she actually owns twelve large armoured junks.

She is rich, probably rich beyond comprehension. She owns a house in Macao which she occupies occasionally, but her home is in one of the villages on the West River.

"What do the words Lai Choi San mean?" I asked Moon. He said that Madame would have to write down the characters of her name. He could not tell me unless he saw them. I asked her to write her name on a piece of paper. She glared at me. I believe that she strongly suspected a trap, or some other devilry. She did not want to do it. Finally, I asked my interpreter whether he thought that she knew how to write. He translated this to her. The trick worked. Scorning to answer my question, she snatched the proffered pencil and laboriously wrote the three characters. Lai Choi San, *The Mountain of Wealth*. Not an unfitting, although not exactly a feminine name. Still, her career was not very feminine either ...

We anchored that night in the shelter of the cape which divides Mirs Bay from Bias Bay. For reasons of his own the captain extinguished all the lights, and our food was cooked over charcoal below deck. It was a very uncomfortable night. Mosquitoes sang their arias in my ears throughout the night; there was not the slightest breeze to blow them away.

Next morning, about half an hour before sunrise, a bit of wind came along and we again set sail. At last we were cruising up Bias Bay. The country around was hilly and unfriendly. The weather became stormy, with occasional rain squalls. A few junks hovered near the shore, and a small village appeared through the haze to the right. The bay is very shallow, and we anchored a mile or so from the shore.

It was understood that I was going ashore to pay a visit to the principal village of Fan Lo Kong. Naturally I asked the captain if he were not coming along to see his uncle, who, according to him, was living in Fan Lo Kong. He shook his head and mumbled something which I did not understand, and busied himself with something of no importance. He would not come along – not this time – but he would let me have as many men as I wanted for a bodyguard. I suggested that I take five men, three to go with me, and two to watch the boat.

A dinghy went overboard, and then the men rowed Moon and me for a little while; but soon the water became too shallow for rowing, and they all jumped out and pulled the boat along. They would not let me wade; I had to stay in the boat. Meantime I studied a sketch map which had been given to me by a native member of the Hong-Kong Police Force who had once been in Bias Bay as a spy. I was very anxious to photograph a house which he had told me of, where all prisoners were kept while their ransoms were being negotiated, and where many people had been tortured and murdered when ransom had not been forthcoming. According to the sketch it was a comparatively small house. I expected to find it on the other side of the village, not very far from the main street.

We landed near a group of small houses, where we were met by a few old men, women, and children. All the young men had disappeared. My ruffians went rummaging in the houses, and for some reason, even to-day not clear to me, they entered one house and came out dragging a small boy who held a baby in his arms. I protested against molesting any of the children, and they finally let the frightened, crying youngster go, but not until he had set up a healthy clamour. This overture was not at all to my liking. It would give the inhabitants an idea that our intentions were hostile, an impression that I was extremely anxious to avoid giving them. I hastened to present the still sobbing boy with a few silver coins; then we marched off towards the village, which was located about a mile from the shore. This was the same village which the British had partly destroyed in March 1927, following an especially atrocious piracy. Though they had demolished over one hundred houses, and had blown up and burned about forty junks, they had only succeeded in demonstrating the futility of such reprisals, for within two months a new piracy had been added to the bloody record of Bias Bay, and before the end of the year there were many more.

So this was Bias Bay. I had heard a great deal of "The Nest," but to me it looked like any other Chinese village, with huts and houses, and walls around the gardens, and the usual domestic zoo of pigs, dogs, and multitudes of ready-plucked poultry taking up every inch of the road. There were, of course, the children, the beggars, and the screeching "honey" carts which spread an infernal smell wherever they passed. Although it had been raining hard, numerous babies were sitting in the middle of the road black with mud. Only upon seeing our approach did their mothers rush out in the road, grab the children and then run madly away. Some women behind heavily-barred windows and doorways shouted curses at us.

They saw me, a foreigner, enter the village with a strange-looking thing, the camera, in my hand, surrounded by half-naked, armed men as a bodyguard. I am certain that they took me for a British official, or policeman, and they had every reason to hate the British, the only people who had ever dared to meddle with their alleged trade rights as pirates, a heritage from time immemorial ...

It was a good half hour before we finally returned to the road which led down to the Bay. There is an open place where this road reaches the village, and here several hundred more persons had assembled. They were expecting us; that was evident. Their attitude was not friendly. They threw sarcastic remarks at us, but they made no move to attack us. I told Moon to order the men not to answer their remarks nor to do anything which might provoke any unfriendly move. My men closed about me. I could see their fingers toying with the breech mechanism of their rifles as we passed through the throng. Something was bound to happen.

Some of the women called out to us in vile language. Then the first stone came flying. It missed us and splashed in the mud a yard or so away. The man in front of me swung around, but I pushed him ahead. A few more stones were thrown at us, and still nothing serious happened. I began to hope that we could make our way through the mob without any accidents occurring.

Then someone hurled another stone, hitting one of my men on the right shoulder. Roaring with rage, he whirled, threw his rifle to his shoulder, and pointed it to the crowd. Yelling, the throng fled in all directions, the children stumbling against each other and the men and women throwing themselves on the ground. Indescribable confusion followed. I expected to hear the crack from the rifle, but to my great relief there was only a sharp click, and I knew the rifle had missed fire. Thank God! I grabbed the man's gun, pushed it aside, and told him to go ahead and behave himself. We reached the road without further adventures.

We had yet to walk about a mile before reaching our boat. The crowd followed along after us until we reached the shore. I stepped into the boat, the men waded alongside, pushing it through the shallow water. Then the fun began. We made a first-class target there on the open water, and the good people of Bias Bay were soon amusing themselves by laying down a regular barrage, in front, behind, and all around us. But they were poor marksmen, or else we were lucky. We passed through it without a scratch.

It was with relief that I found myself safe again aboard our pirate junk. The first to greet me was the captain. He had, of course, heard the shots, and he intimated that he had been on the point of sending a rescue party for us ...

Two days later I was back in Hong-Kong. The junk had taken me as far as the south shore of the island, and from there I had walked all the way to the city of Victoria itself. Lai Choi San had refused to sail into the harbour. Her armed junks were not welcome there I understood.

The trip on Lai Choi San's pirate junk had been

something of a “glorious adventure.” The tropical heat of Hong-Kong was again becoming too oppressive, and I longed to return to the wide, foamy spaces, where pirate junks have their rendezvous, and where the freebooter is a noble man ...

The following day I took a boat to Macao. I met an American on board, and he gave me all the news covering the last three months. There had been a piracy toward the end of September. A Japanese ship, the *Delhi Maru* had been pirated, and at the head of the gang had been a woman! A woman! Could it have been Lai Choi San?

From Aleko E. Lilius, *I Sailed With Chinese Pirates*, New York, 1931.

CHAPTER TWENTY-ONE

AN EPIC FIGHT WITH PIRATES ON BOARD S.S. *HAICHING*

FOUR HOUR BATTLE: SEVENTY CASUALTIES: BRITISH OFFICER KILLED: ONE WOUNDED

Hongkong, Dec. 8.

A dramatic piratical attack has taken place on board the Douglas Steamship Company's steamer, *Haiching*, which left Swatow for Hongkong yesterday in command of Captain O.H. Farrar. Pirates, who came aboard as passengers, attempted to secure control of the bridge early this morning, when off Chilang Point, to the north of Bias Bay.

The Indian guards and the British officers resisted their attempts and much shooting followed, in which the first officer, Mr. R. Perry, and the third officer, Mr. K.A. Woodward, were both wounded, the latter subsequently dying. Several pirates are believed to have been killed as well as two Indian guards.

Failing to capture the bridge, the pirates set the ship on fire, but the captain managed to wireless Hongkong, whereupon H.M.S. *Sterling* and *Sirdar* were rushed to the spot. They put a naval party aboard the *Haiching* and took her in tow when the fire had been extinguished. It later broke out again, but was quenched just as the steamer arrived in port ...

All the pirates who attacked the ship were captured.

Dec. 9.
Escorted by H.M.S. *Sirdar* and H.M.S. *Sterling*, the *Haiching*, which was attacked by pirates yesterday morning off Chilang Point, arrived here under her own steam last evening and anchored in Kowloon Bay. Her superstructure had been partly burnt away.

The police completed their investigation at a very late hour. It was gathered from interviews that the *Haiching* left Swatow at four o'clock on Saturday afternoon, with 300 passengers aboard, amongst whom was one British national and three American ladies, whose names cannot at present be ascertained.

At one o'clock yesterday morning some 20 to 30 pirates, who had mingled with the passengers, appeared from the darkness. Firing their revolvers to the accompaniment of blood-curdling yells, they stormed the bridge, which was very well protected with barbed-wire and locked grilles. At the first sound of the attack, all the officers and the Indian guards rushed to the defence of the bridge and a rapid exchange of shots ensued. After several minutes the ruffians were forced to retire, but not before they had struck a severe blow to the gallant band on the bridge.

THIRD OFFICER WOODWARD KILLED

One pirate, more daring than the rest, crept up close to the grille-gate and shot Third Officer Woodward in the heart and brought down Chief Officer Perry with a revolver bullet in the stomach before he was despatched by a fusillade of shots from the revolvers of the officers and the carbines of the guards. After a brief respite the desperadoes again attempted to storm the bridge. It was pitch dark. The officers switched on their electric torches, which they placed at a distance from themselves, with the light directed on the pirates. The ruse was effective and the screams of the pirates in their death agonies furnished evidence that the bullets of the officers had found their targets.

The pirates were thus repulsed a second time, leaving behind several dead and wounded. The only casualty among the defenders of the bridge was an Indian guard, who was wounded in the groin. In the interval, half a dozen pirates descended into the engine-room and attempted to force the engineers to assist them to find a way to capture the stronghold. The engineers bravely refused and the pirates left them and returned to the deck.

There were, however, no further attacks, and for three hours there was sniping between the two sides. One shot reached its mark and the victim, an Indian guard, was killed instantaneously. Meanwhile the young Chinese radio operator worked desperately with the wireless, eventually succeeding in sending out an S.O.S. signal, which was picked up by H.M.S. *Sterling*, anchored near Bias Bay. The warship immediately proceeded to the scene.

Unsuccessful in their efforts to wipe out the remaining four persons on the bridge who had not been injured – Captain O.H. Farrar, the Second Officer, Mr. R.J. Johnson, and two Indian guards – the pirates resorted to threats to burn the vessel unless the small band on the bridge surrendered. These overtures were answered with a hail of bullets from the bridge.

Using kerosene, the brigands then set fire to the deck,

near the bridge, but fortunately the wind blew the flames in the direction of the desperadoes. The Chinese passengers, thrown into panic, swarmed on the decks, terror-stricken. Women, clasping their children in their arms, jumped overboard, while scores of desperate, yelling Chinese men fought with each other in a rush for the lifeboats, three of which overturned while being lowered, precipitating the occupants into the sea.

At five o'clock in the morning, when the fire was at its height, H.M.S. *Sterling* arrived and boatloads of bluejackets were presently on the deck of the *Haiching* vigorously fighting the flames, which they succeeded in extinguishing. All the pirates were rounded up and securely bound and a strong guard was placed over them.

Shortly before dawn H.M.S. *Sirdar* arrived and the uninjured passengers were transferred to the two warships. The *Haiching* pulled up anchor and, with the two destroyers, made her way slowly to Hongkong, accompanied by several tugs which had been despatched to the scene from Hongkong.

The crippled ship reached Kowloon yesterday afternoon and anchored in the Bay. Then the wounded, 38 in number, pirates included and most of them badly injured, were taken ashore and placed in hospital. Chief Officer Perry is in a serious condition, but he is expected to recover. All the foreign passengers escaped without injuries. All told 12 persons were killed in the fight and it is believed that at least 60 Chinese were drowned.

The names of the other officers in the *Haiching* are as follow:– Chief Engineer, Mr. F.C. Dixon; Second Engineer, Mr. E. Keweld; and Third Engineer, Mr. A. Demello.

The *Haiching* is the first British vessel to be pirated since the steamer *Anking* was attacked by desperadoes in September, 1928, and provides one of the most sensational stories of a bloody conflict on a vessel in Chinese waters – a conflict unparalleled in piracies on the high seas in recent years.

Authoritative shipping opinion asserts that there is an imperative necessity for continuing the anti-piracy military guards on board ships in the China Sea as emphasized by the *Haiching* piracy. This opinion strongly deprecates any movement such as has been mooted for the removal of the guards from ships.

Mr. K. A. Woodward, the Third Officer of the *Haiching*, was buried at sunset to-day with full naval honours. There was a large and distinguished gathering at the graveside.

Admiralty's Admiration
London, Dec. 10.

The Admiralty has cabled Vice-Admiral A. K. Waistell, C.B., Commander-in-Chief, China Station, expressing admiration for the gallantry of the officers and crew of the steamer *Haiching*.

From *The North China Herald*, Shanghai,
Saturday, 14th December, 1929.

THE HAICHING PIRACY

The western horn of Bias Bay is some thirty-five miles, and the eastern end of Hie-chi-chin about ninety-five miles north and east of the busy British port of Hong Kong. It has been asked how pirates can exist within a few miles of a garrisoned British Colony. There are plenty of reasons, but we cannot go deeply into the question here. Suffice it to say that any high-handed action on our part in landing armed forces is naturally much resented by the Chinese Government, and has a bad effect on British trade. Also, on the few occasions when we have sent a force to clear up the district, it has found itself confronted by an apparently friendly multitude of peaceful citizens, all the pirates having betaken themselves to the hills farther inland.

Any merchant ship that runs ashore on the coast of China stands the risk of being boarded by the local fishermen, who all practise piracy as a lucrative sideline. They swarm on board and steal anything removable, and generally take a few of the passengers or officers for ransom. The Bias Bay community are not content with these occasional windfalls. They send out gangs to seize their ship by force during a voyage, the pirates having disguised themselves as peaceful passengers.

Between September 1928 and September 1929 there had been a lull in this 'internal' piracy business, and then, on the 21st of that month, the Japanese steamer *Deli Maru* was seized at night and taken to Hong-hai Bay. The pirates cleared off across country to Fan-lo-kong, their main village, at the head of Bias Bay, taking with them several thousand-dollars'-worth of booty and five passengers for ransom.

Things again remained quiet for nearly three months, and then, on 8th December 1929, the pirates, spurred on by their shareholders ashore, were misguided enough to try to seize the little British steamer *Haiching*.

The *Haiching* is a vessel of about 1500 tons, trading between Hong Kong, Swatow, Amoy and Fuchow. She is one of the three ships in the Douglas Line. The last time this company had a piracy was thirty years ago – the year the *Haiching* was built – but fortunately this long immunity had not left their officers careless in guarding their ships against attack. It would be tedious to give a long technical description of the ship, but it must be explained that the third-class, or coolie, passengers are penned with their baggage and mattresses on the 'tween decks – one deck below the upper deck. They cannot normally get through into the defended portion of the ship, which consists of the bridge, boat deck, and officers' quarters, as this area is defended by grilles and gates of bar-steel. If they find that they need a breath of fresh air, as well they may, they can come up a ladder on to the after well-deck and thence on to the poop, but nowhere else. One Indian guard patrols the two cabin alleyways – with a grille door at the after end of each; one guard patrols the boat deck – above the upper deck; and two guards, off watch, sleep in a cabin near the end of the starboard alleyway.

The *Haiching* left Swatow on the afternoon of Saturday, 7th December, on the last lap of her homeward voyage to Hong Kong. She carried four European passengers, some forty Chinese cabin passengers, and about two hundred and sixty coolies, including women and children. About 1.20 a.m. on Sunday morning the ship was off Chilang

Point, in the danger area, about eighty-five miles from Hong Kong. All was quiet on board, and one of the Chinese cooks was picking his way through the sleeping bodies on his way aft to his galley, when he noticed a group of men standing round an open hatchway which leads into one of the coal-bunkers. The hatch should not have been open and his suspicions were aroused, but the men, on being questioned, said, "*Mo ye,* nothing wrong," so he went on his way mystified but probably too frightened to give the alarm. Anyhow it was none of his business. A few minutes afterwards shots were fired, passengers shrieked, and pandemonium broke out. Cookie, very wisely, went along to his galley in case anybody should suddenly want a four-course dinner.

The pirate gang was about fifteen strong – *at the start.* They were probably all Bias Bay men and had embarked as passengers at Swatow. As unostentatiously as possible they had lain down within easy reach of the bunker-hatch, and seizing their opportunity when all was quiet and the ship was in their home waters, they had gone through the hatch into the coal-bunker. This space was nearly empty of coal as the ship was nearing the end of her run, so they had plenty of room to move about. When all was ready they rushed through the low bunker doorway into the boiler-room and then broke into two parties. One gang held up the third engineer and his men, and the other rushed up the ladders in the boiler-room casing and emerged through a doorway into the starboard alleyway, opposite the guards' cabin.

The intention of the attacking party was probably to kill the two off-watch guards in their sleep, find and overpower the upper-deck guard who might be anywhere on that deck, and quietly arrive on the bridge, having posted men on the officers' cabins. One cannot tell what is in the mind of a Chinese pirate, but that seems to be the obvious way of tackling the job.

Unfortunately for the pirates, Bhag Singh, the Sikh guard, happened to be within a few feet of them as they reached the passage. They fell on him from behind and disarmed him, but omitted to take the precaution of covering his mouth with his turban. The Indian yelled out in his own language, "Pirates have seized me!" and the two men in the cabin awoke and attacked the gang. The pirates were then forced to use firearms and shot down both the men, wounding one in the groin and killing the other outright, the latter having first felled one of his assailants with the butt of his Winchester. From the moment those first shots were fired the piracy was doomed to failure.

The second officer was on watch up on the bridge. Hearing the shots and shouting down in the starboard passage, he seized a revolver, called the Captain, and blew long blasts on the ship's syren – the pirate-alarm for the ship. The Captain was on the bridge in a few moments and started organising the defence. His orders, in case of attack, were that officers and guards were to rush to defend the bridge at the first alarm. The pirates were handicapped by the fact that, on leaving the starboard alleyway, they had to expose themselves on the fore-deck when crossing to the ladder on the other side. Having gained this ladder and reached the boat deck they would be exposed again when mounting the bridge ladder. This was not at all the kind of piracy which appealed to them; things had gone wrong, and anyone who was rash enough to poke his head out was a target from the bridge above. They would have done better to rush the bridge in the early stages instead of giving the officers time to assemble.

Meanwhile the chief officer and chief engineer had rushed from their cabins. They were fired at by pirates and defenders alike. The engineer reached the bridge unharmed, but the chief officer met a man on the lower ladder; they both fired their revolvers at point-blank range; the officer was wounded in the stomach and the pirate fell dead on to the upper deck. The second engineer and third officer, rushing from their cabins under the forecastle, were an easy mark for the pirates in the starboard alleyway; the former was grazed by a bullet, but the third officer, who showed up clearly in his white pyjamas, was mortally wounded but reached the bridge. He died in one of the ship's boats some hours afterwards.

About ten minutes after the attack started the lights went out and the engines stopped, which put the defenders at a disadvantage. The party on the bridge consisted of the four officers and two guards unwounded – Bhag Singh had managed to reach the bridge after the fight in the guards' cabin – and the two wounded officers. The third officer, poor man, was dying, but the other, despite a painful wound, assisted gallantly in the defence. The defenders, who luckily had torches, had to repel repeated attacks, as a party of pirates had managed to get on to the boat deck, probably approaching from aft, round the edge of the grille, under cover of darkness.

There was yet one officer unaccounted for, the third engineer, who had been on watch down below. His absence caused the Captain great anxiety, as he knew the pirates had been to the engine-room. Suddenly there was the sound of a scuffle in the starboard alleyway and the voice of the engineer rang out, "Don't shoot, I'm coming up," and he dashed round the edge of the well-deck and arrived up on the bridge. His escape was miraculous. He had been held up by the men who took the engine-room and ordered to provide them with kerosene, which he refused to do, playing for time in hope of making his escape. The pirates, however, found the tank and drew off some kerosene, with which, without success, they tried to burn the dynamo. They were very flustered and started smashing gauges and lights; then, at the point of a gun, they made the officer stop the engines and dynamo and lead them up the ladders, with a view to using him as a shield when approaching the bridge. He had reached the starboard alleyway with the muzzles of a couple of rifles prodding him in the back, but seizing his opportunity in the darkness of the narrow passage he ducked down and hit the nearest pirate in the face and then ran through the door to safety. A cool hand in an emergency, the third engineer.

The Captain now went down and fetched up all arms and ammunition from the ship's arm-chest, which was in the chart-house under the bridge. Things were now looking better for the defenders; they had got their tails well up, and the slightest movement on the part of the pirates was met by a volley. There were two dead pirates at the foot of the bridge, another man had been killed and fell into the sea as he tried to climb up the foreside of the bridge, while from down below, in the passage, came the sound of groans, testifying to further casualties. About 2 a.m. the officers saw flames shooting out from the chief officer's cabin. The pirates had brought up kerosene from the engine-room and started a fire in the starboard alleyway. The *Haiching* has wooden decks, and the fire, helped by the breeze, spread rapidly, and in a few minutes the sides of the bridge were ablaze.

The object of the fire was probably to drive the officers from their commanding position and keep them occupied while the pirates made good their escape in the ship's boats. They had failed in their surprise attack, they were pitted against men who were much better fighters than themselves, and they were in the main track of shipping, so the best thing that they could do was to try and gain their friendly shore before daylight. They attained their first object; as there was no hope of saving the bridge the defenders came down on to the boat deck and crouched behind the freshwater tanks, bringing the two wounded officers with them.

The woodwork of the Captain's cabin, charthouse, and bridge blazed furiously, and if the smoke had driven aft the defenders would have been in a bad way. Luckily there was a light wind on the beam and the fire blew over to the port side. Things were fairly quiet for ten minutes, and then three pirates made a rush. One of these men had crept along a little ledge on the outside of the ship. The Captain switched on a torch and shot him just as he was climbing over the rails. He fell dead into the sea. The second man was wounded and fell on the wooden deck, where the fire roasted him alive when it spread later along the port side. The third man very wisely hid himself – more of him anon.

Again there was a lull in the action, and then one of the Indian guards spotted some men climbing round the edge of the grille. They were probably trying to leave the boat deck unobserved and join the passengers in the stern. It would be a difficult gymnastic feat in daylight as the grille curves outwards over the ship's side and is fitted with sharp steel points; at night with half a dozen sportsmen doing rapid firing at short range it must have been most unpleasant. It is probable that one or two of the men were hit and fell overboard.

The pirates now kept on firing intermittently from the after well-deck – below the level of the boat deck. The Captain had, by this time, discarded his revolver and got busy with a shot-gun. Standing behind a steel plate on the grille he waited for the flash of a rifle or pistol and replied with a couple of charges of buck-shot. One gets a good "spread" with buck-shot, and the moral effect is said to be very strong. Next day the space behind the steel plate looked like the "best stand" at a big shoot – littered with empty 12-bore cartridges.

The fire was spreading from the port alleyway, the bridge was gutted and the cargo of wood planks in the fore hold was blazing. The Chinese crew, meanwhile, had arrived on the scene from their quarters in the forecastle and were helping the officers. The Captain, thinking that the boats might catch fire at the davit-heads, had them lowered to the water.

There was an ominous silence from the after-end of the ship, and then it was seen that the pirates were trying to lower the starboard lifeboat on the poop, using their torches to clear the tangle of ropes. The passengers noticed it too, and tried to rush the boat, so the pirates fired at them to keep them back. The officers and guards returned the fire and drove them from the boat. The Captain of the *Haiching* was not the type of man to say "Please go and leave us in peace"; no, the pirates had given his ship a lot of trouble and he wanted them to pay for it. This was the last move of the pirate gang, and they then probably threw away their arms and mingled with the passengers, hoping, when help arrived, to remain unidentified.

The Captain had made several attempts to get hold of the European passengers, but they were locked in their cabins, aft, and luckily the pirates had been too busy to attend to them. These people, an Englishman and an elderly American lady and her two daughters, afterwards attended to the wounded in the first-class saloon. As the firing had now ceased the Captain sent the officers, guards, and crew to the boats and made them lie off the ship within hail, while he himself stayed behind above on the boat deck. He sent the second officer to a junk which was near the ship, and told him to stand by in case the fire spread to the passengers in the stern.

One can imagine the Captain's feelings as he sat on a locker waiting for daylight. Now, after all his efforts, having fought against overwhelming odds and saved his ship from pirates, it seemed that he would lose her by fire. To make it worse a ship passed within two miles of the blazing *Haiching* and never noticed her. One thing the Captain did *not* know and that was that under the life-belt locker on which he was sitting was the pirate who had disappeared when his two companions were shot! This wretched fellow was spotted and dragged out alive and kicking, twelve hours later, when the ship was on her way to Hong Kong.

At about five o'clock the deck passengers, terrified by the fire, rushed the lifeboat on the port side of the poop. In their panic they overcrowded the boat and, in starting to lower her, they let go the foremost fall with a run, and a number of people were decanted into the sea. The Captain sent one of the boats to pick them up and transferred them to the junk, having first ascertained that she was registered in Hong Kong and not in league with the pirates.

We now come to the narrative of the wireless operator, Mr. Cheng Yan Tak. His cabin and office are in the starboard alleyway, just abaft the guards' cabin. On hearing the shots outside his cabin he started making S.O.S. signals, in accordance with the ship's orders. It happened that the Chinese wireless stations up and down the coast were very busy at the time. Canton was enjoying one of her periodical civil wars, and the other was alive with messages referring to the movements of troops and warships. The *Haiching*'s feebler efforts were swamped by the high-powered coastal stations, and try as he would the operator could not clear his message. He was in a most unenviable position. The passage outside was full of pirates, and a fire soon started to make matters worse. He knew that the safety of the ship depended on him, and try as he would he could not get his signal through. At any moment he was expecting his cabin-door to be forced and the pirates to arrive. Why they did not go in and smash his instruments straight away is a mystery, as the wireless installation is generally the first thing which the pirates put out of action. When the Captain had transferred to the boat deck he had managed to get a message through to the operator, who came up and joined the officers. About 2.30 he tried to pass his signal again, but without success; he then lay off the ship in one of the boats. About an hour before dawn, at about 5.30, the Captain called the operator alongside and hauled him on board. He found the wireless aerial had been earthing on a steel davit, and this may have been the cause of the early failures. After overhauling his instruments, he made another attempt to make his signal, and got through to the Government Radio Station in Hong Kong at about 5.40 a.m.

The message which spoilt Hong Kong's beauty sleep that calm Sunday morning summed up the situation in a few words: "Douglas steamer *Haiching* pirated and on fire, position off Chilang Point, send help quick, going to sink another hour." The Naval authorities passed this signal to the two destroyers on piracy patrol. H.M.S. *Sterling* happened to be under weigh behind Chilang Point only ten miles away from the *Haiching*, while the *Sirdar* was off Bias Bay some forty-five miles to the south-westward. They both raced at full speed to the *Haiching*'s assistance. The *Sterling* sighted the glow of the burning ship to the north-eastward and was alongside her about six o'clock, the *Sirdar* arriving about seven-thirty. It was most fortunate that there were two men-of-war in the vicinity, as one alone could hardly have coped with the situation.

The *Haiching* was a terrible sight as *Sterling* closed her in the early dawn. She was blazing furiously amidships; three of her boats, packed with terrified passengers, were drifting near the ship, while another boat hung bows-down from her port quarter. A body was hanging on a rope from her stern, a badly wounded man lay huddled up on her accommodation-ladder, while her decks were littered with passengers' belongings, bloodstained clothing, and rubbish.

The destroyer sent an armed guard on board, who mustered all the passengers and sorted out the wounded, and another party was sent to assist the ship's crew in putting out the fire. She then lay alongside the burning ship and played her hoses into the hold. When the *Sirdar* arrived she was sent to search the junks inshore to make certain that no pirates had escaped; she then embarked passengers from the ship and her outlying boats.

The *Sterling* now took the ship in tow while the *Sirdar*, lashed alongside, assisted, with her screws, to keep her steady on her course, as the *Haiching*'s helm was jammed hard-over. The Captain asked to be towed in towards the shore as he was afraid that the fire would gain the upper hand, but it was got under by the *Sirdar*'s hoses after about an hour, during which time both ships had been bumping heavily in the swell.

The *Haiching*'s engineers and firemen went down and found that, except for minor damage, the engines were all right, though the boilers were nearly empty. About 11.15 a.m. the ship was able to proceed under her own steam, and, led by the *Sterling* and using her auxiliary steering gear, from aft, set course for Hong Kong, at a speed of ten knots.

The *Haiching* arrived in Kowloon Bay, Hong Kong, about 6 p.m., and, from then onwards, affairs were in the hands of the police. The passengers were landed in launches, and all those would could not immediately prove their identity were sent to the police-station. After several days of wearisome cross-examination by detectives they were all released except six men. At the time of writing (5th February 1930), there are three men waiting trial for murder and piracy on the High Seas.

The prisoners may consider themselves lucky that they are to be tried in a British court; the Chinese have a very short way with men who are suspected of having the "piracy habit." On this occasion, owing to the darkness and confusion at the time of the attack, there was little chance of their being recognised afterwards.

Upwards of twenty wounded were landed in Hong Kong and eleven bodies were recovered. Besides these there were several people drowned, and two or three pirates are known to have fallen overboard after being shot. The extraordinary thing is that there have been no inquiries made about the missing passengers. Presumably their relatives think that they had better keep clear of the affair altogether.

The gallantry and resource of the *Haiching*'s defenders have created a profound impression in the Far East. If testimony were needed, witness the long line of mourners which followed the naval gun-carriage bearing the body of the Third Officer through the busy, crowded streets to its quiet grave on the hillside in Happy Valley.

From *Blackwood's Magazine,* Edinburgh, May 1930.

TWENTY-TWO

THE TWENTIETH CENTURY PIRATE

FRANK DEXTER

On the wharf at which the steamer was berthed in Singapore hundreds of brown and yellow bodies jostled, screamed, grunted, and gesticulated. A few harassed white wharf officials attempted to establish some semblance of order in this squirming mass of sweating humanity. Their white suits hung limply from their saturated bodies, and the sun struck fiercely at their topees, but many of the Chinese who swarmed on the wharf were naked above the waist. They wore no hats, but the sun had no more effect on them than had the agitated shouts of the officials. Their only thought was to board the steamer which was to take them to their native land. Some were going back to die, but the majority were returning to spend their meagre savings, hoarded through years of ceaseless labour in Malaya or the Dutch East Indies.

Vendors of food and drink sat stolidly beside their goods or argued frantically with prospective customers. Family groups zealously guarded their belongings – bundles of clothes, baskets of food, teapots, buckets of cooked rice, bananas, family treasures, and hordes of children. Suddenly the gangway from the foredeck was lowered, and at the bottom of it the officials mustered in force to regulate the flow of passengers, who, gathering their families and their belongings, pressed eagerly forward. They filed rapidly up the gangway to find a place for themselves on the already overcrowded foredeck, the most favoured positions on which were vigorously defended by those Chinese who had booked from Rangoon to Hong Kong or Shanghai. The overflow disappeared mysteriously to a lower deck, provided for that purpose, and even into the hold. They cared not for discomfort, for the steamer was headed for home.

"Fifteen hundred now," growled the second officer, when we asked the number. "Six hundred in Rangoon and 900 here." The seven white passengers gazed sympathetically down through the bars and steel lattice which separated the rest of the ship from the deck passengers, who by the time the steamer moved away from the wharf were already busy with their chopsticks. "Don't pity them yet," warned the officer. "You may have reason to fear some of them before we reach Shanghai." But the steel seemed to be strong, and the narrow doors through the lattice carried heavy padlocks. Here was no fear of pirates. At night, however, came the first shaking of our faith in those barricades. As we left the dining saloon a dark figure brushed past us. He wore a turban, a uniform, and carried a rifle – a familiar sight throughout the East, for many countries employ Sikh police, imported from India. But the sight of this man and a few of his companions posted at strategic positions throughout our part of the steamer did not add to the enjoyment of our evening stroll, nor aid our concentration on the game of bridge which followed. "Why the army?" asked one of the passengers at last. The second officer, who had joined us, chuckled. "I told you not to sympathise too soon with the deck passengers." He replied. "There may be a few pirates among them, and iron bars do not always keep them out. We have a dozen police on board in charge of a white sergeant."

A little later the sergeant appeared – a Russian in the uniform of the Shanghai municipal police. He carried a revolver in a holster at his waist, and a whistle reposed in a small breast pocket of his tunic. Here was a modern steamer of 7,000 tons in a modern year more closely guarded than a Spanish galleon in the days of Sir Henry Morgan. But we were not in a modern sea. We were modern intruders in a sea which for thousands of years had been the cradle, the nursery, and the home of Chinese and Malays, who earned a precarious living in their crazy junks, the huge sails sometimes flapping lazily in a calm or straining to breaking-point as they ran from a storm to save their precious cargo. These were men and women who did as their ancestors had done, who lived and died in their strange craft, and looked upon piracy as a legitimate business. They could not understand the interference of fussy little destroyers with the business of piracy or smuggling. Some, after repeated encounters with foreign warships, had turned their business into less dangerous channels, but many others remained to attack and loot a helpless ship.

Piracy is thus an organised business in some Chinese waters, and as precaution against these organisations there were the Sikh police, as well as the steel bars on our steamer. The casual junk pirates were not feared by a ship of this size, but the efficiency of the organised bands was very much to be feared. The pirates usually board the ship with the deck passengers, and 10 picked men are sufficient for the task of capturing a ship. Each knows what is expected of him. One is a navigator, another is an engineer, and the third is a wireless man. The others are employed in various ways. All have automatic pistols hidden among their belongings, and at an opportune moment they make a raid on the officers and saloon passengers. If their position on the steamer is not enclosed by barricades their task is easier. One or two attack the officer on duty on the bridge, others repeat the performance in the engine-room and the wireless-room, and the others take care of the officers who are off duty as well as the white passengers.

Rarely are the passengers or officers harmed unless they attempt to obtain weapons with which to defend themselves, and the Chinese and Lascar members of the crew are soon persuaded that they must obey their new masters. The steamer is then headed for some secluded beach, where as much of her cargo as can be loaded on the waiting junks is transferred, and as many valuables as can be found are taken. Officers and white passengers are taken on shore as hostages until the stolen goods are well on their way inland, and then usually they are allowed to return to their ship. If, however, the saloon or second-class passengers include some wealthy Chinese he or she may be taken inland and held for ransom, a business which in China is more efficiently organised and often more profitable than piracy. When the ship is barricaded the task of capturing her is harder, but locks are easily picked, and then the same procedure is followed. Hence the need for an armed guard.

The first night out from Hong Kong on the way to Shanghai and other northern ports is the peak period of the danger to steamers carrying their hundreds of deck passengers. But by the time we left Hong Kong we had become accustomed to our steel bars, our guards, and our passengers. We had no thought of pirates, but we were rudely reminded of them that afternoon, when a British destroyer rapidly overhauled us. She was chasing the s.s. *Helikon,* a small Chinese-owned ship, which was carrying 300 deck passengers. The authorities had learned that pirates had boarded her at Hong Kong, and the destroyer had been detailed to bring the ship back to port. A few hours later we saw her returning in the wake of the destroyer. We heard no more of her until we arrived at Shanghai. There we learned that nine pirates, including three women, had been found among the passengers, and arrested.

A year previously [and again in October, 1932] the *Helikon* had been pirated and taken to Bias Bay, where the compradore and 14 of the Chinese passengers had been taken ashore, and held for ransom. In addition, cargo and jewellery, valued at 1,000 pounds sterling, had been take by the pirates.

Apparently, however, we had no pirates on our steamer, or the guards were too alert and too heavily armed for them to make any attempt to gain possession of the ship. The remainder of the voyage to Shanghai was quiet. The only junks which crossed our path were those which suddenly darted across the bows of the steamer, thus cutting off any evil spirits which might have been pursuing them. Our deck passengers screamed their delight when the steamer turned into the Whangpoo River at Shanghai. Our expressions were of relief.

From *The Argus*, Melbourne, 23rd April 1932.

CHAPTER TWENTY-THREE

NORWEGIAN STEAMER SEIZED AT MIRS BAY

OUR CORRESPONDENT

Hong Kong.
The Master of the Norwegian steamer *Prominent*, Captain H. Jensen, [on charter to Nam Fat Steamship Company of Saigon] was wounded on Friday, when 14 pirates, armed with revolvers seized the vessel in Mirs Bay, and after looting her, escaped in boats, landing at Ha Sha. The vessel was bound for Saigon and was only a few miles out of Hong Kong when the outrage occurred. Although the attack was made with surprising suddenness, a message was sent out and was picked up by No. 4 Police launch, which patrols the district. The launch gave chase but failed to reach the ship before the pirates had escaped to the shore opposite Ping Chau Island, in Mirs Bay. No-one was kidnapped, and the extent of the looting is not yet known. The ship returned to Kowloon Bay on May 27.

The *Prominent* which was rescued from pirates at 11 p.m. on Friday, had been in the hands of the pirates for two days. Her wireless distress signals were picked up by Nos. 1 and 4 police launches. The No. 4 police launch chased the pirated steamer in Mirs Bay and fired a three-pounder shell at the vessel, and the *Prominent*, in the hands of the pirates, attempted to ram the police launch. It is estimated by the water police that the police chase took place in Mirs Bay about 20 miles from Hong Kong.

The master of the *Prominent* was taken to the Kowloon

Hospital immediately on the arrival of the pirated vessel in Hong Kong harbour. He is suffering from a bullet wound in the left leg.

The steamer left Hong Kong on the evening of May 24, on a voyage to Saigon. She has been chartered by Messrs. Larssen, Karsten & Co., local agents for the vessel, to the Nam Fat Steamship Co., of Saigon, for the period of one year. It is estimated that about 100 deck passengers were on board the vessel at the time of the piracy.

The Europeans on board numbered six, namely the Captain, two officers, and three engineers. The Chinese crew totals 38. The local agents of the vessel are unable to furnish any details of the piracy at the present time, as full news has not yet reached their office.

The *Prominent* is a steel-screw steamer of 2,232 tons gross, has a length of 270.6 feet, a breadth of 40.1 feet and a depth of 19.4 feet.

The water police state that at 11.30 p.m. on Friday, the No. 4 police launch was patrolling in the vicinity of Mirs Bay when the *Prominent* was seen entering the Bay. It was known that the ship should not have been in that locality, and the police launch signalled her to stop. As the *Prominent* did not do so, the Police launch fired a three-pounder shell at her. Thereupon the Norwegian officers called out, "Don't fire."

The pirates then escaped by landing at Ma Sha, in Mirs Bay, opposite Ping Chau Island. They took with them two of the Norwegian officers to cover their retreat, as they were pursued by the police. After they had landed they allowed the two officers to return to their vessel.

The Hong Kong police have launches in Mirs Bay which

are still patrolling in the hope of capturing the pirates who attacked the *Prominent*. The pirates, however, have escaped into Chinese territory.

When interviewed by *The China Mail*, on May 27, Capt. H. Jensen, of the ill-fated *Prominent*, stated that the piracy took place because the pirates believed that the ship was carrying a large amount of money in her cargo. He also stated that finding no money in the cargo, they stole $335 in Hong Kong money, 106 Piastres Saigon money, and about three or four dollars in small coinage. The pirates also helped themselves to money and valuables from the persons of the passengers. They selected four passengers and the ship's compradore, whom they had intended to kidnap, but the arrival of the police launch No. 4, caused them to leave the *Prominent* in a hurry and they were unable to carry out their intention.

Captain Jensen stated that the fire of the police launch proved dangerous to those aboard the pirated steamer, as the pirates were desperate and threatened to set the vessel on fire if the police did not desist. The firing from the police launch was so hot that several of the Chinese crew jumped into the sea rather than face the hail of machine gun bullets and the three-pound shells falling on the ship. The second officer who was on the poop attempting to launch a boat was forced to beat a retreat owing to the dangerous fire which he experienced.

The vessel left Hong Kong at 8 p.m. on May 23, after she had been searched for pirates by members of the Hong Kong Police. For the first day the *Prominent* and the

Helicon, a vessel on the same run were running side by side down the China Sea, about six miles separating them. The pirates had intended to make their attack on the night of May 24, but the presence of the *Helicon* caused them to alter their plans. They therefore made their attack at about 2 a.m. on May 26.

The second officer, Mr. George Jensen, was on watch when he was attacked by the chief pirate who threatened him with an automatic pistol. The second officer picked up the pirate and threw him on to the deck below, and followed him down the ladder.

He found, however, that several other pirates attacked him. The noise attracted the attention of the Captain who came out of his cabin brandishing a malacca cane, since he thought that a fight was in progress between some coolies. When he found out that the ship was being attacked by pirates, Captain Jensen joined his second officer in the fight, and received a bullet in the thigh which splintered the bone. The second officer received a chopper gash in the back. The pirates appeared to be novices, except for about four or five out of the total of fifteen, for they were nervous of their weapons and shot badly. Many of them, also, were armed only with choppers and table knives.

The Captain and second officer were at last overpowered. The chief officer had been captured while asleep on the boat deck. The chief engineer was captured in his room and the second and third engineers were taken in the engine-room. The pirates were thus masters of the ship and ordered the Captain to make for Mirs Bay. At 10.30 p.m. on May 26, the Captain was forced to go up on to the bridge, in spite of his painful wound, and on arrival there he found that in spite of their lights all being out they had been sighted by a police launch, which kept them in view with her searchlight. They were then chased to Mirs Bay, where the vessel grounded owing to the desperate nervousness of the pirates. The pirates landed at Ha Sha, and took the chief and second officers with them to cover their flight. The officers after accompanying the pirates over the hill were allowed to return to their vessel.

Captain Jensen was taken to the Kowloon Hospital immediately on the arrival of the *Prominent* in Hong Kong at 8 a.m. on May 27.

The Chief Detective Inspector stated on May 29 that no further developments had taken place in the *Prominent* piracy case. He stated that several of the officers believed that the pirates had formerly been employed on board the vessel. The water police state that the No. 4 police launch left harbour this morning to take up her patrol in Mirs Bay, where she spent all day yesterday. The No. 1 police launch is also patrolling Mirs Bay. Members of the police from the No. 4 police launch which pursued the pirates on the night of May 26, followed them ashore for some distance inland and fired several shots. Though the Captain denies that the *Prominent* attempted to ram the police launch, the water police reiterate their former statement. The police state that none of the three-pounder shells fired by them struck the *Prominent*.

H.M.S. *Wishart*, had been anchored at the scene of the pirates' landing on the night of May 25, but on May 26 was on patrol and did not arrive on the scene until about

3.30 a.m.

Technical knowledge on the part of the pirates is shown by the fact that they disabled the wireless set on the ill-fated *Prominent*, and even went so far as to wreck the emergency set and thus cut off all communication with the outside world. On the morning of May 25, after they had captured the vessel, the chief of the pirates ordered the bo'sun to paint out the red band around the funnel, and also to obliterate the Chinese characters on the ship's side which went to make up the name of the *Prominent*.

The Captain of the vessel relates how after their nefarious work of the night before, the pirates sat down in the ship's saloon, and ordered a substantial breakfast of ham and eggs, and pork chops. They also ordered a bottle of whiskey and dozens of soft drinks, and proceeded to make merry for over an hour. Captain Jensen, who now lies in the Kowloon Hospital with a splintered thigh-bone caused by a bullet wound, states that the officers were not ill-treated by the pirates. The chief pirate had several long conversations with him and it was not until the advent of the police launch, with its deadly machine-gunfire, that the pirates showed any desire to kill the officers. The Captain further states that some of the pirates were recognised by the Chinese crew as they had been tallymen employed by the Jeb Shun Steamship Co., of Hong Kong, during a previous trip of the *Prominent* to Rangoon, when she was chartered by that firm.

Captain Jensen said that the pirate chief had stated that he had spent much money for some time, investigating the cargoes carried by the *Prominent*, and expressed himself disappointed by the fact that they had made a mistake by attacking the vessel on this trip, when she carried no money except the $335 Hong Kong money, 106 Piastres Saigon money and the three or four dollars in small money, which they had taken from the Captain's safe.

From *The Overland China Mail*, Hong Kong, 31 May 1933.

CHAPTER TWENTY-FOUR

THE SECOND S.S. *TUNGCHOW* PIRACY

OUR CORRESPONDENT

BRITISH STEAMER SEIZED

Hong-Kong, February 1st.

The China Navigation Company's steamer *Tungchow,* carrying 70 British and American boys and girls back to the China Inland Mission's School at Chefoo, in North China, from Shanghai, on the conclusion of the school holidays, was attacked and seized by pirates on Tuesday and taken to Honghai Bay, some hundreds of miles to the south and adjacent to the notorious Bias Bay. A Russian guard was killed and a British engineer, Mr. K. Macdonald, wounded in resisting the pirates. The children and the other passengers and the rest of the crew were prisoners of the pirates until the latter abandoned the ship to-day, but none of them was harmed. The British naval authorities, fearing piracy when the ship was reported 24 hours overdue, dispatched H.M.S. *Sandwich* from Wei-hai-wei to search the coast in the vicinity, and H.M.S. *Suffolk* and destroyers from Hong-Kong to proceed along the coast to the north. Aircraft from H.M.S. *Hermes* also took part in the search.

The pirates, numbering about 12, boarded the *Tungchow* at Shanghai on Tuesday and made their attack at 6 p.m. A Russian Guard resisted strongly, fighting four men who finally shot him. The passengers saw him alive 20 minutes later, when the pirates brutally finished him off. Mr. Macdonald rushed from his cabin, only to fall shot in the chest.

The pirates quickly took control of the ship, seized all arms, and turned her southward. For three days they looted her, but treated the passengers with every consideration except for herding them in the saloons. They repainted the ship's black funnel red and white, and also painted on the ship the Japanese name *Toamaru*, which is the name of a derelict ship recently salvaged near Hong-Kong.

To-day at noon the ship stopped near Chilang Point. The pirates summoned a junk alongside and conveyed a load of loot ashore, but before a second trip was possible an aeroplane from H.M.S. *Hermes* appeared, wildly cheered by the children. The pirates hastened ashore in the ship's boat, taking as hostages the chief officer, the Chinese wireless operator, and Chinese passengers. They stove in the boat, leaving the hostages on the beach, from which another boat took them off. The ship then proceeded to Hong-Kong.

Piracies are normal this time of year, when wealthy Chinese are returning home for the New Year. The same ship was pirated 18th December 1925. Spies informed the police last month that the Bias Bay gang had gone to Shanghai, and shipping was duly warned. But the gang bided their time. They amazingly avoided being reported by any ship, and apparently the *Hermes* aircraft, which operated fanwise off Swatow, were requisitioned too late.

The *Tungchow*'s officers are, in addition to the wounded engineer, Captain James Gordon Smart, Chief Officer John Middleton, second officer Harry Pilling, chief engineer

John Roxburgh, third engineer James Ferguson Fry, an Australian. None of the children has suffered any harm.

The Times, London. Saturday, 2nd February 1935.

CHILDREN TELL OF THEIR EXCITING EXPERIENCES DURING THE THREE DAYS THE PIRATES WERE ON BOARD

When the *Tungchow* returned to Shanghai on Thursday, Captain Smart, weary and wracked by his experience, was immediately sought out by the Director and Secretary of the China Inland Mission. They expressed to him their warm and hearty congratulations and their gratitude for his work.

Helen Heal, the daughter of Mr. & Mrs. A. J. Heal, took exception to press reports. "Were you and Daddy some of the scores of anxious parents we read besieged the offices of Butterfield & Swire?" she asked. "I must tell you the papers don't know all that happened. Much of what was in them was junk." She launched into an ambitious tale, but remarked that she saw "Parliament was making quite a fuss about it."

Little eight-year-old Owen Hughes, who had been fired at directly by a pirate, told a most graphic story of the entire trip, to a representative of *The North China Herald* when the vessel berthed at the French Bund.

"Were you afraid when the pirate shot at you?" was the query and the reply came instantly. "No, not afraid, but when the bullet whizzed past my shoulder, I ducked and ran, because I did not know what he would do next."

Beginning his narrative, young Owen said that he was in the smoking room about 5.50 p.m. on January 29. The noise of the shooting alarmed him and he ran out on the deck.

He continued, "The pirates, who had been on the deck below, came up the back stairs (companion way) in numbers and were on our deck in a jiffy. The grille was up (open), and I ran forward toward the dining saloon. I was on the left side of the ship and tried instead of going to the saloon, to enter the door leading to the engine room. On the right side stood a pirate with pistol in his hand.

"He fired at me at once. I drew back, while the bullet whizzed by my shoulder and fell into the sea.

"Then I ran to the dining saloon, where the Preparatory children were having their supper. In a few minutes, a pirate came in. We all stood up and raised our hands. He was not bad, however, and we sat down again. I did not have any supper. I was not hungry.

"About 8 o'clock, I went to bed, but a pirate came later and flashed his torch at us. I did not sleep all night.

"Two days later, I saw the pirate again," he added, "he smiled at me and chucked an orange at me."

Questioned further regarding his assailant, Owen replied that the pirate was a long-haired fellow, whose hair blew in the wind. He was wearing a mauve coloured jacket "of which," he added gleefully, "I got a piece, the day they left the ship. His pistol was a long one, and he carried the stock in one hand and the weapon in the right hand." It would seem that the weapon was a military Mauser.

Owen's brothers supported him in further details regarding subsequent incidents. The pirate chief was a very polite fellow, fragile in appearance, with a clean face. All others looked like ruffians, as compared with him. Although polite, "he took our pocket money," they added.

According to the boys, a big pirate, six feet tall, snatched a scarf from one of the boys. The chief snatched it back again from the fellow and handed it to the youngster, meanwhile brushing his henchman gruffly aside, with a muttered malediction. The malefactor had been shot in the hand – probably by the unfortunate Russian guard, and after the incident, flicked his bleeding member toward a cabin wall, spattering blood over the white paint.

The boys believe that another pirate had been shot in the foot, as later they saw it bleeding profusely.

In a graphic manner, the boys told how the pirates abandoned the ship. They looked like "real gentlemen," it was said. They had rifled the officers' cabins and as one went over the side, he wore a top hat, with a leather fur-lined coat. Others wore sundry articles of foreign make, most of them having cast off their long gowns.

On every hand, a representative of *The North China Herald* heard fragmentary accounts of what had happened. Jimmie Baskett bubbled over with concern to his mother, Mrs. A.S. Baskett, for he had lost all his pocket money. Norman and Lelia Cliff of Hangchow shouted with delight when they caught a cheery welcome from their mother, Mrs. H.I. Cliff, standing with Mrs. W.R.O. Taylor, and joined Evelyn and Noel Taylor in a steady flow of adventure.

Mark Griffin and his sister Fern beamed at their father, Mr. H.M. Griffin, of the China Inland Mission, smiling, but speaking not at all, for Mr. Griffin was decidedly busy.

He it was who had the task of notifying dozens when the *Tungchow* had failed to respond to radio calls. Mrs. Albert Taylor and Mrs. N. Pells were seen listening to the story of Helen Sawyer, while Betty John poured forth her gruesome memory to her mother, Mrs. A.L. John of Nanking, and her aunt, Mrs. Leo Saphiere, and Eve John listened. "I saw a man shot," she announced. "I was scared the first night the pirates took the boat, but not so much afterwards. It was awfully queer. I heard a bang, and then I watched a little red ring come on his shirt." Her mother hurried her away.

Off to one side, another voice was piping exciting news. "The pirate chieftain – he wore a kimono – said that he could pirate any ship that ran along the China coast. You ought to have seen them run, though, when the aeroplane circled us. They were afraid of the British Navy, and we were afraid that they'd kill us if we were found too soon."

Young John Quimby, with his sister standing by, gave a graphic account, while his father and mother, Mr. and Mrs. John W. Quimby, of Phoenixville, Pa., listened intently. His story substantiated the detailed version presented by another youthful passenger, and bristled with accounts of the officers and the pirates. He proudly displayed three empty cartridge cases as his spoils. His father, identified with the Shanghai Gospel to the Jews, followed him closely.

Mrs. L. Larsen had arrived early to greet Jimmie Larsen, whose story was no less vivid, while Mr. and Mrs. F. A. Dinsdale were equally to be congratulated on the tales spun by their three children, Felicity, Peter and Timothy. Like their *Tungchow* parents, the youngsters had taken a balanced attitude. Their stories, far from being disjointed, were matter of fact, minus personal heroics, and altogether reasonable, as exemplified by Miss Helen Heal, and her brother David, children of Mr. and Mrs. A.J. Heal. This little lady greeted her interviewer with assured poise and proceeded to give a chronological account of exactly what had happened. Her face lighted with grim humour as she described the reaction of the doughty buccaneers when a British aeroplane swooped close.

"They jolly well made tracks for shore, leaving a frightful mess behind, and we didn't shout either, as the papers said we did, when the aeroplane arrived. We were too scared. The chief said the children would all be killed if he and his band were captured, so we stayed like mice."

"They played with me," interrupted her eight-year-old brother David, "The pirate all dressed in black came in and laid his pistol down when he saw us playing tootsie toys. There was one toy we weren't using, so he joined us on the floor for awhile, and, when he got tired of the game, he picked up his pistol and went off somewhere."

It was his sister, though, enjoying a promenade on deck, who saw the start of events on the *Tungchow*. She was just starting down to her cabin when she beheld a dark skinned man, dressed in a reddish-brown kimono decorated with circles of red and purple, come on deck, his silken kimono tassel dangling at his side. Brandishing a pistol, he grabbed young Ronnie Weller and shook him thoroughly.

"I wondered whatever Ronnie had done to make a Chinese so furious with him, and then I saw other men following him. It dawned on me that they were pirates and I fled to my cabin, shouting to Joy Hayman to shut the window, which was stiff and stuck. We got it down and put out our lights, so none would know where we were."

Miss Heal laughed at the remembrance. "He couldn't have enjoyed himself under guard, for the cooking improved like magic when the pirates went off."

"Once we sighted one of the big Japanese Marus," said Miss Heal, "and again we were petrified. The captain told us he had promised to deliver the pirates safely to their destination, and had ordered no fighting. We were desperately afraid of meeting a ship, and, so the Captain said, he dodged it. They had said they were expecting their own junk, but it didn't come. Then they shot at another. It proved to be loaded with women, but, before they could board it, their own junk appeared, came alongside and tied up."

She heaved a sigh of relief, and reminded the reporter that the *Tungchow* made Hongkong under a convoy of three British gunboats just as the ship's coal and food was all but exhausted. The trip back was described a frightful bore. The "officers' and everyone's nerves were so jumpy that we weren't permitted to shout or run about at all. If we made much noise we were sent to bed."

"Well," rejoined the reporter, "would you have preferred school or pirates and Hongkong?"

"Hongkong, of course," beamed Miss Heal, "– and we couldn't have got there without the pirates!"

Miss Heal also volunteered her opinion of an attempt by the wireless operator to send a message. "We were told Sparks got a message half through when the pirates stopped him. I'm delighted that he failed, because, if anyone had found us before the pirates popped off, well – they would have killed us all, and we just wouldn't be here."

Several youngsters have specimen Bank of China notes, printed on only one side and unsigned, as well as stamped "specimen." This was the currency the pirates had been "tipped off" to and presumed to amount to a fortune.

The North-China Herald, Shanghai,
Wednesday, 13th February, 1935

THE PIRATE'S STORY.
OUTRAGE PLANNED IN A SHANGHAI HOTEL

Canton. Feb. 12.
While the naval authorities of Hongkong and the military authorities of Canton are continuing to co-operate in an effort to round up the pirate gang who looted the *Tungchow*, details contained in a Chinese letter from Waiyang to-day confirmed the capture of one of the pirates, and also his alleged confession. The man's name was given as Fan Shu-ai, and he was said to have been seized after a hot pursuit by the police of Waiyang district, personally conducted by the magistrate.

It appears that four of the pirates broke into Siaomohsiang village, telling the villagers that a large quantity of "gifts" had been left on the seashore awaiting first arrivals. Upon investigation, the villagers discovered a small fishing-boat tied off the shore, in which were found two pistols, five bundles of banknotes and three suitcases.

Meanwhile, the four men had hurriedly made their

escape, but later the pursuit started by the militia and police resulted in the capture of Fan Shu-ai at Fenghsienkumiao. Apparently the four, with their loot, had made for the shore aboard a small fishing-boat in the vicinity of Haifeng, while others landed near the lighthouse. Each of the four had received as his share of the loot $30 in foreign banknotes, $200 in unendorsed Bank of China notes, and one pistol.

The alleged confession of Fan Shu-ai disclosed that a gang of ten participated in the looting of the *Tungchow*. Armed with four pistols and disguised as travellers, they left Pingshan, Lienshan, and Chishih in separate parties on January 17. They arrived in Haifeng district that same night and proceeded by train the next morning to Swatow, where they remained for one night before boarding the *Tungchow*, and they arrived in Shanghai on January 24.

Putting up at the Ping An hotel for several days, they perfected their piracy scheme and finally boarded the *Tungchow*, which was to carry 70 children to school in Chefoo. According to Fan Shu-ai's alleged confession, the gang first seized nineteen pistols aboard the *Tungchow* and then shot two foreign officers. Their subsequent raid resulted in loot of about $1,300 in foreign banknotes, five boxes of unendorsed Tientsin Bank of China notes, a number of overcoats, fur coats, blankets, and other personal effects.

The leader of the pirates, Fong Tung, is still at large, but the authorities are making every possible effort to capture him, as he is believed to be the brains behind several piracies which have occurred recently. Fong Tung is a native of Haifeng district, which he has terrorised for years, making his headquarters at Bias Bay.

Messrs. Butterfield & Swire alone have offered H.K. $2,500 for the capture of this man, while the Canton military headquarters have offered a further $1,000, making the total rewards for the capture of the entire gang almost $10,000. On February 6, the provincial authorities offered a reward of $5,000 for the capture of leaders and members of the gang and recovery of the loot, within one month of that date; $3,000 for the apprehension of members of the gang and recovery of the loot; and $2,000 for the capture of the leader.

Canton Feb. 13.
An official bulletin, issued to-day, gives the following as the names of the *Tungchow* pirates still at large:- Fong Tung (nicknamed "Big Head"), Chen Kuo-ching ("Flower Pig"), Huang Kuan, Kan Chun, Chan Tanhsien, Wu Ti-hua, Ou Chu, Chen Tiyin, Tan Tsu, and Chen Ti-ti.

According to a Chinese report, Tsai Teng-hui, Commander of the Pirate Suppression Corps in the Bias Bay district, received secret information some time ago that "Big Head," the leader of the gang, was plotting another piracy, but was unable to follow his movements.

Commenting on the number of pirates who infest the Bias Bay region, Chinese circles here express the opinion that most of them at one time or another were seamen on coastal steamers, turning pirates because they lost their jobs. They are believed to have met success in seizing ships because of their thorough knowledge of the arrangement, condition, and habits of coastal vessels.

Considerable interest was aroused in at least five Shanghai hotels bearing the same name of Ping An, last

Wednesday, following receipt of the report that one of the *Tungchow* pirates had confessed to the gang having perfected their scheme in a hotel of this name after their arrival in the *Yochow* from the south on January 24. Interest particularly ran high in the Ping An Hotel in Rue Chu Pao San, where it was ascertained that, among more than forty guests who registered there on that day, 21 arrived in the *Yochow*. Of this number, twelve wore uniforms and claimed to be military policemen travelling from Canton to Nanking. The party left the same night. The remaining nine guests came in four different groups and occupied four separate rooms. Two left the hotel on January 26 and returned for a brief stay after two days. The remaining seven left on January 25.

When a representative of *The North China Herald* visited this hotel, none could give a description of the nine guests and their movements. It was said, however, that the majority spoke a southern dialect.

According to a report from the south, five of the ten pirates are thus described:–

1. The leader: 26 years. Tall and well built, with long wavy hair.

2. Aged 20. Short and thinly built. Pronounced small hands. Sallow complexion.

3. About 30 years. Tall and stoutly built. High cheek bones and dark complexion. Had the appearance of a boatman and a bullet wound on the back of left hand.

4. About 35 years. Tall and stoutly built. Dressed in dark blue clothing, socks, pullover, trousers, and wearing a European style overcoat.

5. Aged 40. Medium height and thinly built. Dressed in

blue buttoning-up jacket, wearing a native cap and muffler. Looks like an opium smoker.

It has been widely reported in the south that another gang of pirates has proceeded to Canton with the ultimate object of pirating a ship from Shanghai.

Canton. Feb. 16.
It was officially announced to-day that the pirate suppression headquarters at Bias Bay were despatching further troops to Niumien, Hokow, Hsintsai, and Yacho, in the Waiyang district, to round up the pirate gang who looted the *Tungchow*. The authorities also have issued a warning to all inhabitants of Waiyang district against providing refuge for the outlaws, under pain of death.

Canton. Feb. 18.
The local military headquarters to-day announced the despatch of further troops to Bias Bay as an increased precaution against further piracies being committed. It was stated that one regiment stationed at Waichow was now under orders to proceed to Bias Bay to reinforce the anti-piracy forces there.

From *The North China Herald*, Shanghai, 20th February 1935.

GLOSSARY

This book has a wide range of nautical flavours (to be expected with so many different authors and periods), and this glossary is included to render clear any obscure parts of the text and clarify too other things in the minds of those readers unacquainted with the language of the sea.

Abaft Behind or towards the stern of a vessel.

Aboard/On board On, or in, a vessel.

About A turning point.

Aft Behind. Towards the after or stern part of a vessel.

Ahead In front of a vessel. Opposite to abaft.

Ahoy An interjection. 'Ahoy,' preceded by a vessel's name, is the customary way to hail a ship.

Aloft/Lay aloft In the upper riggings or on the yards. Lay Aloft is the order to go aloft.

Amah A Chinese wet nurse or female servant.

Amidships Generally speaking, the middle portion of a vessel.

Astern Behind. In the after part of the vessel; behind the vessel; in her wake.

Aweigh Spoken of an anchor when it has been lifted from the ground. See also *Way*.

Barong A long thin-edged knife or sword used in the Far East.

Barque/Bark General speaking, a three-masted merchant vessel.

Beam The width of the vessel at her widest part; the term is derived from the beams of timber extending across old ships.

Bearing The direction, or angular distance from a meridian, in which an object (perhaps an island or ship) lies. Properly belongs to the art of navigation.

Beheading In China, beheading was the standard punishment for many crimes, including piracy.

Berth A bed, bunk or space for a hammock on board ship.

Bilge That part of the hull of a ship inside and adjacent to the keel.

Bilge water Water that has collected in the bottom of a ship and is generally offensive and very dirty.

Binnacle The fixed case and stand in which the steering compass of a vessel is mounted.

Black Flag The old flag of pirates. The Jolly Roger is a pirate flag in popular legend and movies.

Blue Jackets Seamen in the Royal Navy, when short jackets were worn during skirmishes on land and battles at sea.

Boarding The act of going on board a vessel using force, as in battle or piracy.

Bow The sides at the fore-part of a vessel, distinguished one from the other as the starboard bow and port bow.

Brig A vessel with two masts (fore and main), both of them square rigged.

Brigantine The same as a brig except that it has fore and aft mainsail.

Broadside The firing of all guns on one side of a warship at the same time. Often used by naval ships against pirate fleets.

Bulkhead A partition of almost any material.

Bulwarks A parapet around the deck of a vessel, serving to keep passengers, crew and cargo from being swept overboard.

Carronade A gun of great destruction power but short range.

Chinese Braves Chinese foot soldiers during the many civil wars in China proper.

Compradore A Chinese agent engaged by foreign establishments of all kinds to take charge of its Chinese servants and household duties.

Companionway The entrance to a ladder or flight of stairs leading from one deck to another.

Coolie An unskilled labourer or porter in or from the Far East, often used in pirate ships as slaves. They suffered a high rate of mortality.

Corvette A small warship of the 18th and 19th centuries.

Cutlass A short sword used by naval seamen and pirates.

Cutter A small sailing boat. In various navies cutters were also large rowboats propelled by as many as ten oars, useful when chasing pirates in shallow waters.

Deck Generally speaking the covering of the interior of a ship, either completely or over only a portion.

Flagship That ship of a fleet which flies the Admiral's flag.

Flotilla A fleet of small ships, pirate and naval. See also *Squadron*.

Fo'c'sle/Forecastle The quarters of the crew on board ship, generally in the bows.

Frigate In the days of sail, a fully rigged ship with 24 to 38 guns on a single gun-deck; used for scouting and raiding pirate dens and junks in waters of the Far East.

Gangway A narrow platform or bridge passing from one deck of a vessel to another.

Gig A small ship's open boat used in port, sometime known as the Captain's gig.

Gingall A large musket much used by pirates; the gun was mounted on a swivel.

Grappling iron A small anchor of several arms used in close action by navies and pirates for seizing the rigging of an enemy's vessel and dragging the two together preparatory to boarding.

Gunboat A small warship used for minor naval duties.

Halyard A rope by which a sail, flag, or yard is hoisted.

Hatch/Hatchway An opening in a deck of a vessel through which persons or cargo may descend or ascend.

Havens Pirate captains selected hidden harbours among the many islands and river estuaries along the southern coasts of China and Indo-China. These were safe and convenient havens for the constant repairs and periodic cleaning of their junks. The preferred hideaways were near major shipping tracks, where merchant ships were frequent.

Helm/Helmsman The helm is the steering apparatus of the ship. The helmsman, or man at the helm, steers the ship.

HMS Her or His Majesty's Ship.

Hold The inner space in which cargo is stowed.

Imperial Customs Service/Chinese Maritime Customs Service A huge Chinese government tax collection agency staffed by British, European and American nationals.

Jolly-boat A small ship's boat corresponding to a dinghy.

Junk A ship common in China and Japan. It is ungainly in shape, but often remarkably seaworthy. It is driven by sails often made of grass matting, bamboo or rattan and stiffened with thin bamboo poles. Junks were of various sizes and were armed with cannon. See also *lorcha, prahu*.

Knot A knot is a measurement of speed – one nautical mile per hour. Sometimes, though erroneously, it used as synonymous with a nautical mile.

Kowtow In China, to kneel and touch the forehead to the ground as a token of homage, worship, or deep respect; showing obsequious deference.

Ladrones Chinese pirates or water thieves with no settled residence on shore, but who live constantly on their vessels.

Ladrone Islands Situated in the South China Sea, to the south-east of the Pearl River estuary, Macau and Hong Kong, the islands were once the haunt of thousands of pirates.

Larboard The old term for 'port' or the left-hand side of a vessel, no longer in use because of its close resemblance to 'starboard' in sound.

Lascar An East Indian seaman.

Launch The largest boat belonging to a Royal Naval ship.

Lee The lee side of a vessel is that side opposite to the one upon which the wind blows.

Lorcha A small vessel whose hull is of western build but whose masts and sails are Chinese. Pirates found these craft useful among the islands.

Luff A manoeuvre in the wind.

Mandarin An influential official (civil or military) in the Chinese Empire. Also, the language spoken in official intercourse through two-thirds of China proper.

Marine Corps See Royal Marines.

Miasma Believed to be a poisonous vapour or mist made up of harmful particles which caused disease. This theory was held until the 1870s by most Europeans.

Monsoon The seasonal trade winds of certain latitudes in the Indian Ocean, China Seas, and West African coast. The wind blows in one direction for six months (in some cases three months) then in the opposite direction for the same period. The rainy season accompanying the south-west monsoon.

Opium A bitter brownish addictive narcotic drug that consists of the dried juice of the opium poppy.

Opium Wars The wars waged by Great Britain on China (1840–42 and 1856–60), to enforce the opening of Chinese ports to opium from British India, which paid for Britain's imports from China, of porcelain, silk, and, above all, tea.

Packet A small passenger or mail ship.

Pinnace A Royal Naval open boat once propelled by oars, now fitted with an engine and used for general purposes.

Piracy Felony on the seas or in harbour. Various acts are now considered piracy, such as violence, and boarding against the will of the master. Acts of piracy frequently occurred in the China Seas, on the coast of West Africa and elsewhere. Today piracy is still found in the Indian Ocean, off the east coast of Africa.

Pirate A robber on the high seas.

Pirates of the South China Seas Pirates were very strong and well organised on the southern coast of China at the beginning of the 19th century. There were an estimated 25,000 men with 500 or 600 junks. Most of the vessels were between 70 and 150 tons, some up to 200 tons, carrying twelve guns. Merchant ships and coastal towns and villages were liable to attack, unless they had previously paid for exemption. At one time the pirates were under the rule of a woman, widow of a former pirate chieftains.

By 1809 they had increased to 70,000 with 1800 ships, and the Chinese government sought the help of the Portuguese Navy. A policy of cutting off supplies by keeping all vessels in port, combined with quarrels among the pirate leaders, broke their power. This calm period did not last however, and by the 1820s pirates once again began to prowl the South China Seas and rivers of China proper. The Portuguese were later joined by the British and American navies in the suppression of piracy.

Poop Properly, an extra deck on the after part of a vessel.

Port The left hand side of the vessel when facing forward.

Prahu A swift Malayan sailing vessel much used by Chinese pirates and some merchants. Pirate warships were built sharp in bow and wide in the beam, most had one large sail and up to a hundred rowers who sat cross-legged on a lower deck. The upper deck carried the crew of fighting pirates. By the 19th century many prahus carried brass cannon fore and aft as well as numerous swivel guns along the side.

Proa/Prau A genral term used for all types of vessels in the Far East from sampans to square rigged ships.

Rig The manner in which the masts and sails of a vessel are fitted and arranged in connection with the hull.

Rigging The system of ropes on a vessel by which her masts and sails are held up and operated.

Rover A pirate or plunderer.

Royal Marines/RM A corps of soldiers, trained in warfare ashore and afloat serving on board ships of the Royal Navy.

RN Royal Navy.

Sailor On shipboard, one who is making a voyage. A crew member who is qualified to go aloft and tend the sails. A sailor is not necessarily a seaman. See also *Seaman*.

Saloon The main cabin of a merchant ship.

Sampan A boat of the Far East, often propelled by an oar over the stern, the larger ones carrying a mast and small sail.

Schooner A fore-and-aft rigged vessel with two or more masts.

Screw Steamer An early steam ship fitted with a propeller.

Seaman A man who has served a certain number of years at sea. A complete seaman is called *able-bodied* and rated A.B.; one having served a fewer number of years, an *ordinary seaman;* one only beginning his career, a *landsman.* See also *Sailor.*

Ship In general, a sea-going vessel, larger and distinct from a boat. Ships carry boats.

Shoal water A shallow place in the water.

Sloop of War An old naval term, once given to ships of war below the size of corvettes and above that of brigs.

Specie Coin money.

Squadron Part of a fleet of naval ships under a flag officer, usually an admiral or commodore. See also *Flotilla.*

Starboard The right hand side of a vessel.

Stern The rear end of a vessel.

Stinkpot Usually an earthenware pot filled with very smelly, offensive and suffocating materials thrown onto the deck of ships by pirates before boarding.

Storm A wind whose average speed is 48–63 knots. Among seafaring men the term has little reference to wind, and is generally understood to mean rain, or thunder and lighting.

Supercargo A person who superintends transactions relating to a vessel's cargo for the ship's owner or master.

Tack To tack in sailing is to change the course of a vessel from one direction (or tack) to another by bringing her head to the wind.

Taffrail / taffarel The sternmost rail of a vessel, around the stern.

Tiffin One of the meals once supplied to officers on board a merchant or Royal Mail passenger liner; a sort of 'high tea' or an early light lunch.

Typhoon A violent storm in Eastern seas.

USN United States Navy.

USS United States Ship.

Vessel Any ship or boat; in navigation, a general term for all craft larger than a rowboat.

Watch To stand a watch on board ship is to be on duty for a given time, usually, but not always, for four hours.

Way Momentum. It is important to note the difference between this and the term 'weigh', the two being often confounded. A vessel in motion is said to have *way* on her, and when she ceases to move, to have *no way*. But a vessel *under weigh* is one in the act of weighing her anchor, or having weighed it, during which time she has no way on her.

Weigh To lift the anchor from the bottom is to weigh anchor. See also *Way*.

Windlass The machine or crank in the bows of a vessel, used for heaving in the anchor cable.

A. Ansted, *A Dictionary of Sea Terms*, Glasgow 1920, Reprinted 1991.

W. Clark Russell, *Sailor's Language – A Collection of Sea-terms and their Definitions*, London 1883.

Samuel Couling, *North-China Branch of the Royal Asiatic Society*, Oxford University Press, London 1917.

CONVERSION TABLE

1 inch	25.4 millimetres
1 foot (12 inches)	30.5 centimetres
1 yard (3 feet)	0.914 metres
1 chain (66 feet)	20.1168 metres
1 mile (1760 yards)	1.61 kilometres
1 nautical mile	1.852 kilometres
1 nautical league	5.556 kilometres
1 mile per hour	1.61 kilometres per hour
1 knot	1.85 kilometres per hour
1 pint	0.568 litres
1 gallon	4.55 litres
1 ounce (oz)	28.3 grams
1 pound (lb–16 ozs)	454 grams
1 hundredweight (112 lbs)	50.8 kilograms
1 ton (2240 lbs)	1.02 tonnes

Note: tonnage in ships is usually a measure of volume, not weight.

First published in 2010 by
Fremantle Press
25 Quarry Street, Fremantle, Western Australia 6160
(PO Box 158, North Fremantle, Western Australia 6159)
www.fremantlepress.com.au

Editorial assistance Naama Amram
Cover design by Ally Crimp

A catalogue record for this book is available from the National Library of Australia

ISBN: 9781921696077

Fremantle Press is supported by the Western Australian State Government through the Department of Cultural Industries, Tourism and Sport.

Fremantle Press respectfully acknowledges the Whadjuk people of the Noongar nation as the Traditional Owners and Custodians of the land where we work in Walyalup.

www.ingramcontent.com/pod-product-compliance
Lightning Source LLC
LaVergne TN
LVHW041106080826
845145LV00007B/1701